Call School

Rural Education in the Midwest to 1918

Paul Theobald

Southern Illinois University Press
Carbondale and Edwardsville

Copyright © 1995 by the Board of Trustees,
Southern Illinois University

All rights reserved
Printed in the United States of America
Designed by Faith Nance
Production supervised by Natalia Nadraga
98 97 96 95   4 3 2 1

Library of Congress Cataloging-in-Publication Data

Theobald, Paul, date.
    Call school : rural education in the Midwest to 1918
/ Paul Theobald.
        p.   cm.
    Includes bibliographical references and index.
    1. Education, Rural—Middle West—History—19th century.
    2. Education, Rural—Middle West—History—20th century.   I. Title.
LC5147.M55T44   1995
370.19′346′0977—dc20   94-26920
    ISBN 0-8093-1859-8   CIP

The paper used in this publication meets the minimum requirements of American
National Standard for Information Sciences—Permanence of Paper for Printed
Library Materials, ANSI Z39.48-1984. ∞

For *Susan Ann Theobald* 1943–1975

Contents

Preface   ix
Acknowledgments   xi

Introduction   1

1. The Kingdom of God in the Wilderness:
   Education and Religion in the
   Antebellum Midwest   6

2. Transience and Free Schooling in the States
   of the Midwest   32

3. Community Gatekeepers: The School Board
   Men of the Rural Midwest   65

4. Recess, Recitation, and the Switch: Students
   and Teachers in Midwest Country
   Schools   102

5. Rural Meets Urban: Country Schools, State
   Departments of Education, and the Country
   Life Commission   153

Conclusion   177

Notes   187
Bibliography   227
Index   243

Preface

In the fall of 1988, I attended a conference on rural education in Bismarck, North Dakota. Having made prior arrangements with very congenial representatives of North Dakota's State Department of Public Instruction, I took a day off to visit an operating one-room school. The teacher, aware of my coming, had her day well planned. Shortly after I arrived, a young pupil fairly begged the teacher for the chance to "call school." When this was granted, the child ran quickly to the door and quite literally called "school" to the children playing in the yard. As they hurried in to take their seats, they whispered to one another about my presence. I began to feel much like a county superintendent of old as I sat and listened to first through eighth graders recite various lessons. Change happens slowly in the countryside. Tradition lingers.

There are reasons for this, of course. I ask the reader to look beyond the pejorative connotation we often attach to being "slow to change" or to "clinging to tradition" and to look for the sense behind these propensities. In many ways the story that follows is the story of a shift from an agrarian world view to an industrial one, that is, the story of people in conflict over whether one should look to the past for present-day direction or to speculate about a possible future for the same reason. The latter view reached an ascendancy of sorts in the American countryside during the Progressive era. The jury is still out concerning the wisdom of this development.

Acknowledgments

I wish to express my appreciation for the use of materials from the following sources: Illinois State Historical Library, Springfield, Illinois; Indiana Historical Society Library, Indianapolis, Indiana; Minnesota Historical Society, St. Paul, Minnesota; Nebraska State Historical Society, Lincoln, Nebraska; Office of the Burleigh County Superintendent of Schools, Bismarck, North Dakota; Olmsted County Historical Society, Rochester, Minnesota; Rock County Historical Society, Janesville, Wisconsin; South Dakota State Historical Society, Pierre, South Dakota; State Historical Society of Iowa, Iowa City, Iowa; State Historical Society of North Dakota, Bismarck, North Dakota; University of North Dakota, Country School Legacy Collection, Grand Forks, North Dakota; and Wisconsin State Historical Society, Madison, Wisconsin.

My sincere thanks go to my wife and children for supporting me through this rather long and arduous process. The work kept me away from home far more than it should have. I think it appropriate as well to mention a few of the superb teachers of my past who were instrumental, indirectly, in the publication of this book. It is difficult for me to imagine ever reaching this point without having had the good fortune to be under the tuition of Dan Bell, Gerald Hrabe, and Dave Jewison, three genuinely humane high school teachers blessed with exceptional talent.

Further, my work as an undergraduate was enriched by two excellent historians at St. John's University in Collegeville, Minnesota, David Bennetts and Bill Franklin. Clarence Karier and James Anderson, two of the University of Illinois's finest historians, deserve special mention as well. Last, I would like to thank several of my colleagues who have contributed greatly to my professional growth: Dale Snauwaert, Gaile Cannella, David Leo-Nyquist, Mike Johnson, Ed Mills, Vicky Newman, Alan DeYoung, Paul Nachtigal, Jeanne Connell, Todd Dinkelman, Yvonna Lincoln, Carolyn Clark, and Ron Rochon.

Call School

Introduction

Rural educational history has been marked by pervasive resistance to state-sponsored schooling and school initiatives. In order to understand the reality of the one-room school experience in midwestern farming neighborhoods—the goal of this book—one must first understand all the dynamics that undergirded this resistance.

Free public schools were the first systematic industrial imposition on agrarian life in the United States. The creation of this system accompanied the East Coast transition from merchant to free market capitalism, with all its social and political upheaval. The British industrial legacy called "charity" schooling evolved in America into a tax-supported system intended, among other things, to alleviate the crisis of idle urban youth. Secular, state-directed schooling, one should remember, was a response to industrial problems, specifically, the notion that concentrated population led to a crisis among children. In addition, it was supposed that immigration could possibly usurp the American democratic process. Many believed that a Roman pope could dictate United States policy by directing the vote of Catholic Americans. These were not rural concerns, and thus a secular solution proposed by many of New England's urbanites, the common school, was frequently resisted by the Midwest's rural yeomanry.

With this much in mind, however, I suggest that perhaps too much has been made of attempts (especially nineteenth-

1

century attempts) to "urbanize" rural schooling in this country. Pinpointing a motive for such a goal is difficult. Before 1918 the nation was predominantly rural, and it was abundantly clear that rural residents did not share the problems of the city. If common schools were at least partially successful in the eastern states as a result of their potential to solve urban problems, this much of the pro-common school agenda was missing in rural areas. It should be no surprise that the rural embrace of the concept was more neutral, less enthusiastic. If common school architects had tried to sell the concept in rural areas by advertising a calculated attempt to urbanize rural schools, one can easily see that resistance would have been far greater than it was. Instead, the concept was sold in the Midwest by imbuing local districts with broad power over curriculum, pedagogy, and funding.

Liberal tenets such as individualism, competition, efficiency, and specialization are what propelled schools in the United States toward an industrialized culture. Traditionally, agrarian societies espoused communalism, cooperation, tradition, and diversification, tenets that still may be seen in rural schools today. For the most part, however, they were replaced years ago by the industrial values that proponents thought would yield universal human progress and betterment. Change swept through all American institutions as a result of the widespread belief that the United States would show the rest of the world the meaning of the word *progress*. When the interior plains were opened for settlement, a host of unprecedented circumstances played themselves out. The result has been a convoluted and complicated history that, at least in the Midwest, historians have only recently begun to appreciate.

Two circumstances seem to me most crucial to understanding the rather unenthusiastic rural embrace of common schools. The first is the role of religious competition and expansion in the plains states. According to my findings, inter-Protestant competition resulted in both pro- *and* anti-common school sentiment among various groups. I recognize that in the pages that follow I have not told the full story in this regard; indeed, to do so would be a book-length project on its own. Nevertheless, chapter 1 is devoted to advancing this hypothesis because we cannot come to understand rural resistance to common schools and subsequent state department of education initiatives without understanding the totality of the agenda both supporting and opposing the common school. The dominance of one religious tradition in the founding of state school systems across the Midwest is too pervasive to dismiss. The intensity of inter-Protestant rivalry during the midwestern states' formative years is also beyond dispute. Taken together, these circumstances suggest that religion—Protestant religion, in fact—was sometimes a part of the antebellum anti-common school agenda and sometimes a part of the pro-common school agenda. But again, I make no claim to having the last word on this subject. I have devoted a chapter to this analysis because it suggests another lens through which we can observe the anatomy of rural resistance. In many ways rural resistance represents a profound contribution to the history of education in the United States. If almost all schools in this country before 1900 could be accurately described by Michael Katz's label "democratic localist," it is because overcoming resistance to sell the common school concept in rural areas required the extension of broad powers to the local district.

The second circumstance deserving fuller exploration is the incredible impermanence of life on the plains. The Midwest was occupied by a mobile society. Even a casual glance at the region's history quickly reveals this fact. But to date, the record of midwestern rural educational history seems to treat the region as if it were comprised of steady farmers who created intergenerationally stable neighborhoods in part by establishing noncontroversial churches and schools. The majority experience in the Midwest was a transient one. The second chapter of this book is devoted to sorting out the educational implications underlying this fact.

The first two chapters provide a framework for understanding the enduring tendency of rural school districts to keep the initiatives of a centralized state department of education at arm's length. With this in mind it is easier to make sense of the day-to-day experiences within the small rural schools of the Midwest. The attention will shift, therefore, in the third chapter to the intermediaries between the state and the children, the school board men who came to control the affairs of the local district. While every school board handled matters differently, there were clear trends related to various issues that developed over time and across geography. Barring women from a voice in school affairs, for example, was a particularly telling circumstance, as was the fate of non-landowners, most often tenant farmers, in terms of the educational circumstances provided for their children. A score of other issues demanding action from the school board men of the Midwest provide a clear picture of the experiences surrounding the day-to-day operation and maintenance of rural one-room schools.

The fourth chapter shows one-room schooling experiences through the teachers' eyes and to some extent through the students' as well. Both rural school pedagogy and curriculum meshed well with the mixture of Puritan and Lockean thought that made up the ideological milieu of the plains.

The fifth chapter explores the relationship between local districts, intermediate school authorities (such as township and county superintendents), and state departments of education. It focuses on the experiences of rural schools during the Progressive era when an intelletual concern for the state of the American countryside was at its peak. To this end, the schooling agenda of President Theodore Roosevelt's Country Life Commission is also examined. The reform movement that ensued from the Commission's work lost its momentum by 1918. It was at this point as well that the number of small rural schools peaked and began a rather rapid decline. For this reason I have decided to conclude this study of the history of Midwest rural education at 1918.

The book was written so that the reader might come away with a more accurate understanding of what occurred in midwestern country schools—and, more important, the ramifications of what went on in these schools—than could be gleaned from any other single source. What is presented in the pages that follow, however, is not *the* history of rural education in the midwestern states. That work has yet to be written. This is *one* history of rural education in the Midwest, one that I believe readers will find useful and one that will mesh well with the work of other recent rural historians, thereby contributing to a larger picture while increasing our understanding of the region.

1

The Kingdom of God in the Wilderness

Education and Religion in the Antebellum Midwest

According to Richard Jensen in *The Winning of the Midwest*, "Religion was the fundamental source of political conflict in the Midwest." Analyzing similar data, Paul Kleppner added in his political history of the Midwest, *The Cross of Culture*, that "the more ritualistic the religious orientation of the group, the more likely it was to support the Democracy; conversely, the more pietistic the group's outlook, the more intensely Republican its partisan affiliation." Jensen and Kleppner contend that religious competition in the Midwest ("pietists versus ritualists") has defined its political history. David Tyack and Elisabeth Hansot use Kleppner's and Jensen's distinction and add that pietist Republicans were generally pro-common schoolers while ritualist Democrats were generally anti-common schoolers. In their analysis, Roman Catholics and a few Lutheran groups were labeled "ritualists" while the rest of Protestantism in the United States, especially Baptists, Methodists, Presbyterians, and Congregationalists, were "pietists." Although these groups competed against one another for souls in the voluntaristic milieu of the midwestern plains, according to Tyack and Hansot, "they called a truce at the schoolhouse door."[1]

Viewing educational history in general terms, the interpretation of a pan-Protestant common school crusade competing against Catholics and an occasional Lutheran group seems to suitably account for incidents like the Cincinnati Bible war (an outburst of resentment and court litigation that followed the Cincinnati Board of Education's decision to exclude the Bible from public schools) and the consternation over the Edwards and Bennett laws in Illinois and Wisconsin (laws designed to deal severe blows to parochial education in these states). But for the historian focusing on *rural* education in the Midwest, the notion of a pan-Protestant/Republican crusade for free schools leaves some questions unanswered.

If the prototype for a pro-common school advocate in the rural Midwest included belonging to the Whig/Republican party and one of the Protestant denominations labeled pietist, there should have been very little resistance to common schools in the rural Midwest. After all, most churchgoing, antebellum rural midwesterners were Baptists and Methodists, who, according to Kleppner and Jensen, adhered probably to Whig/ Republican politics and, according to Tyack and Hansot, espoused pro-common school views. Casual examination of Midwest school records show, however, that rural resistance to common school legislation and almost all subsequent state department initiatives was widespread. Although in every other respect I agree with the themes advanced by Tyack and Hansot in their study of educational leadership *Managers of Virtue*, my disagreement rests with the idea that Protestants more or less uniformly embraced common schools. As the quotation from Jensen that began the chapter indicates, religion was the lifeblood of nineteenth-century midwestern politics. It was also the lifeblood of arguments concerning formal, free education. Consequently, understanding all sides of the debate over common schools requires a review of the origins of the nineteenth-century midwestern religious scene.

The English Puritans who in the 1630s fled the tyranny of Charles I and Archbishop Laud ascribed to the tenets laid out by theologian John Calvin. Simplified, Calvin's contribution included the notion that the earth's population could be divided into two camps: one composed of an elect predestined for salvation and the other, the non-elect bound for hell. The sixteenth-century Dutch theologian Jacobus Arminius quarreled with Calvinist theology and suggested that the behavior of an individual might qualify one to become a member of the elect. Thereafter, the religious notion of "free will" was equated with Arminian theology. However, Arminianism was not immediately popular. The conservative, Calvinist-reformed traditions remained the only viable Protestant alternative to the established Anglican church until the eighteenth century. [2]

The creation of an urban underclass after two centuries of enclosure in England's countryside resulted in large numbers of persons without a church. The aristocratic Church of England was not a likely spiritual home for the new urban masses, and the dissenting Calvinist sects offered only the likelihood that salvation was reserved for others rather than oneself because of so little material progress on earth. John and Charles Wesley, among others, embraced the tenets of Arminianism and refined a methodology whereby the unchurched, the poor, and the new urban working class might find individual salvation. A "Methodist" version of Arminianism came to the United States via George Whitefield in the late 1730s. [3] Whitefield, of course, is generally credited with exciting the colonial religious fervor we now call the First Great Awakening. However, many evangelical revivals during the 1740s were instigated by graduates of William Tennent's "log college" established in Nesahimy, Pennsylvania, in 1726. Working within the Calvinist tradition, Tennent, his son Gilbert, James Davenport, Jonathan Edwards, and others seriously criticized the efficacy of strict denominationalism and rigid orthodoxy of most Presbyterian and Congregationalist ministers. To bring the people to God, the United States' first generation of pietists rejected the intellectualism of Edinburgh, New Haven, and Princeton, believing that sophisticated Biblical exegesis alienated the common farmer and the shopkeeper. For this reason, Tennent constructed his log college to train ministers who could communicate God's message in simple terms.

Yet in the American colonies, as in Europe, Christianity remained a territorial affair. Roman Catholics settled in Maryland, Congregationalists in Massachusetts, Anglicans in Virginia, and so on. As settlement extended beyond the Appalachians following the American Revolution, however, the first sizable Christian experiment with the separation of church and state was underway. The souls of the frontier settlers were there for the first denomination that could claim them, and as a result, a religious crusade for the West ensued. The purpose of this chapter is to demonstrate how this denominational rivalry affected the campaign for free common schools in the midwestern states. This analysis warrants, however, a clarification of terminology. This is no easy task, as referents like *Puritan* and *Calvinist* are subject to vastly different interpretations. Nevertheless, some explanation is in order.

The Congregationalists and Presbyterians represent the two most important denominations as far as the establishment of free schools in the Midwest is concerned. Originally Calvinist in their theology, the majority within these denominations had moved by the nineteenth century a considerable distance from the Confessions of Westminster, the historic source for Calvinist doctrine. Technically, perhaps, it is scarcely correct to refer to them as Calvinist except as they represented the legacy of the Calvinist tradition in the United States. They also represented the Puritan legacy in this country even though John Cotton or John Winthrop would have hardly recognized the nineteenth-century version. References to the Puritan or Calvinist heritage of common school reformers like Reverend John Pierce or Reverend Caleb Mills are accordingly not meant to imply that they were advocates of sumptuary laws or that they believed in predestination. These are descriptive labels that handily differentiate their religious tradition from others.

While in British terms Methodists might deserve the label Puritan, American Methodism deviated significantly from the theology of John and Charles Wesley. A far more individualistic, far less corporate Methodism took root and thrived on the American plains. In this respect Methodism paralleled the Baptist faith, which also experienced tremendous denominational gains in the West. However, doctrinal differences separated Baptists and Methodists, such as the Baptist denouncement of "infant sprinkling." These denominations often are referred to as pietist because of their consistent use of the revival to gather converts. The term *pietist* will be used to refer to Baptists and Methodists generally, as well as a few other sects that dissented from the Calvinist tradition. But by the nineteenth century, Presbyterians and Congregationalists were also staging revivals and consequently are also often referred to as pietists. This is why use of the labels Puritan and Calvinist is necessary. Further complicating matters is that some Baptist groups were so heavily ritualistic and dogmatic that they hardly deserve the pietist label. Orthodox Calvinists were also better described as ritualists than pietists. Episcopalians and Unitarians, differing in theological perspective, shared the similarity of not traversing the Appalachians in large numbers and being essentially nonplayers in the religious drama of the nineteenth-century Midwest. They are also similar in that neither could meaningfully be called either Puritan or pietist. While Episcopalians are sometimes defined as ritualists, Unitarians might fall somewhere at the other end of the spectrum.

The last group to consider are those sects that created their own denominational identity in the West by breaking away from mainstream Presbyterian and Congregational churches. Cumberland Presbyterians and the followers of Barton Stone and Alexander Campbell who created the "Disciples" tradition are the best examples in this regard. These groups, as a result of their extremely simplified theological outlook and emphasis on individual conversion, are here identified generally by the label of pietist because of their many similarities to the religious approaches made popular by frontier Methodists and Baptists.

These pietist groups created a distinction between "experiences of the heart" in terms of a spiritual conversion or rebirth and the emphasis they saw in established churches on "experiences of the intellect" manifested in conformity to church creeds, confessions, and ritual. Early American Calvinism within Presbyterian and Congregationalist churches was heavily doctrinal, emphasizing a strict orthodoxy. In contrast, America's first generation of pietists pushed for a strict orthopraxy in a less didactic, more devotional church.

The pietists advocated simple religion rather than the strict emphasis on catechism of established Congregational and Presbyterian churches. Their experimentalism resulted in a subjective knowledge of God obtained through inward means. In contrast, the communal tradition of early Calvinism suggested that it was not enough to come to know God on one's own, but that it must be accomplished communally through formal educational measures. For the pietist, the "invisible" church was inward, within one's self, and dependent on the experience of conversion. The "invisible" notion suggested a "priesthood of all believers" that was sometimes played out among pietists through rejection of any hint of hierarchy or the need for a specially trained pastorate. Ritualists like the early Calvinists preferred the "visible" church that harbored some role greater than the salvation of individual souls, extending their efforts to unbelievers and to attempts at establishing a (visible) national church.

Gilbert Tennent pushed the Puritan tradition in America to the limit when he accused ministers who were not born again of being the equivalent of "'moral negroes.'"[4] (He also illustrated eighteenth-century racial thought among ordained clergy.) The log college graduates and other pietistic Calvinists of the First Great Awakening created a rift in the dominant tradition of American Protestantism that did not heal until the end of the nineteenth century. The religious legacy that evolved in the Awakening's twenty-year period had far greater impact on defining the pietism of the midwestern plains than the previous century of Puritanism had. Certainly, the Great Awakening withered away, and the established clergy successfully defended themselves from the attacks of men like Gilbert Tennent and James Davenport. However, the seeds were sown for a new version of American Protestantism. During the Revolutionary era, the Methodists and Baptists had been the two smallest denominations in the country. By 1840 they were the two largest.

Methodists and Baptists were not the only groups concerned with spiritual life on the frontier. Presbyterians were also zealous in their efforts to expand into the interior. Indeed, the famous Kentucky revivals of 1801 that signaled the beginning of America's Second Great Awakening took place in Presbyterian churches. However, doctrinally wedded to the Confessions of Westminster, Presbyterians found themselves handicapped in their battle for souls on the plains, as Sydney Alhstrom explains: "Presbyterians were committed to a concept of education and instruction. The doctrinal system of Westminster formularies was ill-adapted to the simplifications of frontier preaching; it demanded a genuinely 'teaching church,' a catechetical system, sustained preaching, and a well-educated ministry." Many Kentucky preachers found the ritual of Presbyterianism so restrictive that they adopted certain Arminian tenets (such as encouraging rebirth experiences through the practice of revivals) or broke away from the organized Presbyterian polity altogether.

The log college legacy of the Tennents is reflected in the spread of Cumberland Presbyterians on the midwestern plains. The Cumberlands was a revivalist sect that got its start primarily in Kentucky but thereafter spread rapidly into Ohio, Indiana, and Illinois. The group was expelled from the greater Presbyterian union in 1809 because it refused to halt the practice of licensing uneducated ministers. Followers of Presbyterian clerics Barton Stone and Alexander Campbell represented other groups disillusioned with the intellectual tradition within Calvinist theology. A nineteenth-century Indiana doctor, relating his pioneer experiences in the Hoosier state, described a typical religious pattern that swept up his parents along with thousands of other early immigrants to the Old Northwest: "Not a very great while after coming to Indiana my parents united with the New Lights [the followers of Barton Stone]." Furthermore, he added, "My father was a thoughtful man, and early became dissatisfied with the Calvinist creed. My mother went along with him rather. But if she had been favorable circumstanced she would never [have] been anything but an Episcopalian, but circumstances make all the difference in the world."[5]

Of course, these circumstances did not go unnoticed. As early as 1801, Presbyterians and Congregationalists recognized the growing strength of Methodists and popular Baptists as well as the disaffection in their own ranks. They reacted by developing a "Plan of Union," which was to be the basis for interdenominational cooperation in establishing Calvinist churches throughout the Old Northwest. "Presbygationalism," however, never proved to be an effective vehicle for Puritan expansion in the West. The inroads that the concept did make usually resulted in an advantage for Presbyterians, for they had accommodated Edwardsian evangelical theology to a somewhat greater degree and thus were more popular on the frontier. The Plan of Union did mark the beginning of an extended period of Congregational-Presbyterian cooperation in which ministers ordained under the auspices of one church generally were accepted as pastors for either denomination. But this was not particularly helpful in the West. In fact, most Calvinist growth on the frontier took place in a spirit of compromise considered unacceptable on the seaboard.[6] Rejecting ministerial education requirements was the first and most divisive compromise. As John Mack Faragher has noted, midwesterners "insisted on a ministry linked directly to folk culture, separated neither by formal training nor professionalism."[7] The American Home Missionary Society, created in 1826 as a Presbyterian-Congregationalist cooperative effort to accumulate Puritan converts in the West, was an outgrowth of the Plan of Union. Several common school architects in the states of the Middle West began their careers as Puritan home missionaries.

One significant aspect of the spread of American pietism in the first years of the nineteenth century was the tension between faith and formal education.[8] This is a major theme in Richard Hofstadter's *Anti-intellectualism in American Life*. Methodists, popular Baptists, Stonites, Campbellites, and Cumberlands gained most of their converts from the western regions of the seaboard states. Settlers from these areas had been the first to cross the Appalachians and create farms and villages in the Midwest. They clung tenaciously to the pietist legacy of religion as a social leveler while similarly harboring the notion that formal education needed close scrutiny, lest the spirit of inquiry erode one's endowment of religious faith. They rejected strict doctrine and denominationalism manifested in various church rituals, including the memorization and recitation of commandments, creeds, and prayers—that is to say, rejection of a common pedagogical structure in early American schools. To pietists, religion was more a matter of heartfelt preaching, praying, singing, testimonials, conversions, and right living than intellectual discourse and rigid adherence to ritual.

The emotionalism that typified camp meetings sometimes bordered on comical, as witnessed by itinerant revivalists who recounted their experiences in autobiographies. Peter Cartwright, the well-known Methodist minister in Illinois, wrote that he once had an audience of over five hundred simultaneously experiencing the "'jerks.'"[9] Western revivals were noted for the popularity of some kind of physical manifestation as proof of a Holy Spirit-inspired regeneration. When a bodily appendage would convulse uncontrollably, the convert was said to have experienced the jerks. Others laughed uncontrollably for prolonged periods or barked in a strange fashion. The "falling exercise" occurred when an individual simply would fall prostrate on the ground and lie still or writhe about screaming as if in agony. Many frontier Presbyterians, Congregationalists, and Episcopalians who opposed this kind of religious "excess" were quick to denounce it as evil, further intensifying inter-Protestant rivalry.

When Kentucky Presbyterian minister David Rice (founder of Transylvania Seminary, which eventually evolved into Transylvania University) found a camp meeting too emotional or too "Methodistic," he would promptly make his exit with the remark, "'High sail and little ballast.'" Cartwright admitted that events sometimes got out of hand: "'It became necessary to post guards to prevent affected couples from going into the woods. In their hysteria some women would throw themselves on the ground, tear open their clothes, and hug and kiss everyone around them.'" One church historian concluded that "some of the women who were the most persistent victims of the 'falling exercise' were the ones prone to forget the edict of virtue." In fact, Presbyterian minister John Lyle actually kept a list of young girls whose pregnancies he attributed directly to camp meetings. [10]

Calvinist ministers who encountered this type of religious expression often found it distasteful. Because this form of evangelism was not conducive to the "teaching religion" of mainstream Presbyterian and Congregational churches, these groups felt it was their duty to provide a kind of educational renaissance on the frontier. Timothy L. Smith concluded,

> The young Congregational ministers sent out by the American Home Missionary Society after 1827, especially the members of the famous Yale Band, professed amazement at the ignorance they found in Southern Illinois when they first encountered frontiersmen from Kentucky and Tennessee who had no Puritan tradition in education. The smoothly operating Roman Catholic schools in St. Louis and Vicennes seemed to them an alarming contrast to the educational neglect of children which they observed in Methodist, Baptist, and Presbyterian families. The missionaries immediately reacted by shifting their emphasis from a primarily pastoral and evangelistic ministry to an educational one. [11]

The religious and educational evangelism of the Calvinist ministers who came West as "missionaries" was not always welcome. Strict Calvinism was a hard sell on the frontier. The notion of predestination was especially distasteful. It was obvious to a few early nineteenth-century Puritan leaders that changes had to be made if church growth was to occur. Lyman Beecher, Charles Grandison Finney, and Nathaniel Taylor represent the leading dissident voices at this time in the Presbyterian church. Each accepted various Arminian tenets and embraced the revival or "camp meeting" as an acceptable characteristic of "New School" Presbyterianism. These men represent the most effective Puritan figures of the Second Awakening, and it is largely a result of their efforts that historians today often lump Presbyterians, Congregationalists, Methodists, and Baptists together as pietists. Lyman Beecher was a pietist, but he was hardly interchangeable with a Methodist cleric like Peter Cartwright. Beecher, Taylor, and Finney were harassed by "Old School" authorities and brought before church courts on charges of heresy. Finney eventually left the Presbyterian church, but Beecher and Taylor never relinquished their attempts at reforming Calvinism to keep Puritanism a viable alternative in the Midwest. Beecher's move to Lane Seminary in Cincinnati is indicative of this Puritan concern for the frontier. The West was to become the last bastion of appropriately Puritan Anglo-Saxon stock. Of course, this was the theme of Beecher's anti-Catholic tract, A *Plea for the West*. The reform agenda was crucial to Beecher and other "Protestant cosmopolitans," as Carl F. Kaestle has referred to them, not only because Catholics were swarming "like the locusts of Egypt," but because the "vulgar" Protestants—that is, the Cumberlands, Methodists, and Baptists—were growing in such large numbers. [12] According to Sydney Ahlstrom, "the degree to which Congregationalists and Presbyterians considered themselves the chosen means for bringing learning, culture, and religious sophistication to the frontier is difficult to exaggerate." [13] Significantly, Lyman Beecher became the patriarch of a leading family of "Protestant cosmopolitans" with those very intentions. Son-in-law Calvin Stowe was an early architect of Ohio common schools. Edward Beecher was influential in beginning the Illinois common school crusade. Henry Ward Beecher proved to be influential in making peace with Darwinian thought, and Catharine Beecher helped to create an organization that sent appropriately Puritan women to teach in the common schools of the West. [14]

With the pietist fervor of the Second Awakening came high-spirited debate over the efficacy of common schools. It is interesting to note, as Tyack and Hansot point out, that the leaders of the free school movement were individuals who could pay for any kind of education they chose. Why, then, were they so driven to provide common schools for all? In answering this question, it is useful to examine some of the characteristics of those leaders. Focusing on the Midwest, it is easy to create a list of well-known common school architects. Reverend John Pierce and Isaac Crary of Michigan, Ninian Edwards and Reverend Edward Beecher of Illinois, Reverends Calvin Stowe and Samuel Lewis of Ohio, Reverend Edward Neill of Minnesota, and Reverend Caleb Mills of Indiana make up a list of eight. Seven were Calvinist by religious tradition, being members of either Congregationalist or Presbyterian churches. Lewis, a Methodist, represents the only exception. Further, six of the eight were ministers. These and others of similar religious persuasion influenced educational issues in their states to a far greater degree than the population of their denominations warranted. As Reverend Amory Mayo recalled looking back at his career as a common school advocate, "'The old-time Congregational clergy were, to a great extent, the organizers, administrators, and teachers of the common school, and without a fair estimate of their service we shall fail to understand many things in its original constitution.'"[15]

For Beecher and other Protestant cosmopolitans bravely carrying forward their Puritan heritage, the future of the nation was to be determined by what happened in the West. If they were to ensure that the region would be appropriately Christianized, literate, and imbued with republican values, these things would have to be accomplished through common schools. The population of Puritans was too small to be effective through traditional church-related channels. By adopting pietistic measures, they might establish a foothold in terms of church membership, but it would have to be through common schools that they would meet the rest of their designs. As Beecher claimed so vehemently in *A Plea for the West*, "'We must educate, we must educate, or we shall perish in our own prosperity.'" These words were repeated by thousands of rural midwesterners as they recited this selection from Beecher in one of Reverend William H. McGuffey's readers.[16]

Ruth Miller Elson, Barbara Finkelstein, and Lloyd Jorgenson have variously documented the role of Presbyterian and

Congregationalist ministers in the production of common school textbooks. The absence of Methodists, Baptists, and other Protestant groups in this arena is even more pronounced than their absence from the politics of schooling. [17] It suggests that the common school crusade in the Midwest was the creation of a vanguard of intellectuals concerned about the future of Puritanism and thus the spiritual welfare of Americans on the frontier. While clearly members of all Protestant groups were represented in support of the free school campaign, to suggest that "Protestants in the United States were unified in support of the common school" seems to ignore some subtle differences and some not-so-subtle animosity among various Protestant denominations. [18]

As noted earlier, resistance to the common school concept was widespread in the rural Midwest. An Indiana legislator made it known that when he died he wanted it etched into his gravestone: "'Here lies an enemy of free schools.'" [19] A state-wide referendum on property taxes for schools was put before Indiana voters in 1848. The results of this vote indicated a marked propensity among those in the southern areas of the state to reject the referendum. This could be attributed to these areas being populated chiefly by southerners from Kentucky and Tennessee where there was no "tradition of public education," which made these settlers "wary" and "apathetic." [20] Doubtless, there were many reasons to favor either side of the common school issue. Curiously, however, the feature of Midwest history that according to Jensen and Kleppner wields the most explanatory power—religion—seldom is mentioned. This may be because southern settlers were Protestant and objection to common schools on religious grounds would require reinvestigation of the interpretation of pan-Protestant support.

Kleppner and Jensen seem to be correct about the primacy of religious conflict in the history of the Middle West. Certainly no one would question the highly religious nature of the common school crusade. It stands to reason, then, that decisions about whether to support the concept of free schools stemmed in large measure from an individual's view of the "fit" between one's religious framework and the way free schools were touted to function. Supporters and opponents of common schools came to their respective positions partly as a result of deep-seated philosophical commitments to certain procedures, structures, or forms. The catechetical nature of the Puritan experience in the United States predisposed its legatees to an education-based view of life on earth. Their ancestors, after all, established Harvard College just six years after their arrival in Massachusetts. On the other hand, groups that broke from this tradition in the frontier regions, like the Cumberlands, Stonites, and Campbellites, along with the escalating numbers of Methodists and popular Baptists, often were indifferent to the particular form of formal education embodied in the common school concept. Thus, they were not in a hurry to embrace it. [21] Other Christian groups, like the Mennonites, Amish, and anti-mission Baptists, because of their allegiance to certain structures, went beyond indifference and were sometimes openly hostile to the concept. Even some Old School Presbyterians were distressed enough by the seemingly Arminianized leadership of common schools to start their own parochial school movement.

The religious indifference or hostility toward the structure of common schools allowed the "old-time Congregational clergy," as Reverend Mayo referred to them, to create a school system amenable to their distinctive views. This sort of educational hegemony was quite likely enough to discourage many non-Calvinist pietists from supporting the notion of free schools for all. Congregationalist minister Caleb Mills, who later served as Indiana's common school superintendent between 1854 and 1857, initially opposed the election or appointment of one "education czar" for the entire state. Speaking of such a position, Mills wrote, "'Let him be elected by popular vote, or appointed by Executive authority, or chosen by joint ballot of the Legislature, the question would be immediately asked by thousands, not is he qualified, but is he *Presbyterian?*'"[22] Many rural Hoosiers were wary of placing dominion over the common school curriculum into the hands of an individual steeped in the Calvinist tradition.

The rural Methodist circuit rider and Lyman Beecher may both have been pietist in their insistence on a conversion experience and in their enthusiasm for revivals, but they were most likely miles apart in their cultural opinions of how to build a Godly society in the West. Indeed, skepticism was widespread about the rigidity and stuffiness of New England religion, and many midwesterners were not excited about the possibility of the Puritan message spread in the schools. Writing in 1858, a rural Illinois schoolteacher commented in his diary that "western people think Yankee religion is a cold and passionless affair." He went on to explain that "the difference principally lies in forms of worship. The Western man enters a New England church and finds pews rented or sold; finds an organ or melodeon and choir, and when the minister kneels in prayer, is shocked to find that he kneels alone. All this seems strange and he is ready to exclaim 'If this be Yankee Methodism, Lord save me from it' . . . now when these forms are brought here with New England immigration they meet with resistance."[23] It should be noted that these were the words of a midwestern Methodist who harbored an aversion for Yankee forms or structures within his own denomination. The fiercely competitive, voluntaristic atmosphere made even the smallest of differences in belief or practice a major offense. This is why subscription schools in the antebellum Middle West were often religious extensions of local churches, taught by preachers, frequently, or controlled by a small board of the same denomination. Alexis de Tocqueville, after traveling widely through the United States during the early 1830s, wrote that "almost all education is entrusted to the clergy."[24] One very early Kentucky resident complained in 1787 that "'from the cradle'" youth were "'enlisted in the service of some sect or interest.'" He noted further that "'every neighborhood encourages schools under different teachers according to prevailing doctrines'" where they inculcate their particular vision of "what is to the best advantage of pupils in after life." John Donald Pulliam, in his study of the educational history of antebellum Illinois, found that the administration and supervision of fron-

tier schools were "almost entirely in the hands of clergy. Ministers had the training, time and willingness to look after schools, and a very large number of teachers in Illinois had some connection to organized religion." The religious education in a rural township school may have been enough to reference it as the "Methodist school" or the "Baptist school." Peter Cartwright, initially from Kentucky, moved to Illinois because of hatred for slavery, saying, "'I'd rather my children went to a Calvin school in a free state than a Methodist school in a slave state.'" However, he also despised "'the diabolical hatred that a rigidly enforced predestination education could impart against the Methodists.'"[25] Cartwright was not reticent about his hatred for Calvinism. In his autobiography he was scarcely able to disguise his contempt describing a visit by a

> fresh, green, live, Yankee from down East . . . called by the Home Missionary Society to visit the far-off West—a perfect moral waste, in his view of the subject; and having been taught to believe that we were almost cannibals, and that Methodist preachers were nothing but a poor, illiterate set of ignoramuses, he longed for an opportunity to display his superior tact and talent, and throw us poor upstarts of preachers in the West, especially Methodist preachers, into the shades of everlasting darkness.[26]

At one point during the 1850s, Cartwright participated in a bit of a literary sparring match in several central Illinois periodicals. Accused by three Calvinist clergy of anonymously submitting a few slanderous essays attacking the Puritan faith that were widely published in the vicinity of Springfield, the three offended clerics wrote a reply to Cartwright pseudo-anonymously authored by devils of hell. "Unitarianism suits our purposes to a notch," they wrote, "so does Infidelity, Deism, Shakerism, etc. . . . but the above-mentioned sects attack too openly to be useful." These devils much preferred "Arminianism," because "it comes in more subtly, has much zeal, so much of apparent goodness and besides, it is so congenial to human nature that the consequences are not easily discovered, and consequently better suited to our purposes." So congenial, in fact, that these devils believed that "Arminianism in the effect of doctrine, borders on atheism."

Cartwright responded vehemently. To the charge of Arminianism bordering on atheism, he complained that "a falsehood more bold, more brazen, and more daring, was never before uttered by man nor devil." He contended that far from embracing Arminianism, the devil truly was happy when the "blasphemous trash" called Calvinism "is spread far and wide." Referring to the education-based structure of Puritan churches, Cartwright acknowledged the hegemonic influence of "prejudices in education," a device, in his view, keeping Calvinism alive in the United States. As a parting jab Cartwright mused, "As a filthy snail will always leave a trail of slime behind, so has it happened to the filthy reptile, Calvinism."[27]

Much of the success of common school reformers in the antebellum Middle West was accomplished without the aid of rural Protestants who saw in the Presbyterian or Congregational leadership a likelihood that Puritan dogma and doctrine would permeate the entire affair. To counteract perceived sectarianism in Calvinist-controlled state departments of education, Methodists, Baptists, and other Protestant groups lobbied in state legislatures for comprehensive local control of the new free schools.

The famous Social Gospelite, Washington Gladden, looking back on his antebellum youth, was struck by the ferocity of the sectarian rivalry of the age, noting that ministers of neighboring churches "were hardly on speaking terms."[28] Cartwright spared no pejoratives when referring to members of other congregations. Presbyterians were "'wicked and high-strung predestinarians,'" Mormons were "'outlaws and murderers,'" and even Baptists he considered "'indecent.'"[29] In his 1873 autobiographical novel *The Circuit Rider*, Edward Eggleston characterizes a young Hoosier Methodist itinerant who hides his religious persuasion from a young Presbyterian

girl. When she discovers his Methodism, she is overwrought
with anger:

> "Morton, if you are a Methodist, I never want to see
> you again," she said with lofty pride, and a solemn
> awfulness of passion more terrible than an oath.
> "Don't say that, Patty," stammered Morton.
> "I do say it, Morton, and I will *never* take you back."[30]

The inter-Protestant sectarian conflict of the antebellum
Midwest was divisive enough to prohibit any kind of consensus
over what might be the Protestant *paideia* in the schools. And
whereas the dimension of anti-Catholicism in the form of opposition to the immigration of papists was perhaps enough to
sell the common school reform agenda in the East, these circumstances were generally not as troublesome in the antebellum West. However, this is not to suggest that anti-Catholicism
did not exist. In fact, Lyman Beecher's rationale for leaving
his Boston pulpit for Lane in Cincinnati was so that he might
contribute to saving the West as a bastion of American Puritanism free from the influences of the "priest-ridden dregs of hu-
manity." The vehemence of Beecher's anti-Catholic pulpit de-
nunciations has been linked by more than one historian to the
1832 burning of the Ursuline convent.[31] Despite constitutional
lip service to England's Toleration Act of 1690, seven colonies
carried anti-Catholic legislation into state law. As states enacted disestablishment legislation during the 1790s and the
first years of the nineteenth century, these strictures against
Catholics were dropped. But the anti-Catholicism visible in
the common school crusade in some ways hides the extent of
the bitter ecclesiastical battle for souls among the dominant
Protestant groups in the United States, a battle that Jensen
and Kleppner contend became a key contextual feature in the
history of the Midwest.

In Europe and, to a lesser extent, the United States there
was a religious backlash to what many saw as a dogmatic drain
in the rise of pietistic Protestantism.[32] The liturgical movement

at Oxford University during the 1830s and 1840s doubtless affected certain American Unitarians and Episcopalians. The conversion of Episcopal Bishop Levi S. Ives of North Carolina to Catholicism was one well-publicized example. Unitarians Isaac Hecker and Orestes Brownson were two other Catholic converts more controversial because of their visibility in the public sector. If anything, however, the growing interest in Catholic liturgy at home and abroad seems to have intensified anti-Catholic reaction to Irish immigration. These developments were followed closely by widespread efforts to curb public aid to Catholic schools as well as growing allegiance to the American (Know Nothing) political party in the 1850s.

Heavy concentration of Catholics in eastern cities also provoked religious concerns about the problems of industrial urbanism. Horace Bushnell's *Christian Nurture*, published in 1847, was an attempt to erode the primacy of pietistic Protestantism's conversion experience by denying the concept of Original Sin. His emphasis on "nurturing" youth led him to advanced ideas about the importance of playgrounds and city parks, heralding a later "Social Gospel" movement. Bushnell, despite membership in the Anti-Romanist Christian Alliance, was far more ecumenical in his theology than his revivalist counterparts, Beecher and Finney. This, combined with his concern for America's growing urbanism, quite naturally brought him into contact with the American Sunday School Union (ASSU).

The Sunday school concept was developed in eighteenth-century England largely through the work of Robert Raikes in Gloucester. Raikes attempted to offer the working children of England a chance for a basic education in reading and religion on their one day each week away from the factory. Initially, the concept worked similarly in the United States. The ASSU was created in 1824 to function as a kind of clearinghouse for nondenominational Sunday school materials, but the highly sectarian nature of American Protestantism made this kind of operation difficult. Local and state associations evolved, as well as denomination-based societies such as the Episcopal Sunday School Union and the Methodist Episcopal Sunday School Union, ultimately reducing the ecumenical focus of the original concept. As Sydney Ahlstrom reminds us, the Sunday school movement was never "so ecumenical an endeavor as it might sound. In New England especially, the state organizations were for all practical purposes Congregational agencies."[33] The publications editor for the ASSU wrote a series of "letters" from his office in Philadelphia that were published in the *Boston Recorder* during the spring of 1838. He complained about the general absence of Union publications north of the Hudson River, which left him with the impression "'that they are not sufficiently elevated in style or matter for the favored children of the north, and that New England people are disposed on the whole to supply their own wants in their own way.'"[34]

It is a curious paradox that the genesis of public education in the United States was so overwhelmingly a religious affair while the development of Sunday schools was first quite secular, a response to industrial and urban conditions. The interplay between the two institutions, however, particularly as the story unfolded in the midwestern states, produced a rather dramatic turnabout. As formal schooling became increasingly secular, Sunday schools became increasingly religious. The spread of common schools had a profound effect on the nature of Sunday school instruction. Cognizant of these circumstances, Lloyd P. Jorgenson concluded that "as public schools gradually became more numerous during the early decades of the century, it became less necessary for the Sunday schools to provide instruction in secular subjects. The Sunday schools [then] became more and more closely tied to the various denominations, and their work became more and more exclusively religious."[35] Sunday school leaders called for a universal system of common schools, while common school leaders called for religious Sunday schools even on the remote frontier. Speaking before a Calvinist congregation in St. Paul, former Minnesota territorial superintendent of schools Reverend Edward Neill claimed that "though the common school is important, it is of no great moral efficiency unless there is a Sunday school entirely distinct from the State in operation by its side."[36]

The Sunday school provides a key to understanding the eventual acquiescence of "Protestant localists," as Carl Kaestle has referred to them, with respect to their tolerance for centralized and often Calvinist-controlled state departments of education. Some ritualist Protestant groups, many of the "vulgar" pietistic denominations, and even some Catholics came to accept common schools as a positive addition to the landscape.

The two most renowned common school leaders in New England, Horace Mann and Henry Barnard, were not pietists or clergymen. [37] Both were lawyers who happened upon their careers in education by being well-situated in their respective state legislatures, as Clarence Karier has pointed out, with respect to "the right social, economic, and political conditions." [38] However, Karier does not contend that favorable "religious conditions" elevated Mann and Barnard into their roles as common school architects. That these men were not Calvinists and yet were able to lead Connecticut and Massachusetts in creating free school systems suggests that in New England the stakes were not nearly so high in the battle for religious (and consequently *educational*) hegemony as they were in the West. Unitarianism may have swept through some Calvinist churches, but by and large, the old saying that Unitarians preached to "the fatherhood of God, the brotherhood of man, and the neighborhood of Boston" was not totally inaccurate. [39] New England was a stronghold of Puritanism and although inroads were being made by Unitarians, the popular denominations, and Roman Catholics, the future of the Puritan heritage depended heavily on the results of the religious crusade for the West.

This is not to say that Mann and Barnard encountered no resistance in their attempts to create nonsectarian common schools. Congregationalist clergy and schoolmasters sensed great danger in the new innovations and the kind of pedagogy of love that Mann was trying to advance. The Calvinist view that humans were born predisposed to evil and required a spiritual rebirth contradicted Mann's embrace of Rousseau's and Pestalozzi's concept of innate human goodness. Ques-

tions concerning classroom authority and classroom punishment could not be separated, according to opponents of Mann
and Barnard, from larger theological debates concerning authority and punishment. Nevertheless, it is noteworthy that
Mann and Barnard were decidedly successful in Massachusetts, Connecticut, and Rhode Island (where Barnard also became the leading school officer) in establishing ostensibly nonsectarian free school systems. This could not have happened
without the approval of a significant number of orthodox Calvinist ministers. In fact, two members of the first Massachusetts Board of Education fit that description, who not only
accepted the will of the legislature in establishing the board,
but also defended it from the attacks by the schoolmasters,
Roman Catholics, and other disapproving clergy. [40]

As Carl Kaestle and Maris A. Vinovskis have shown, "com-
merce and manufacturing" seem to have been highly corre-
lated to the extension and promotion of schooling in Massachusetts. [41] Midwestern states were debating the pros and cons
of free schools at precisely the same time as the New England
states, but under circumstances similar to those in the rural
western areas of the East where opposition to the common
school concept was strongest. Problems associated with immigration, urbanization, and industrialization in the East
helped to generate support for common schools. But this dimension of the pro-common school rationale was less powerful
in the antebellum Midwest, where the problems of the city
were not nearly as troublesome or divisive. Thus, the midwestern battle over common schools (as with other political
questions) was to a greater degree a religious battle. And this
was precisely the terminology used by the common school
fathers of the antebellum Midwest.

It may prove helpful to examine circumstances in Illinois
surrounding the establishment of their free school system as
a counterpoint to the way the story unfolded in New England.
Specifically, the careers of Methodist minister Peter Cartwright
and Baptist minister John Mason Peck are instructive. [42] Peck
was born into a Congregationalist family in Litchfield, Connecticut, and converted to the Baptist faith after moving to

New York in 1812. In 1817 he traveled to Missouri as a missionary called by the First Baptist General Missionary convention. After working for nearly three years to promote Baptist schools in St. Louis, Peck was recalled to New England. Working next for the Massachusetts Baptist Missionary Society, he was sent to Illinois in 1821. Like Cartwright, who left Kentucky because of slavery, Peck seems to have chosen to return to Illinois rather than Missouri because the latter had entered the union as a slave state in 1820. At any rate, in Illinois he began an extended career as an advocate of Baptist schools, Sunday schools, Bible and tract societies, temperance reform, and to a lesser degree, common schools. [43]

As a New Englander, Peck's Baptistic views were not always welcomed, even among frontier Baptists. Helen Louise Jennings reported Peck's distaste for the emotionalism of western revivals that seemed to typify Cartwright's ministry. Peck frequently lamented the high number of illiterate Baptist preachers. He wrote that "'the radical evil, which lies at the bottom of other evils amongst western Baptists is *the deplorable ignorance of the ministry.*'" In their turn, a group of Illinois Baptists wrote that "'John M. Peck is to be considered a dangerous foe, . . . could he succeed in blending the church and state together, our religious rights would be gone, and our governments overturned.'" These critics referred to the fact that Peck was a constant observer of Illinois legislative affairs and worked tirelessly to receive any kind of state aid or charter that would strengthen the fledgling Baptist academies and seminaries he founded in Illinois. As Jennings contends, Peck's connection with his denomination "was always prominent in spite of the many and varied projects with which he was concerned." [44]

Peter Cartwright, born in Virginia and raised in Kentucky, started his career as a Methodist minister there. Harboring an extreme distaste for the institution of slavery, he eventually moved his family northward into Illinois, where he led a very public life, serving two terms in the Illinois legislature as chair of the committee on education. Cartwright knew well the process whereby religious groups could tap the state school fund if they promised not to discriminate on the basis of sect or denomination. In this manner Cartwright was able to encourage and sometimes preside over the creation of nonsectarian, yet Methodist-controlled grammar schools. In the years shortly after statehood in what was once the territory of the Old Northwest, schools often were created and governed under the auspices of a local church. [45] Frequently, the school promoters would petition the state legislature for financial assistance coming from the lease or sale of the sixteenth section of land in their township, while promising to keep their school enterprise open to children of all faiths. The Illinois legislature granted such a petition in 1820 by passing "An Act to Encourage Learning in White County." The law was written as follows:

> "Whereas, there is a society of Christians called 'Cumberland Presbyterians,' who have erected a house for worship on the sixteenth section of township five south, range eight east of the third principle meridian, and whereas the said house may serve to have the gospel preached therein and likewise may be used for a school house, for the township, be it enacted, etc., that two or more of the county commissioners are hearby authorized and required to lease five acres of the sixteenth section . . . to the trustees of the township for ninety-nine years, for the use of said society of Cumberland Presbyterians and for the use of the schools of said township. Said school shall be under the direction of the trustees of the township and of said society of Cumberland Presbyterians. There shall be no preference of sect and the Cumberland Presbyterians shall be entitled to hold divine service in the said house during the period of said lease." [46]

Like Peck, Cartwright and other religious leaders also worked to promote denomination-based colleges. While there is a great deal of glowing rhetoric concerned with diffusing Christian morals and principles throughout the growing republic, little biographical evidence from the lives of men like Peck and Cartwright suggests that the strength required to conduct their numerous educational activities was derived from a vision of a "united Protestant front." A standardized, nonsectarian common school system for the nation's general educational well-being may have motivated men like Mann and Barnard, but it was not the inspiration of these Illinois clerics. Peck worked to advance a Baptistic version of Christianity just as Cartwright worked to advance a Methodistic one. In the antebellum Midwest, schools clearly were an extension of religious work.

The standard-bearers of the religious crusade to preserve the Puritan heritage in the West also entered Illinois. A group of seven Calvinist theology students from Yale (consequently often referred to as the "Yale Band") moved to Illinois in 1830 intending to create a "Presbygational" college equipped to prepare ministers of the Puritan tradition. Illinois College in Jacksonville became the fruit of their labors. Newton Bateman, whose family migrated to Illinois from New Jersey when he was eleven, entered Illinois College intending to become a minister. Before he finished, however, he changed his plans and instead became the principal of a Jacksonville high school. When the Illinois legislature decided at last in 1855 to standardize a system of free common schools across the state, it was not the Methodist Peter Cartwright nor the Baptist John Mason Peck who received the call to become the state superintendent of schools. Instead, after a brief interlude under the direction of former governor Ninian Edwards and William H. Powell, they chose a Jacksonville resident, an individual from the Illinois stronghold of Puritanism, Newton Bateman. Bateman was elected to the state superintendent's office in 1858 and remained in that position long enough for his contemporaries to begin to refer to him as "the Horace Mann of the West."

The pattern in Illinois was little different from circumstances in Ohio, Indiana, and Michigan. While David Tyack, Mary Gordon, and Timothy Smith have persuasively demonstrated the role of Protestant clergy in founding the common schools of the West, there seems to have been little attention paid to the pervasiveness of a certain religious tradition in decision-making circles. Encumbered by forms and structures not readily adaptable to frontier conditions, outnumbered by the explosive growth of the popular denominations, there was a certain utility to the Puritan embrace—and control—of non-sectarian free schooling. Understanding this, I believe, is a prerequisite for coming to terms with antebellum rural resistance to the common school concept. As Kleppner and Jensen argue, religion has been a key variable in the political history of the Middle West. The region's educational history has been no different.

To date, this history suggests two extreme interpretations for widespread rural resistance to the common school concept. Richard Boone, an early Indiana historian, chastised resistant rural dwellers as "hating and puerile." In a similar vein, Paul Monroe claimed that "rural democracy was willing to stay in its ignorance and its restricted environment, provided it was left alone." To these historians, resistance to common schools was an expression of the worst in humankind. A more recent interpretation, however, describes rural resistance as the very best sort of human expression. Yeoman farmers stood up to the "professional educators" in state department offices and insisted on creating schools that suited their own purposes, making it "doubtful," according to Wayne Fuller, "that there was a better example anywhere of the effectiveness of democracy than the Midwestern rural independent school districts."[47]

I find both interpretations unsatisfactory because they ignore the religious dimensions underlying both pro- and anti-common school agenda. The pervasiveness of religious concerns in the political, economic, and social life of the Middle West is not disputed by historians. This chapter has explored the ramifications of this circumstance as it related to the general region-wide embrace of the common school concept. The next chapter will engage another commonplace notion regarding midwestern history and explore its effect on the acceptance of free schools, that is, the incredible amount of impermanence among settlers, the almost ceaseless western movement of migrants.

2

Transience and Free Schooling in the States of the Midwest

Writing an educational history of the heartland is a controversial affair. It seems that when something is said about the "'most distinctively American part of America'" people tend to perk up and listen.[1] It is almost as if two camps exist and people want to know right away where to put someone. For example, a historian might be asked whether he interprets rural resistance to common schools as an expression of an allegiance to democracy or as an expression of an undemocratic tendency. Or a historian might be asked whether she believes that much had been achieved when most midwestern states codified free school laws by the outset of the Civil War or whether, quite to the contrary, she is disillusioned because it was not until the Civil War that these states recognized the value of a free educational system. Because the Midwest is often thought of as a region that prizes education so highly, a region that fosters a kind of hard-nosed work ethic, and so on, the ideological stakes are high. Any history that defies conventional wisdom is likely to receive heavy criticism.

These questions are complex. Certainly there was much that required the attention of the leaders of Midwest states during the early years that would have appeared more important than establishing schools. Yet according to Carl Kaestle, the midwestern states were still wrestling with the common school concept well after other northern states had created relatively stable systems.[2] Similarly, in response to the first question, skepticism over who would control public schools may have been a reflection of democratic principles, or it may have been the opposite. Perhaps the reality of the past lies somewhere between the extremes of the interpreted past.

The purpose of this chapter is to examine the high rates of mobility across the midwestern plains and analyze the interplay between the persistence of transience and the schooling provided in rural neighborhoods. David B. Tyack and Elisabeth Hansot have noted that in the farming areas of the nineteenth-century West "only about one-third of the people remained in the same place from one census to the next." Other work indicates that this estimate may be high. Exact mobility rates, however, even if they could be determined, are not required for our purposes. We need simply to acknowledge that transience was commonplace and determine whether rural schooling played a role in this feature of midwestern life.[3] To do this it may be worthwhile to pose yet one more discerning question. The first provisions made for education in what would become the Midwest were probably those few words included in the Land Ordinance of 1785: "There shall be reserved the lot No. 16, of every township, for the maintenance of public schools within the said township." And two years later, the Northwest Ordinance declared, "Religion, morality, and knowledge, being necessary to good government and the happiness of mankind, schools and the means of education shall forever be encouraged."[4] Were the architects of these ordinances trying to increase the attractiveness of western settlement by making it appear that there would inevitably be schools for their children? Or were they more concerned with the possibility of an unruly citizenry too distant to effectively control if schools were not provided to "republicanize" the "lawless" frontier settlers? Put another way, one might ask whether the history of rural education in the Midwest began in an attempt to control midwesterners or in an attempt to provide an opportunity for them. The impermanence of the Midwest rural experience may suggest an answer.

Regardless of the goal Congressional legislators had in mind, the Land Ordinances accomplished very little. Most states squandered the school funds derived from the sale or rental of the sixteenth sections. According to Carl Kaestle, these funds were used to support projects other than schooling, and generally, "the funds from the school lands were insufficient and ineffective."[5] Nevertheless, westward expansion picked up speed as the nation entered the new century. It is important to examine the circumstances trans-Appalachian migrants faced in order to assess whether the fifty years worth of debate over free schools was a short time or a long time, or whether the resistance to free schools was a manifestation of democracy or something closer to its opposite.

There can be little doubt that the abundance of land seemed to suggest more than ample opportunity. For example, there were 13,000 people in Illinois before federal lands sales began there in 1814.[6] "Squatter's rights" was a prevalent slogan in the early years of Old Northwest settlement. But even aided by preemption legislation, squatter's rights were no guarantee of eventual land ownership. The purchase of land required cash, something always in short supply on the northwest frontier. As a result, transience was extremely common. Some historians have explained the ceaseless movement of settlers with a "speculation" hypothesis. Said one, "Like the big speculator, thousands of small farmers were convinced that they could make more money by getting land cheap, or for nothing, and holding it for increased prices, than by the slow, hard work of farming." John Mack Faragher's recent study concerning life on the Illinois prairie suggests that the purchase of land for profit at resale is a contestable interpretation of the high mobility rates across the Middle West. Such an interpretation suggests that trans-Appalachian migrants had the financial resources for initial purchase, and as noted earlier, even in New England, the ownership of a freehold estate was the goal of young farmers, rather than a universal condition.[7]

For those who made their living farming in the seaboard states, the West is best perceived as an alternative, rather than an opportunity. Although the migration often amounted to a breaking of kinship ties, the traditions and values of preindustrial America went west with the settlers. Prominent among those values was the supremacy of the family as the primary institution in society. Young New England men who "worked out" contracted to pay parents a portion of their wages to offset the loss of production in the household economy. Likewise, girls who went to work in textile mills also sent a portion of their earnings home. This sort of preindustrial *mentalité* accompanied those migrants who crossed the Appalachians. According to James Henretta, "lineal family values were *more* important than individualism in the new farming communities of the Old Northwest."[8]

According to most historical scholarship in the United States, westward movement was the result of "pull" rather than "push" forces. There was abundant land out there (if one could rationalize taking it from native Americans). With hard work a person could own a piece of it. This was the kind of rhetoric that cast the United States as "the land of opportunity." But this suggests an interesting definition for the word *opportunity*. Close historical inspection reveals that those who broke away from the primacy of familial ties and went west searching for land could expect to live in a single-room dwelling with an average of six other persons, could expect to have to hew down huge trees and grub out stumps to create fields to grow crops, could expect to go without churches and schools for extended periods, could expect to walk great distances to visit neighbors or to wash clothes in a stream or to bring back water for household and livestock.

Still, if the majority of those who endured these hardships were subsequently able to acquire legal title to a farmstead and a more comfortable lifestyle, we might be correct in interpreting the West as an opportunity for the common person. However, that the move west and the inevitable hardships that followed did not, in most instances, end in the establishment of a freeholding suggests that the West is better viewed as an alternative than as an opportunity. Once again, recent historical study seems to promote this supposition. James Henretta, among others, has documented the "steady increase in the number of permanent tenant farmers" in the eighteenth-century North:

> The renewed expropriation of aboriginal lands during the early nineteenth century brought a partial reversal of this trend. Massive westward migration enabled a rapidly growing Euro-American population to *preserve* an agricultural society composed primarily of yeoman freeholding families in many eastern areas, and to *extend* these age and wealth stratified communities into western regions. This movement did not, however, produce less stratified communities in the Northwest states, nor did it assure universal ownership of land. Within a few decades of settlement the wealth structure of the frontier states was nearly indistinguishable from that in the agricultural areas of the more densely settled east. [9]

The initial generations on the frontiers of the Old Northwest were the focus of Faragher's study of rural life in nineteenth-century Illinois. There is a tendency to view the agriculture of the interior plains as preeminently commercial, with the profit motive as the driving force in the Old Northwest. This interpretation naturally follows from the notion that those who gave up farming in New England to move to the West did so by rejecting preindustrial agricultural traditions through tacit acceptance of industrial values concerning profit, material accumulation, recognition of an economy larger than the household, and recognition of markets more expansive than neighboring counties. This explains the prevalence of mono-crop agriculture on the frontier. It explains why Cincinnati, Milwaukee, Minneapolis, and Kansas City were the leading milling centers of the nation in succession, as farmers persistently moved west planting wheat, the only reliable cash crop of the Old Northwest. This interpretation is consistent with other explanations (such as speculation theory) of the dramatically low decennial persistence rates in census records across the prairie states. Frontier settlers were mobile because they rejected preindustrial tradition; they followed profits. In keeping with a Turnerian interpretation, this mobility was fertile ground for politics of the average person, for establishing a degree of legitimate democracy unheard of in recent times. [10]

By synthesizing the work of Henretta, Faragher, and other "new rural historians," however, an alternative interpretation can be advanced. Their work indicates that the first few generations on the interior plains experienced a life of incredible hardship. The initial opening of federal land sales encouraged settlement far in advance of available credit-extending institutions. Without the resources to purchase a farm, squatting on unoccupied government land became accepted practice. At times, through threat of violence and coercion, informal "squatter networks" discouraged would-be buyers of federal land occupied by an illegal tenant. A federal preemption law in 1841 made it possible for squatters to buy their farms at $1.25 an acre, but this was not particularly helpful, for most squatters lacked the cash to pay for it. Even after lending institutions were available, without possessing any land as collateral, squatters found it difficult to obtain credit.

Early settlers tended to seek out what Faragher called a "juncture of environments." That is, the first areas to "fill up" were those possessing forest, prairie, and preferably some source of navigable water. The prairie was considered useless land compared to forest soils, for it was generally assumed that the quality of the land could be assessed by the size and vitality of the plant life it supported. Tracts of huge trees were thought to possess uncommonly good soil. [11] The prairie was used generally as communal grazing and as a source of winter feed for livestock. The forest, in contrast, provided some protection from inclement weather, winter fuel, building materials, and fields for crops once the trees were removed and the stumps grubbed out.

This is not to suggest that the frontier farmer ignorantly left valuable crop-production acres idle because of preindustrial folk wisdom. There were many early attempts to farm the prairie acres. Surprisingly, however, clearing forests produced better results than attempting to plow up the thick, root-strewn prairie sod. Wooden and iron "shovel plows" that ideally "jumped over" roots and rocks and did a fair job in forest soils were absolutely useless on the deep root systems of prairie sod. Farmers sometimes hired young men who had developed reputations for effective sodbusting. These men typically owned two to six oxen as well as large, heavy wooden plows. But at $1.50 to $2.00 per acre, the costs of hiring this work done was prohibitive for many. One Illinois farmer wrote to his friend to explain, "'Were I in yr place I would not cultivate my ILL. lands—you could not get a man [to] make fence, break the ground &c. without paying a high price.'"[12] It was not until John Deere's famous steel plow and other lighter, more durable models were introduced in the late 1830s and early 1840s that the cultivation of the prairie became possible. Up until this time, most "farmers continued to break timber soils with wooden plows, harrow fields with tree limbs, and thresh wheat by driving their horses over grain strewn on the barn threshing floor."[13]

When the prairie sod was successfully opened, wheat thrived on the rich soils. To be exchanged for cash, however, the wheat had to be brought to market. River traffic was the only viable option in the early years of frontier settlement. The distance that settlers were willing to move out into the prairie expanse was calculated by the rigors involved in taking quantities of wheat to navigable rivers and, later, railroad terminals.[14]

Clearly, ready markets were scarce for the first few generations of frontier pioneers. Theirs was a world of barter, exchange, communal exploitation of government prairie and timber, and work so demanding that lives were recognizably shortened by the rigors of frontier exertion, particularly for women. Land ownership eluded most of the early settlers because they lived in a world without cash, and cash was needed to buy land. It was natural, then, for farmers to plant wheat. If it could be brought to a market, it would yield cash, and cash would yield land, land would yield more wheat, and if circumstances were right, parents could hope to set up the next generation to succeed them. However, logistics were everything. According to Clarence Danhof, "Since wheat could not be profitably hauled any great distance by wagon, only well-located farmers enjoyed the advantages of being able to negotiate with more than one buyer."[15] Location was an advantage of the early settler, but as noted earlier, it was not a guarantee of success.

The physical labor required to get more acres under production was immense. At this task, a single family moving west was at a much greater disadvantage than an extended family of brothers, sisters, in-laws, and unmarried adult children who moved west in one enclave. "It is likely that many, if not most, of the single men and families who came without associates passed through the community," said Faragher of the central Illinois Sugar Creek community. "A lack of kin, as well as a lack of funds, seems to have accounted for their lack of permanence." Even those families that possessed abundant labor resources were constrained by the intricacies of wheat cultivation. No more wheat could be planted than that which could be harvested in a three-week period, or the grain would begin to irretrievably fall from the plants. Equipped with a sickle or a scythe, top cutting production for one man was less than an acre a day. There were talented scythemen who could accomplish much more than this, and they roamed the Midwest during the harvest weeks looking for work on large farms. But once again, the wages these laborers commanded were often prohibitive for small operators.[16]

According to Henretta, Faragher, and others, by the 1850s the states of the Old Northwest had passed through the initial few generations of transition en route to reproducing the "age and wealth stratified society" of the rural East. Squatting had almost disappeared. Faragher suggests that it was replaced, "not by universal republican ownership, but by tenantry and the rural proletarianization of the poor." Using a microanalysis of the Sugar Creek, Illinois community, Faragher related that "of the forty-six heads of squatter families of 1830, only nine succeeded in buying Sangamon County land over the next decade, and most left the county." By 1850, it was clear that the story of settlement in Sugar Creek was characterized by "the improvement of one segment of the community and the stag-

nation or decline of another." Faragher saw "architectural testimony" to the differentiated society in the coexistence of log
huts and I-frame clapboard houses. For Faragher, it was largely
the acquisitiveness of the persistent from the first few generations that proletarianized a large segment of the rural poor.
Given that the experience of the majority in the Old Northwest
was one of failure in terms of acquiring a freeholding, it is not
surprising that the demand for land in the trans-Mississippi
west should become a national political issue. [17]

According to Faragher, two groups coexisted on most of the
Northwest frontier: "a majority with high levels of mobility,
who farmed for a time before pushing on, and a significantly
more permanent landed minority who rooted themselves in
the community during the first two decades of settlement." [18]
How did one group become persistent, settled, and successful
while others were forced to move, resettle, and move again?
As noted earlier, the presence of a kin network system mul-
tiplied the amount of work that could be accomplished on
fledgling farms when it was perhaps the most significant variable that could eventually bring about land ownership. As in
New England, kin networks were extended by strategic marriage arrangements between landed families. Sibling-exchange
marriages, where two brothers married two sisters or some
combination producing the same effect, was also inordinately
prevalent on the frontier. In such a way the "continuity required for community institutions was supplied by these core
families . . . who came to control a large portion of the real
property." [19]

Historical interpretation that idyllizes the communal aspects
of rural life may well disguise as much, if not more, than it
informs. Even the barter and exchange feature of early settlement can be misinterpreted. There is an underlying assumption in many historical accounts that presupposes that everyone
was able to produce something and consequently had something with which to barter. However, "some goods could not
be purchased at any price because they were spoken for by
friends, neighbors, or kinfolk." [20] According to the understanding reached by Faragher, "community did not work to the

benefit of all; rather, it was a device that allowed some men and women to succeed and prevail while others, the majority, failed and pushed on."[21] And the school and church were the most visible elements of midwestern community.

In a study of generational succession in frontier Minnesota, Kathleen Neils Conzen documents the successes and failures of parents who worked lifetimes, literally, to provide land for their children while allowing themselves some support in their old age. Conzen and other rural historians have begun to reject popular interpretations of geographic mobility as a quest for social mobility. Successful preindustrial agriculture was not accomplished by a constant search for a better farm; rather, it was accomplished by the stability inherent in a family economy bound by mutual responsibility. According to Faragher, "farm families usually trained and encouraged their children 'to succeed *them*,' rather than 'to succeed' by rising in the social system."[22]

The preservation of a lineal heritage tied to ancestral land is a preindustrial legacy. The quest for material success in some external economy apart from the household is an industrial legacy. Historians who consciously or unconsciously value the acquisition of material success or production for a national economy will misinterpret a great deal of the rural experience. For instance, the tendency to view rural schools as "laboratories of democracy" from which came "the majority of the Midwest's political and professional leaders" ignores the results of rural schooling for most rural children.[23] If the prevailing parental concern was a desire to see the next generation succeed them, then this has implications for examining the rural school experience.

Equipped with the insights drawn by the new rural historians, it is easier to see a certain utility in the highly sectarian nature of the frontier religious experience, the resistance to centrally controlled common school systems, as well as the racism, anti-intellectualism, and xenophobia that has typified much of the rural Midwest. In contrast to the South, there were no legal barriers to stipulate who was not welcome or who was not allowed to become a part of a given community.

The openness of the Old Northwest necessarily served to intensify efforts at community guardianship. The establishment of institutions, like churches and schools, sometimes worked to insure the preservation of property for those who were persistent community members. Faragher described the situation in Sugar Creek this way:

> The development of a community was not contradicted by the regular turnover in the population of the creek. The community, in fact, assured the success of the persistent and the continuity of their culture amid flux and change. Community did not "break down" with the approach of the modern world, community, in fact, provided the means of making a transition to it. Like the society that bound the households together, cultural sentiments along the creek were essentially traditional and conservative. [24]

The move of American settlers from east to west was not so much a consequence of "pull" factors, or a rejection of antiquated preindustrial subsistence agriculture as it was a result of "push" factors, such as the settlers' lack of land ownership accompanied by the encroachment of industrial entrepreneurial interests. Close examination suggests that the move west was accomplished by the settlers' deferring to preindustrial tradition rather than rejecting it. For most, the move west was a series of stops and starts. Unsuccessful in one location, the settlers moved to another. One Yankee farmer who found himself in Minnesota after several attempts to settle elsewhere in the Middle West commented that he was "always settling, never settled."[25] Writing to his Congressman, another Minnesota farmer described his imminent dispossession at the hands of railroad interests this way:

> "I settled on this land in good Faith Built House and Barn Broken up Part of the land. Spent years in hard labor in grubing fencing and Improving are they going to drive us out like tresspassers wife and children give

us away to corporations how we can support them. When we are robed of our means. they will shurely not stand this we must Decay or Die from Woe and Sorrow We are loyal citicens and do Not intend to intrude on any R. R. Corporation we Beleived and still do Beleive that the R. R. Co. has got no legal title to this land in question. We love our wife and children just as dearly as any of you But how can we protect them give them education as they should wen we are driven from sea to sea."[26]

As the transients of western society continually moved on, they inevitably found themselves in states and territories of the trans-Mississippi West. Unlike their more successful predecessors in the Old Northwest, there was no longer a shortage of bankers and creditors available to secure mortgages on the arid prairie soils settled after the Civil War. In many instances, speculators from the emerging urban centers of the Northwest states preceded settlement and spelled out exacting terms for those who would follow. The Dakota Territory land scheme provides a good example. Just out of Minnesota jurisdiction, a group of settlers near Sioux Falls set up a mock government, elected officials, and began to petition Congress for territorial status. Initially, it appeared as if frontier democracy could be epitomized by no better example. As it turned out, however, the self-governing squatters of Sioux Falls were land agents organized by Minnesota Democrats. According to Patricia Nelson Limerick, "Their plan was to get to Dakota early, create paper towns, organize a government, persuade Congress to ratify their legitimacy, and enjoy the benefits of dominating a new and developing region."[27] Such was the legacy inherited by many of those dispossessed in the Old Northwest who came to settle at the very edge of territory suitable for rainfall agriculture. One Dakota newspaper reported, "We are so heartily disgusted with our dependent condition, with being snubbed at every turn in life, with having all our interest subjected to the whims and corrupt acts of persons in power that we feel very much as the thirteen colonies felt."[28] That a recent his-

torian of agrarian protest could suggest that the strength of
the Dakota Territorial Alliance was "an anomaly" when compared with the Alliance's relative weakness in the states of the
Old Northwest reflects an inadequate understanding of the
dynamics at work in the peopling of the interior plains. A
strong Dakota Farmers Alliance becomes a completely predictable phenomenon when viewed within the context provided by the recent work of rural historians.

Transients who owned no land were never likely candidates
for orchestrating the construction or creation of a school. Their
lack of permanence prohibited this kind of investment. Extant
school records indicate that the creation of schools was generally left to landowners, those individuals who survived the
rigors of establishing viable farms on the frontier and in many
instances had enough land to spare a small donation for the
schoolhouse site. These individuals tended to be prominent
church members, and often there was no more to creating a
school than calling together their equally well-situated neighbors to discuss the possibility of attracting a male teacher who
would be paid "by the scholar." Such a meeting was called on
8 January 1820 in the tiny Indiana hamlet of Bethlehem in
Hamilton County. The minutes of that meeting illustrate the
manner in which thousands of subscription schools received
their start:

> At a meeting of the citizens of the town of Bethlehem
> and its vicinity at the house of Rev. William Robin-
> son—for the purpose of adopting a plan for erecting a
> building for a school house . . . it was Resolved that a
> Brick house thirty feet by twenty and one story high
> be erected on the Public Square in Bethlehem for a
> School house and which may be used as a meeting
> house, the Presbyterians to have the preference until
> the society can erect another for themselves. That each
> subscriber to said building be entitled to a vote in ap-
> pointing trustees . . . whose numbers shall not exceed
> five, to take charge of the house and also have charge
> of the school under such regulations as may be agreed

on by those who subscribe scholars. Those Trustees shall be authorized, should they deem it proper, to open the doors to ministers of other societies beside Presbyterians but not to interfere with the regular time or usual hour appointed by the minister of the Presbyterian church.[29]

Of the sixteen individuals who signed the petition, several indicated that they would pay with work, smithwork, produce, lime, or hauling. Cash was always in short supply.

The religious persuasion of the teacher for a subscription school was not unimportant, but few localities could be assured of a steady stream of potential teachers from the appropriate religious denomination. Residents in Kaskaskia, Illinois, advertised back East for a Presbyterian cleric who could minister to their congregation and "'teach a small school.'" Another rural Illinois community placed an advertisement in the *Baptist Tract and Youth Magazine* in 1831 looking for a pastor for their local congregation. Popular Baptist preachers were not paid for their ministry, but this group indicated that if the individual responding to the advertisement would teach school as well as preach, he could earn an income of twelve dollars per month.[30] If Baptists or any other religious group wished to attract funds from the state based on the sale or lease of the sixteenth section, they generally had to form a district, elect trustees, procure some funds of their own (sometimes through tax, most often through subscription), promise there would be no discrimination on the basis of sect, and begin the process of formal recordkeeping and reporting. Inter-Protestant rivalries and anti-Catholic antipathies often kept children out of schools waiting, in many instances, for the numbers that might make their own church-related school feasible. Under such conditions there is little wonder why so few rural midwesterners received an education in the antebellum years. Abraham Lincoln is typical in this regard. While growing up in Kentucky and Indiana, Lincoln had a total of three months of formal schooling.

An examination of the early legislative efforts to provide schools in such states as Michigan, Ohio, and Indiana reveals a marked tendency to continue the New English tradition of religiously-oriented academies and seminaries. The first piece of legislation in Indiana related to schooling was the "County Seminary Law" passed in 1818 that provided for state funds from fines and other unpredictable sources to help members of one or another denomination establish a seminary in their county. These schools were to provide a classical education for young scholars aged four and five years all the way up to young men in their twenties. Though many such seminaries were chartered in Indiana, a majority of the rural seminaries failed shortly after opening or never got started. The state efforts at directing the establishment of these schools and providing funds for their continued existence were poor at best. [31] Nevertheless, the sentiment strengthening the connection between religion and education in Indiana remained enduring over many decades.

The history of higher education in Indiana and in other Midwest states reflects this linkage. In Franklin, a town of about 5,000 in 1870 and the largest community in rural Johnson County, the presence of Franklin Baptist College so disillusioned area Presbyterians that there was a drive to establish a Presbyterian college in the same village. Failing in their attempt, they nevertheless succeeded at establishing an academy for precollegiate instruction. The current trend in educational history seems to suggest that in this fiercely competitive sectarian age, "schoolhouses remained neutral territory."[32] Yet there is evidence that indicates that schoolhouses, while they certainly evolved into neutral territory, were not construed as such in the Midwest from the outset. As late as 1890, the Franklin *Jacksonian* reported that "'there are strong indications that a Presbyterian will be chosen [as State Superintendent of Public Instruction],'" and found it necessary to add that "'there is more than half concealed kicking from other denominations.'"[33]

The evolution toward a pan-Protestant "truce at the schoolhouse door" seems to have begun when the states of the Midwest began to seriously debate the merits of a tax-supported common school system. Iowa established a free school system upon statehood in 1846. Wisconsin, Minnesota, Kansas, and Nebraska did as well, all accomplishing this ahead of the slowest of the Old Northwest states, Michigan, which established a statewide free school system in 1869. Indiana's free school law was passed in 1852, Ohio's in 1854, and Illinois' in 1855. The Dakotas made provisions for free schools upon statehood in 1889.

Despite legislation being on the books and the power to tax real property being officially extended to duly elected school trustees in newly formed districts, many residents objected to the notion of free schools and seemingly did what they could to stop them. In Wisconsin, early state superintendents were flooded with mail from local board members who wished to know more about their legal authority in the district. A fairly typical inquiry was concerned with what the board could do in the event the taxable residents of a district would not approve of any tax levy: "I desire your opinion and instruction, whether or not, the power exists by which the 'District Board,' independently of a District Vote to that effect, may levy a tax in order to pay the teachers, by them, employed."[34] Another wrote to complain that

> at the present time [there is] considerable difficulty in regard to the District School, much of the wealth of the district is in the hands of individuals, who have no children to send to the School, these men are endeavoring to have the school supported by paying by the scholar and are endeavoring to make the people believe that such may be done . . . there is a great struggle between the two classes of individuals, and what we need is a decisive voice from you . . . that will put to silence the voice of those who are trying to deprive the parents and children of our village of the benefits of wholesome lives.[35]

The entire board of a joint district in Iowa and Dane Counties, Wisconsin, collaborated to explain to the state superintendent that "ever since the board took office in Oct. last they have been very much annoyed and obstructed in their duty by party spirit among the voters in the district. One party supporting the school and school system by raising and paying taxes and the other by preventing a levy and defeating the collection of taxes already voted."[36]

As Wisconsin districts were forming in response to the education provisions in Wisconsin's Enabling Act, Indiana submitted the question of passing a free school law in the Hoosier state. Exactly 140,410 voters responded to the question. Fifty-six per cent of the votes were in favor of free schools. As an example of how deeply opposition to free schools ran, however, it should be pointed out that there were reports in some locations of reputable citizens appearing "at the polls armed to intimidate the advocates of free schools."[37]

A year after taking office as Indiana's state superintendent of public instruction, Caleb Mills repeatedly complained about rural districts clinging to their subscription schools. "In Many townships," he wrote in 1855, "where there have been no public schools becaus[e] the funds have been appropriated to the erection of school houses, the trustees, in their reports, have dismissed the subject of schools with the apologetic remark, 'we have had subscription schools' and given no details of even the *substitute* for free schools." He added that "ninety townships failed to report last October and no communication has been received since that period, relating to their educational affairs." Mills was an indefatigable opponent of subscription schools. As he continued to receive notice that rural districts sustained subscription schools, he never failed to ask "the troublesome question," that is, "who paid the tuition of the poor children of the district whos[e] parents were unable to subscribe?"[38]

It was difficult for rural midwesterners to consent to tax themselves enough money to support a school that would benefit the children of those who paid no tax, particularly when there were enough teachers around who were willing to take in a group of pupils in exchange for payment by the scholar. A rural Hoosier wrote to a friend in 1858 to explain that "our public school has been stopped for want of a tax to carry them and the trustees are renting the rooms out to different teachers and they are taking schollars on the pay system. Sally, Theresa, and Sarah is going to school to an Irishman by the name of Kenady in our room over the woolen store."[39]

While some (like the Indiana legislator who wanted etched into his gravestone, "Here lies an enemy of free schools") objected to tax-supported schools to their last breath, most of those who resisted the initial organization process ultimately acquiesced. In the early years, local law enforcement officials were kept busy informing those who refused to pay school tax that their property would be seized and sold at public auction if they continued to hold out.[40] Eventually, the taxes were paid. But sometimes it was a matter of timing. Thirteen disgruntled taxpayers in Dodge County, Wisconsin, explained that while consenting to a tax at the annual school meeting, they understood that it would be collected in the fall. They drafted a petition that read, "Now, the persons whom we elected to office, have taken steps contrary to our wishes & previous understanding, and have now threatened to levy distress on our small means of support, and deprive us of our little means of subsistence, if we do not pay a *Tax in Money* forthwith." These residents let it be known that they would pay the tax in the fall if the crops were good, "but a money tax of the above amount to be collected *now* . . . would not only in the meantime deprive us of the bread from our mouths, but would ruin some of us forever." The tax levy was for $124 split thirteen ways, depending on the valuation of personal property of each household. It seems likely that the six individuals may have overstated their case.[41]

With a voice at the annual school meeting, those property owners who opposed free schools could at least lobby their neighbors to keep expenses low. They could have some say in what would be taught in the local school and who would teach it. They could also capitalize on any irregularities committed by the duly elected board. If a motion was made incorrectly, its carrying vote could be declared void. If proper notice was not given before a school meeting, the property owners could demand that all action taken there be rescinded.

The correspondence records of state and county superintendents across the Midwest are filled with questions concerning
precedent over the most minute details of school district procedure and operation.

As logic would suggest, the first school boards were composed of taxable residents with children to educate. [42] The in-
evitability of legally-mandated free schools meant that those
who opposed the idea were eventually forced to make some
choices. Many opted to participate by becoming board members; others simply attended annual meetings and paid careful
attention to the actions of local board members. Those most
suspicious of free schools soon discovered that the legislators
who put together the school laws left a great deal of power
and control in the hands of long-standing taxable residents,
with or without children. William Beadle, a superintendent
of public instruction for the Territory of Dakota, wrote in his
annual report for 1882 about the problems this power sometimes caused. "Small communities of early settlers secure the
organization of districts large in area in order to erect and pay
for their schoolhouse by taxes on people who can never share
the benefits." Beadle went on to explain,

> The district school meetings are not of advantage to
> school. They are very often scenes of disorder and wran-
> gles between factions. Schoolhouses are located and
> removed and relocated, as the varying strength of fac-
> tions permits. A regular meeting votes taxes for schools.
> A special called meeting annuls the vote. Rich and
> populous districts have been controlled against schools
> by the secret combination of those who had no children
> to educate. [43]

There seems to be a tendency among some historians to make
light of the "wrangling," as Beadle called it, within local school
districts. Conventional wisdom, at least, contends that democracy is not pretty. It is a large leap of faith, however, to assume
that ugly scenes at the annual school meeting were the manifestation of democratic action. More likely the reverse is true.

Keeping close watch over the affairs of the local school, the board men of rural Midwest were able to see to it that schooling served their interests well. In the early years of statehood in the Old Northwest, the link between education and religion allowed schools to obviously display exclusionary intentions. Constitutional rhetoric concerned with the separation of church and state notwithstanding, antebellum schools were sometimes inextricably linked to sectarian interests. In many areas of the Old Northwest, it would have been just as unthinkable for a devout Methodist to send his children to a Calvinist school as it would have been to send them to a Catholic one.

Across the Midwest during the 1850s, farmers faced an institutional imposition not of their own making. They were charged with the education of the neighborhood children, no matter what their faith or convictions. This alone was enough to produce resistance to free schools in some localities, and when this was coupled with the fact that some of the farmer's tax money would be used to educate someone else's child, resistance became widespread. There was no natural connection between the knowledge imparted in schools and the wisdom required to maintain a productive farming household. The intricacies of animal husbandry, planting, cultivating, and harvesting were passed on through tradition, neighborhood knowledge, and the few agricultural periodicals that gained ever wider readership as the century progressed. There was a kind of pastoralism in midwestern agrarian ideology that left little doubt that the good life was one of intimate labor with soil. Biblical metaphors confirmed the primacy of the agricultural way of life: the Lord was a shepherd, the people were His flock. In preindustrial agrarian life, schooling played a small part. Its rather tenuous existence was in large part a product of religious developments during the sixteenth and seventeenth centuries. And as such, preindustrial schooling in the United States was fundamentally a catalyst for spiritual rather than economic or material growth. Daily Bible reading was prevalent on the American frontier and remains today a distinctive characteristic of the American Protestant.

The connection between Horace Mann's common school system and the procession of Catholic immigrants responding to industrial developments in eastern cities like New York, Philadelphia, and Boston was noted in the previous chapter. But these were urban concerns. Although reducing sectarian differences in the process of American schooling possessed a certain utility for some on the East Coast, this was much less apparent in the antebellum Midwest. On the surface of things, the common school notion looked to many midwesterners as if it possessed the power to alleviate any advantage schooling might play in solving intergenerational questions concerning community settlement. If tenant farmers were unable to send their children to school because of the subscription fee or because of the distance to the schoolhouse or because of an undesirable religious affiliation, they were less likely to remain in the neighborhood and were therefore less of a competitive threat (in terms of buying neighborhood land) to the increasingly tightly connected networks of persistent families. Common schools, on the other hand, could perhaps diminish any of these advantages. Also, it was not readily apparent that formal schooling passed on any useful knowledge or skills when stripped of its religious dimension. In fact, the popular denominations characteristically rejected the scholarly life and saw severe limitations in the benefits of extended formal study. To the extent that a common school experience would contribute to a growing spirit of nationalism, however, it was seen as desirable. But in areas where immigrant socialization was not a problem, the promotion of patriotism hardly seemed to justify the institutionalization of free schools.

Pervasive resistance to free schools in the rural Midwest is generally not disputed by historians. While some attribute this resistance to a fundamental allegiance to democratic principles, others, like Faragher and Henretta, are not so inclined to view democracy and community as synonymous. With the exception of rhetoric in the halls of state assemblies, there seems to be little evidence to suggest that such democracy existed in nineteenth-century Midwest rural neighborhoods. Even midwestern political rhetoric was sometimes openly undemocratic. Indiana Senator John Petit remarked that he considered the idea that all men are created equal "'a self-evident lie.'"[44] While the talk of rights and equality served men like Thomas Jefferson and other revolutionaries well, its usefulness quickly disappeared as Americans migrated into an inhabited interior.

The architects of Midwest frontier community—of frontier neighborhoods—were driven by the tangible assets that accompanied ownership of land. This was as true for the settler from Virginia as it was for the settler from Massachusetts, or from Norway, Ireland, or Germany. Undertaking the dramatic move across the Appalachians was deemed to be more desirable than urban employment. Moving farther west was a popular response of those who failed to achieve legal title to a farm in the East. When they arrived in the Old Northwest they clung tenaciously to the values and beliefs of agrarian life. In this regard the rural church served agrarian society well. Drought, hail, blight, grasshoppers, and other agricultural calamities intensified the human propensity to speculate about the power of a divine authority. Rural midwestern society was intensely religious. If one expected to successfully call for divine intervention in the affairs of the world, one needed to adhere faithfully to "right" behaviors. This was particularly true of the pietistic denominations of the plains states.

Until the imposition of the common school movement, schooling had been a small part of the contract between dutiful Protestants and God. Since the ability to read the Bible was considered essential, schooling was seen as an effective means to this end. Additionally, if the school was controlled by like-minded individuals, undesirable behaviors might be squelched, and desirable ones, promoted. The theology of the popular denominations that spread across America's interior plains was based largely on behavioral prescription and proscription. The proper Christian for some, as an example, was one who attended church, read the Bible, and refrained from public song and dance. Schooling, if locally controlled, could enhance and contribute to these behaviors and values. However, the noncontroversial religion advocated in the common schools was troublesome for many among the popular denominations of the plains. It was all the more difficult to accept as it became obvious that the movement received its force from the leadership of one particular religious tradition. As noted in the previous chapter, accommodation was eased by the evolution of the Sunday school concept. But to understand the nature of rural resistance to centralization and common schools, we may find it useful to look at the circumstances surrounding the origins of three Midwest school districts.

In rural Rock County, Wisconsin Territory, a general store was constructed near the property belonging to Ezra A. Foot in 1845. Foot periodically kept a school in his home for local children. With the construction of a Methodist church in the vicinity, the area around Foot's property became a social center of sorts for a portion of Center Township. In the summer of 1847, Foot decided to create a common school district under Wisconsin Territorial law. He called his neighbors together in his home to discuss the creation of the new district. [45]

At the first meeting of District 6, Center Township, Foot described the patch of his land that he intended to donate to the district. The newly elected district officers were instructed to see to it that a good "post and rail fence" was constructed to mark off the boundaries. Foot consented to build the fence for $8. He was also chosen district "collector." Before the meeting adjourned, plans were discussed for the construction of a twenty-by-twenty-six-foot schoolhouse during the following summer.

The summer of 1848 came and went, and still District 6 had no schoolhouse. A short term of two-and-a-half months was held in Foot's home, but there was apparently a great deal of resistance to any attempt to levy a tax on district residents. Finally in October 1848, a vote was passed to raise $200 to build a schoolhouse. By January 1849, however, it was apparent that $200 was insufficient to complete construction of the building. A levy for $75 more was passed. Another two-and-a-half-month winter term commenced, once again in the home of Ezra Foot. The summer of 1849 came and went, and still the schoolhouse remained unfinished. During the fall, a district reorganization was planned in the hope that the ability to generate taxes for school purposes would improve. In November 1849, District 6 officially became Joint District 1 of Center and Plymouth Townships. Despite a greater resident population, Joint District 1 had no better luck in its attempts to pass a levy. A special meeting was called by the Center Township superintendent to settle squabbles over the selection of district officers and to enact a tax levy.

On 5 December 1849, interested residents met with their board members and negotiated a tax levy that would permit the district to complete the school, build two privies, and pay for a teacher for winter term. Board member F. A. Beach was awarded the contract for constructing the privies. However, when the 1850 summer term ended, no privies and no instructional amenities such as a blackboard, a map, or a globe were available for the children.

The idea of a free public school did not go over well in this portion of Rock County. Out of thirty-two school-age children in the district, only nine were attending school in the summer of 1850. Sometimes there were fewer. In the first four or five years of its existence, Joint District 1 struggled with low attendance and contested tax levies and the resulting indebtedness. But things began to change in the summer of 1851. Foot built two privies and was reimbursed $15 for doing so. The district also acquired a blackboard and hired a male teacher to begin a nine-month school term in the fall. Yet school attendance remained poor. For some months the average attendance was as low as five.

In the early 1850s circumstances changed dramatically. A few business establishments gathered around what was now known as Footville as rumors spread that a rail line would soon pass through the vicinity. It arrived in 1855, and as a result the schoolhouse initially constructed in 1849 was no longer large enough to house the many students. On 2 October 1855, Footville residents "voted that the District Board be authorized and instructed to purchas the basement of the M. E. Church and fit it up four a district School Room or School House."

Footville grew into a thriving little village over the course of the next sixteen years. Eventually, the student attendance outgrew the basement of the Methodist church. At the annual school meeting in 1871, a new schoolhouse was considered, and a committee of five was appointed "to confer with the official members of the M. E. Church in regard to the disposal of the present school room." A two-story building was constructed, and two teachers were hired each term. Ezra Foot remained a district board member from the board's inception in 1847 through 1878. In time Footville became an incorporated village, and the environs surrounding it constituted an independent village school district.

Early in November 1858, a few residents of Elgin Township in Wabasha County, Minnesota, got together to form a new school district under the auspices of the free school clauses in Minnesota's new state constitution. As in Rock County, Wisconsin, local residents had supported a subscription school conducted in the home of Gurden Town, an early settler, who was instrumental in beginning the drive for a free school district. But it was not an easy task. On 10 November 1858, at Town's home, an initial meeting was called to create boundaries for the district and select board officers. One week later, again in Town's home, residents met and argued about whether the district should try to support a school for the upcoming winter term. The motion to support such a school lost. However, those who attended the meeting that night decided to post notices that read, "Special meeting called at the house of Gurden Town, Nov. 24, 1858, for the object, First, of locating a Site for a School house[.] Second, building a School house."[46]

At the 24 November meeting it was decided that the district should lease a half-acre of land from Joseph Leatherman, a district board officer. Also, a tax of $150 was levied "to build a 16 × 20 school." However, a vocal element in the district opposed the creation of a free school district. On 4 April 1859, gathering once again in the house of Gurden Town, they managed to "revoke the details passed on Nov. 24." It was decided that the 1859 summer term would once again be held in Town's home. Little progress was made in 1860. The district existed on paper, but it possessed no schoolhouse and no property on which to build one. In April 1861, however, an acre of board member Leatherman's land was finally purchased, although the existing records did not stipulate what price was paid. In September 1861, three years after the district was formed, a tax was levied and collected, albeit it was only seventy-five dollars. With this money the construction of a small, fourteen-by-sixteen-foot log schoolhouse was begun. On 31 December 1861, the board met with residents to raise "$25 to buy a stove and finish the schoolhouse." But this motion lost. Before the meeting was adjourned, a second motion to raise twenty dollars for the same purposes carried.

In a very short time, the district outgrew the small log schoolhouse. After six years of conducting school there, residents voted to raise five hundred dollars by tax to construct a new school. This brought the opponents of the district out in full force. On 28 March 1868, a more modest plan for a new school passed, and three hundred dollars was levied on the taxable residents of the district.

In Brookings County, Dakota Territory, several residents of Oakwood Township met in the summer of 1878 to form District 3. A small collection of businesses had gathered near Oakwood Lake; a post office was established there, and the early circumstances looked a great deal the like the genesis of Footville thirty years earlier in Wisconsin. The residents around Oakwood, however, were never the recipients of a railroad, and as a result their fledgling village eventually died out. [47]

Joshua Downing was part owner of Oakwood's Downing Brothers General Store. The first school meeting was held in his establishment on 13 July 1878. At the meeting, Downing donated "suitable ground for the school house site." Arrangements were made to construct a twenty-by-twenty-foot schoolhouse and to hire a female teacher to conduct a fall term. As the months went by, however, it was clear that neither a fall term nor a schoolhouse would soon materialize. On 16 November 1878, it was decided that Downing "be appointed a committee of one to solicit aid to maintain a winter school." Meeting in the Oakwood Hotel six days later, Downing "reported the amount of money pledged to maintain a term of school." A winter term commenced in December, and eleven pupils attended regularly, but where the schooling was conducted is unclear. Most likely it was held in the home of a district resident. This type of early school funding was a mixture of taxation and subscription. Residents without children attending school generally did not pledge to contribute to the winter term. Those with one child and 160 acres were probably asked to contribute more than those with one child and 80 acres. By the spring of 1879, it was clear that while this method might serve as a temporary expedient, constructing a schoolhouse of any size would require larger sums than the district could ever expect to acquire through pledges.

On 1 April it was decided that the district residents would sell bonds to build a schoolhouse and eventually tax themselves to meet their subsequent obligations. Bonds were sold, a schoolhouse was built on the Downing site, and a fall term began in the new school. In March 1880, a district census was taken, and it was determined that 115 children between the ages of 5 and 21 were residing in the district. Of that number, 39 were attending the new school regularly. The district was of such size that it was not feasible for half of the children to attend the school. As a result, those residents taxed to pay bond obligations from which they received no benefit were angry about the circumstances. They apparently came to a special district meeting on 17 July in great numbers. At the meeting it was "moved and carried that the District will not recognize said school house bonds dated on the 16th day of April, 1879. Moved and carried that the school board be authorized to imploy good and competent councel in behalf of the district provided the Bonds are put into court for collection."

District 3 records include passing remarks concerning litigation against the district brought by dissatisfied bondholders. Although the matter dragged on for years, the district was eventually forced to pay off their obligations. Meanwhile, many district residents went without the benefit of a school. A village called Bruce grew during the early 1880s on the eastern side of the district, and residents there petitioned the district board to build another schoolhouse. They were told that if the community built the schoolhouse through subscription, District 3 would thereafter sustain the school's needs.

In 1883 Dakota Territory adopted a township school organization system in all localities where independent districts did not exist. Those areas that had already formed districts were left with the option of collapsing into a township organization or keeping their independent district status. Oakwood decided to switch to the township system. A township-wide school board took up the governance of four schools in 1884, one in Oakwood, one in Bruce, and two others. To handle all the affairs of the schools, the township school board members found they had to meet every month. By 1887 it was decided that the four schools ought to compose subdistricts, each with its own local board. Although the township board remained intact, questions of whether the schoolhouse should be used for public meetings, whether outside scholars could attend or at what price, and so on, were decided by subdistrict boards at annual or special meetings. The residents of Oakwood Township, South Dakota, eventually dispensed with the township system when four independent school districts were created in 1900.

The notion of a township system to govern the affairs of local schools was at least as old as the common school concept itself. Thomas Jefferson included a version of such a system in his "Bill for the More General Diffusion of Knowledge" offered to the Virginia assembly on three different occasions. Horace Mann favored township school organization though he was vigorously opposed in this regard by rural residents of Massachusetts. Not surprisingly when the Old Northwest states made provisions for common schools, considerable discussion ensued regarding the appropriate governmental form for rural schools: small rural districts or larger township systems. Ohio and Indiana decided to adopt township district plans when they embraced the common school concept in the early 1850s.

The township system has been castigated and characterized as an evil plot by professional educators to centralize or ur-

banize the administration of rural schooling. [48] To explore the
validity of this interpretation, we may find it useful to identify
who the advocates of the township system were, what was to
be achieved through township organization, and how local residents
under this system benefitted.

As noted earlier, the common school reformers of the antebellum
Middle West were predominantly clerics of the Calvinist
tradition. Most reformers being ministers, and many politicians
as well, the term *professional educators* scarcely seems
applicable to such an early phase of evolution. It may have
been that some of these advocates hoped a common school
system would eliminate thousands of local school board members
belonging to popular denominations at odds with Puritanism.
Perhaps they hoped that a broader electoral base would
benefit Calvinist elements in the local population. But given
midwestern demographics, this would seem to have been a
remote hope at best. Townships, after all, remain one of our
smallest political entities. To infer that a shift from small districts
to township organization was centralization, as some have
done, is misleading. Bureaucratic centralization suggests that
decision-makers are remote and unknown to the people whom
these decisions affect. Townships were not so big that a person
living on one side for any length of time did not know a person
living on the other side. Township systems were neighborhood
systems. The advantage that most early reformers saw in township
organization was that it permitted equitable distribution
of local funds to all neighborhood schools. Additionally, the
matter of schoolhouse location might be handled in a way that
would reduce the distance some children had to travel due to
inequitable circumstances.

While the form varied from state to state with respect to
township systems put into place, a few common characteristics
suggest how the concept worked. Townships were divided
into subdistricts depending on the size of the township and
its population. Board members were elected to the township
board at large, and one trustee was elected by the voters of
each subdistrict. (In Ohio, however, there was a small, three-man
subdistrict board.) Voters of the subdistricts met at least

annually and discussed the needs of the subdistrict and directed their representative (the subdistrict trustee) to present these needs to the township board. As a result, township board minutes are filled with requests from "subdirectors," as the subdistrict trustees frequently were called, for furniture, books, brooms, stovepipes, paint, plaster, blackboards, globes, water buckets, and dippers. In most instances, the township boards approved subdistrict requests. In one instance in Iowa, the township board put a thirty-dollar monthly salary cap for hiring male teachers in the district. When a subdistrict trustee complained that he could not hire the teacher the subdistrict wanted for that amount, this subdistrict was authorized to spend thirty-seven dollars per month. It happened just as often, however, that the subdirectors would push for lower salary caps. In subdistrict 2 of Lockridge Township in Jefferson County, Iowa, the voters resolved "that the subdirector use his influence to get the teachers tax levy as light as possible consistent with the wants of the school."[49]

Eventually, Iowa, North Dakota, and South Dakota made provisions to implement the township system. All of these states, however, gradually gave townships the right to go back to the system of small independent districts. Minnesota, Wisconsin, and the Upper Peninsula of Michigan gave local districts the option to disband in favor of township organization. In areas where settlement was sparse, such as the northern reaches of these states, the township system was popular.

Interpreting farmer resistance to township organization as a gut response to a system inherently undemocratic is, once again, misleading. Clearly, midwestern farmers who resisted common schooling probably preferred close neighborhood control over schooling emanating from a slightly larger neighborhood. But why? What did the township system do in states like Indiana and Iowa? The system made it possible for children in districts composed of marginal farmland to receive the same funds as children living in districts composed of highly productive land. In many instances, the system increased the walking distance for some children who had lived close to the schoolhouse in order to reduce the walking distance for others.

In short, advocates of township organization set out to bring an element of democracy to a system that often worked against it.

This is not to suggest, however, that the township system was particularly successful in this regard. For example, when eight male heads of household representing fifteen school-age children living more than two miles from subdistrict 2 petitioned the Fairview Township board for the creation of a new subdistrict, "the question was argued at some length but a final vote failed to cary—some members claiming it to be an unjust demand, exaggerated in its presentation and that most signers were transient residents." Tenant farmers fared little better with the township system than they did with the independent district system. The point here is that too much has been made of the "imposition" of the township system. It was little more than simply a different form of neighborhood control over local schools. There were no substantial changes made to rural schooling as a result of its adoption. The township trustees were the same farmers that sat on earlier independent district or subscription school boards.[50]

When one examines what little the township system accomplished in Indiana, the only midwestern state where an effective township system developed, the goals of the reformers become clear. "Indiana spent more money on teachers' salaries and school buildings than most of the Midwestern states," noted one historian.[51] Indiana had one of the best records of all midwestern states for teacher retention.[52] Yet the Hoosier state fared less well compared with neighboring states in terms of adult literacy rates and the average length of school terms. While it is clear that Indiana educational reformers were not out to reduce the length of school terms or increase the amount of adult illiteracy, they did determine purposefully to use the township organization to alleviate the tremendous inequalities that existed between neighboring districts. Should a child be prevented from obtaining the quality education provided in a neighboring district merely because those who controlled the school in her district opposed the common school concept? Most advocates of the township system in state departments of education across the Midwest did not think so. Their solution, however, judging by the township district experience in Iowa and Indiana, did not produce the desired results.

This examination of circumstances surrounding the lack of permanence and free schools in the Midwest suggests that the decades of struggle over whether or not to establish a common school system was neither an extraordinarily long period of time nor an extraordinarily short one. The view that the debate was short when one considers all the extenuating circumstances of frontier life should be juxtaposed against the view that it took so long to establish free schools because many rural dwellers were "hating and puerile" and wished to be left alone in their "ignorance," as those early educational historians (cited in the first chapter) viewed these circumstances.[53] Once again, the reality probably falls somewhere in the middle.

Concerning the question of democracy, we now see that many variables emerged to shape rural resistance to free schools. A certain utility to controlling local school affairs, via the auspices of one denomination or via a subscription system, had very little to do with democracy.[54] But we ought not dismiss all connections between resistance to free schools and an impulse for democracy. This becomes clearer if we look once again at a question posed at the beginning of this chapter. What was in the minds of those who authored the Ordinances of 1785 and 1787? Were they trying to sell land or protect their vision of the newly created nation? The Calvinist clerical fervor for free schools suggests something more in the common school concept than a boost to real estate sales. Those farmers who rejected the centralized, urban, and often Calvinist-directed state departments of education may have resisted not because the system would have hindered their ability to control who received what kind of education, but because their neighborhoods were genuinely opposed to the values espoused by the architects of the free school systems. Given a homogeneous neighborhood, the issue of control at the local level may have been insignificant. In such instances, raising the flag of local democracy to protest the common school concept would have been a legitimate expression of democracy.

After the Civil War, resistance to free schools faded relatively quickly across the Middle West. But various reforms associated with the concept continued to meet with resistance from rural districts until well into the next century. Generally, however, the business of such districts became routinized, almost predictable. At the annual school meetings, the white male taxable residents would meet, elect or reelect at least one district school board member to a three-year term, decide how much money to tax themselves for the coming school year, decide how many months they would keep a school and whether the teacher they would hire should be male or female, and decide whether they should standardize textbooks, as well as deciding who would supply the fuel for the coming year, if they should build a privy, if they should move the house to a new location, or if they should repair the building or issue bonds to finance a new one. The ramifications associated with these decisions will be examined and analyzed in the next chapter.

3
Community Gatekeepers
*The School Board Men
of the Rural Midwest*

Many accounts of the rural school experience in the nineteenth and early twentieth centuries seem to depend heavily on the assumption that neighborhood efforts to protect local control over schooling were necessarily more democratic than the centralization that came out of the Progressive era. As a consequence, they have celebrated local rural districts as "invaluable laboratories of democracy" and local school board members as "democratic localists." But if we take the word *democracy* to mean that all or even most of the people in a given locale had some decision-making power in the affairs of the school district, then utilizing the term *democratic* as synonymous with majority participation in rural school governance is at best a misnomer.[1]

The most obvious shortcoming in this regard was the exclusion of women from the affairs of the school district for most of the nineteenth century. As the teaching profession feminized, women's enforced silence on educational issues became a paradox increasingly difficult to rationalize. Frontier regions were the first to extend to women the right to vote at school district meetings. Dakota Territory provided for this in 1879 and two years later made it legal for women to hold the office of county superintendent of schools. Wisconsin extended the right of women to vote at annual school meetings in 1885; Kansas followed in 1889. However, Wisconsin denied women the right to vote in these elections if they were classified as paupers.[2]

Generally, the states of the Midwest first made provision for women to become board members or county superintendents and then debated the pros and cons of extending the right to vote at school elections. Indiana provides a good example. In 1891 a law was passed making women eligible to hold school offices. However, the state superintendent of instruction doubted the constitutionality of this law. He wrote that a female county superintendent "'will find herself confronted by our state constitution,'" which indicates that one may not become a county officer if he is not an elector. Women were not electors. In fact, it was not until after the nineteenth amendment was ratified in Indiana that women were allowed to vote in school elections. In this regard Indiana is the extreme instance. In general, however, the older states of the Middle West were the slowest to move toward democracy in the local school district. Illinois made provisions to include women in 1891, Ohio in 1904. However, several states, including Ohio, limited the voice of women to the election of board members and restricted their voting privilege "on such questions as special tax levy, bond issue, erection of buildings, etc." Michigan first extended the vote on school affairs to women in 1893. However, a year later the law was found unconstitutional. It was 1909 before another bill of this sort was passed and allowed to stand.[3]

While the states of the Old Northwest were debating whether to allow women to vote at school elections, the states of the trans-Mississippi West were receiving valuable contributions from women in capacities far more influential than that of teacher. Sarah Christie Stevens was elected superintendent of Blue Earth County, Minnesota, in 1892, running on the "Alliance and Prohibition" ticket. Stevens was prominent in education circles and was a moving force in the Minnesota temperance movement.[4] Linda Slaughter became the Burleigh County superintendent of schools headquartered in Bismarck, Dakota Territory, in 1877, several years before the legislature made provision for female school officers. Like Stevens,

Slaughter went on to become the leader of the state's temperance movement. In 1869 Iowan Julia Addington became the first woman in the United States to hold the position of county superintendent. Laura J. Eisenhuth became North Dakota's state superintendent of schools in 1893, the first female to hold this position in the states of the Midwest.

Despite these noteworthy examples, female county superintendents were rare in the states of the Old Northwest during the period under study. Indeed, females only infrequently ascended to positions on local school boards before the 1920s. In a school district just outside Madison, Wisconsin, an all-male school board saw fit to pass a motion requesting that the "Social Civic Ladies have refreshments for the next school meeting."[5] And this was in 1912. The mechanisms that perpetuated a patriarchal, agrarian social system were indeed pervasive.

One historian of Midwest rural schools has said that "it is doubtful that there was a better example anywhere of the effectiveness of democracy than the Midwestern rural independent school districts."[6] A close look at the treatment of women, particularly in the older states of the Midwest, seems to suggest that this historian had a peculiar definition of democracy if it entailed the systematic exclusion of half the population. Even if we refrain from severely critiquing the exclusion of women from the concerns of the school district, the supposition of democratic school districts and schoolmen is still problematic.

Women were not the only excluded population. Generally, during the period under study, participation in school district affairs was limited to white, male taxable residents. Tenant farmers, black or white, were legally prohibited from voting in school elections or at school meetings in most states. Iowa Territory's 1840 school law clearly specified the qualifications for voting in the local school district: "Every white male inhabitant of the age of twenty-one years, residing in such district, liable to pay a school district tax, shall be entitled to vote at any district meeting."[7] Ohio, Michigan, Indiana, and Illinois had similar qualifications during the antebellum years. Participation in the affairs of the school district required property qualifications for white males at a time when such restrictions had been removed from general elections.

Though the rhetoric of school legislation during the 1870s and 1880s began to sound more democratic, state governments exercised caution in extending a school voice to the mobile of midwestern society. Conditions for rural blacks improved after the Fourteenth Amendment was ratified, at least on paper, until *Plessy vs. Ferguson* allowed districts the right to segregate children into separate schools. Wisconsin opened up the vote at school meetings to any who had the vote in general elections but added that for school elections, the prospective voter needed "a fixed and permanent abode as contradistinguished from a mere temporary locality of existence." The status of tenant farmers was subject to the correct interpretation of this clause.[8]

Indiana opened the affairs of the school by including "all taxpayers, male and female, except married women and minors . . . who are *liable* to pay tax, either poll or property." Though these stipulations passed through the legislature in 1873, they did not significantly alter the status of poor tenant farmers with respect to the farmers' participation in the local district. Michigan retained the property qualifications through the 1870s, dispensed with them in the 1880s, but stipulated, as was often so for women, that "a person who has no property within the school district liable to assessment for school taxes has no right to vote when raising of money by tax is in question." Minnesota extended participation in school district affairs but kept a few key provisions reserved for "'freeholders, or those holding real property'" beyond the turn of the century. "'These only are authorized to call special meetings; to sign petitions for change of district boundary; to sign petitions for rehearing in change of district boundaries, and to sign petitions to consolidate districts.'"[9] In creative ways, a minority among those who lived and worked in the rural Midwest kept the institution of schooling theirs to control and manipulate. The affairs of the local church, too, were under their watchful eye.

A Baptist congregation in Attica, Indiana, expelled Laura Martin in 1871 "'for dancing, breaking promises, and unfaithfulness.'" Just as church elders could come together and expel a member from the local congregation for anything from "'failure to attend worship regularly to moral delinquency,'" these same men held similar power with the local school, a point that will be taken up in the next chapter. [10]

In this way it could seem like an act of generosity when a district clerk in rural Chippewa County, Minnesota, wrote in his minutes in 1889 that it was "moved and carried that those present who are not legal voters in the Dist. be admitted to a seat in the house and allowed to take part in the debate." In rural Stanton County, Nebraska, however, a newly elected board member discovered that he had failed "to qalifie for office of Director on account [of] his election being made illegal by bringing in voters Andrew Baker and others being nontaxpayers of the Dist." The existing records of local school boards are skimpy at best; however, sometimes they hold clues to discussions not explicitly "written up" in the clerk's minutes. On 7 August 1900, a board clerk in rural Dane County, Wisconsin, wrote that "another [in] the district wanded free tex boocks, vot was lost." [11] The Populist demand for free textbooks might be acceptable in the Dakotas or Nebraska, but the established farmers of Wisconsin wanted no part of this. Most local Wisconsin districts, governed as they were by families of long standing, continually rejected petitions to buy texts for all the district's schoolchildren beyond 1918.

The clerk's record book at District 5, Township 6, in Jasper County, Illinois, reveals something of the effect of allowing women a voice at the annual school meetings. It is difficult to say how widespread this phenomenon was, for most clerks took no notice of who or how many attended their annual meetings. The District 5 clerk, however, did both. Throughout the 1880s and early 1890s the school meeting generally transpired with between five and ten people in attendance. After 1895, however, there were very often as many as forty people present, over half of them women. [12] It is possible, perhaps likely, that the newly acquired voice of women in school affairs elevated the concern of all involved.

School affairs held much to be concerned about. For example, when a joint district was formed between parts of Lodi and West Point Townships in Wisconsin, trouble ensued over where to locate the schoolhouse—or to use the language of Lodi school superintendent W. M. Bartholomew, "a *war* commenced some wanted here some there, till finally a compromise was had and that thing fixed." However, a few were not in favor of the compromise. Bartholomew explained that "some were still disposed to fight and try to disorganize the district" and "prevailed on the new superintendent of West Point to set off a new district running on the town line, and thus destroy the joint district and cut off the probability of either having a school."[13] Incidents such as these reflect the failure of certain individuals in rural Midwest society to act in a democratic fashion. Ironically, it often took an undemocratic, centralized, bureaucratic school governance system, in this instance the appointed office of the state superintendent, to persuade local residents to behave democratically.

In 1868 George Nichols gave an acre and a half of land to District 3 of Blooming Grove Township, Dane County, Wisconsin. In return, of course, the schoolhouse was moved to this site. This was common across the states of the Middle West. However, the donation of land was usually little more than a ploy to get the schoolhouse near one's home, and very infrequently was it given in an effort to situate the school in the center of a district. In this instance several of the residents were upset with the Nichols location. A special meeting was called to rescind an earlier vote to move the school to Nichols's land. The special meeting, curiously, was held in the home of George Nichols. The motion to rescind did not carry. One resident, Alexander Campbell, was so irate over the decision that he went to the schoolhouse and broke down the door to gain entrance, although what he wanted therein is not known. At the next annual meeting it "was agreed and ordered that the board prosecute Alexander Campbell for tresspas." Campbell later became a candidate for the school board but was never successful at winning election. [14]

In Sugar Grove Township, Dallas County, Iowa, a group of petitioners from subdistrict 8 asked that their schoolhouse be moved to another location. D. F. Rogers and S. Edmondson were the spokespersons for the petitioners at school board meetings throughout 1870 and 1871. Refused by the township board, they petitioned the state superintendent. Learning of this, the township board wrote to the state superintendent reminding him that "the power to locate [a] school house site is vested exclusively with the [township] Board of Directors subject only to their power." The state superintendent agreed. Dismayed, Rogers obtained a writ of mandamus requiring the attendance of the township board president and vice-president at a special meeting to be held 18 March 1871. On that day the township board clerk noted that "D. F. Rogers and S. Edmondson could not be satisfied until the secretary read all the minutes of the past year upon which they could not find much to make capital out of and finally left very much dissatisfied with the meeting." When they were gone, a sarcastic motion was made by one board member "that the citizens vote Mr. Rogers thanks for his eloquential speeches before the board and his trouble in serving the writ of mandamus." Another quickly added an amendment to this, "that D. F. Rogers take the position of Constable Supervisor and guardian in general for the Township of Sugar Grove, Dallas County." This motion and amendment was "approved by many citizens." [15]

It is likely that no issue caused more conflict with regard to rural schooling than the question of where to locate the schoolhouse. Its equitable placement near the center of the district was a goal not often accomplished. Those with power and wealth enough to give away land had an advantage over others with respect to where the school would be situated. It is remarkable how often the site of a school was successfully changed so that it would be situated on land owned by a school board member. [16] One historian of Midwest rural education has written that "in the vast majority of Midwestern school districts . . . many a small schoolhouse came to sit where it sat not because it was centrally located but because of other considerations, which frequently delayed the building and led to community fights that left bitter memories long afterward."[17]

Just across the township from the Nichols school, Joint District 9 constructed a schoolhouse on land belonging to board chairman Christian Uphoff. To the south of the Nichols and Uphoff schools, in Rock County, Wisconsin, Ezra Foot began the process of forming a district in Center Township by donating a parcel of his land for the schoolhouse. Board chairman O. A. Thompson of rural Chippewa County, Minnesota, led a successful effort to change the site of the school to a parcel of his land. The examples are endless. In fact, the exceptions in the historical record are those incidences where democratic processes appear to have worked. For example, a special meeting was called in District 34 of Chippewa County "to consider a petition to move the school to the centre of the district." Regrettably, the records of this event are so sparse that it is not possible to discern whether the petitioners were successful.[18]

A schoolhouse in Marion Township, Olmsted County, Minnesota, was inequitably located on the western side of District 59. The children of one family in the district were forced to walk over three miles if they wished to attend school. The parents tried to send their children to another public school only two miles away, but this district felt it could not accommodate any "outside scholars." As a result, the children did not attend any school, and the parents were exempted from compulsory attendance laws because they did not live within a "reasonable distance" of their district school.[19]

States with township systems sometimes solved the problem of outside scholars, caused by families living a considerable distance from the school, by electing to construct a new road that would accommodate the children of these families. This alternative emerges frequently in the school records of Iowa and Indiana but is almost nonexistent in states that maintained schools using the independent district system. But again, because the township had the power to build roads does not mean that this solution was often embraced. In Lucas Township of Johnson County, Iowa, a group of petitioners requested the construction of a road "for the proper access to the schoolhouse in subdistrict #5 as there is at least 15 or 20 persons of school age that are allmost deprived of all school privileges for they cannot get to school in a less distance than 2 and a half to 3 miles by the nearest road." After some discussion, the board tabled this request. The matter came up every year for several years, and in each instance the request was either defeated or tabled. Even in Iowa and Indiana, then, the problem of outside scholars remained. In Fairview Township of Jones County, Iowa, the district board resolved "that all schollars residing out side of the Fairview Twp that come to our schools shal obey the rules of the school or take their books and go home."[20]

Every rural district was sooner or later forced to formulate a policy concerning outside scholars. The issue is raised at some point in almost all existing school district records. Sometimes a tuition fee was charged, sometimes these pupils were admitted free, and sometimes they were not admitted at all. The fickle nature of rural boards on this issue was sometimes very troubling to teachers and students, as the remarks from rural teacher Sarah Huftalen's diary indicate: "Verna is greatly concerned now to know if she can come here (being outside the district) for 2 more years. So I think it Mrs. Hood has told her they would need to walk straight because I did not have to have them [in the school]. And Mr. Cocking said enough the other day to make one think that the board will intend to enforce last year's minutes [of the annual board meeting] in regard to those living outside [of the district]."[21] Clearly, the structure of rural education meant that the children of some farmers would have to walk farther than others. The often strange configurations in districts suggest that their evolution was a result of power dynamics rather than democratic action. The localism of midwestern rural ideology had great potential for exclusion and was likely more often used for this end than any other. Those who lived on the edge of certain districts may have simply been unlucky. Or they may have been tenant farmers, or immigrants, or members of a locally unpopular religious denomination.

In some states that received heavy foreign immigration into rural areas, such as Minnesota and Wisconsin, the policy on outside scholars became almost synonymous with "foreign" scholars. The few Norwegian or German families in a district would probably be found living either on the edge of a district or a good distance from an inequitably placed schoolhouse. Consequently, the parents of foreign scholars often found that the school in a neighboring district was closer than their own, but these children were not necessarily welcome there. "No foreign scholars," wrote one district clerk in Minnesota. A Wisconsin clerk noted that his district resolved "to receive no foreign scholar into the school for the next year unless they board in the district."[22]

At different times and in different places foreign immigrants represented the majority population in the school district. This caused problems of another sort. Obviously, in this situation foreigners could control the school board. Interpreters were sometimes needed at the annual meetings. Yankee settlers often felt oppressed by the decisions made by immigrants who spoke another language. Asa Felt, a township superintendent in Wisconsin, wrote the state superintendent to describe the circumstances in his "Norwegian district," as he called it. Felt explained that there were "several American families—residents of the county for six years—who have during that time been entirely deprived of the benefit of school." These residents wanted their property "set off into an adjoining district."[23]

Where Yankee and foreign factions were about equal, difficulties frequently became unmanageable, as in District 2 of Herman Township, Dodge County, Wisconsin. Nicholas Bernard and Bartholomew Ringle were German immigrants who served as district treasurer and clerk, respectively, during the early 1850s. Z. Child, a Yankee, was the board director. As winter term approached in late November 1851, the board members found themselves without a suitable applicant for the position of teacher. Ringle, who had been a teacher for many years in Germany, obtained a certificate from the township superintendent and together with Bernard, hired himself as the district teacher. Child, the Yankee board director, was furious that his colleagues would take such action without his consent.

Accusations were made. Child wrote to the state superintendent and complained that Ringle "could not speak good English [and] did not understand grammar." He noted also that there were "17 American and 15 German scholars" and that "this number is Nearly correct." He was adamant in asserting that the wishes of the district were for "an English school not a forked-tongue one." Child found a sympathetic ally in the person of George Fox, the township superintendent who had granted Ringle the teaching certificate. Fox wrote to Ringle explaining that when he issued the license he "had not the least idea that you would force your self upon the District against the will of so large a number."

When Ringle and other German residents appealed to the state superintendent, their description of the circumstances was quite different. First, they went door to door across the district counting the number of school-age children. Their tally amounted to twenty-nine German and seventeen American scholars. They also pointed out that four-fifths of all tax money raised in the district came from German households. They noted that when Child was chosen as board director, he claimed to some "that he could rule over the district," and that another opponent of Ringle claimed that "he would go against the school as long as he lived." Thirty male German residents signed a petition saying that "we are all well satisfied with Mr. B. Ringle to teach our District School." Additionally, Ringle had the support of three Yankee families. He explained to the state superintendent: "Director Child stated before me and [in] some other places that they are Americans and the land belongs to them, and we are Germans and have no rights in this country. Now if we have no right except paying money, I know the oppinion of our people, but Mr. Sutlief, Mr. Godfrey and Mr. Cole are Americans and each of them have children [sent] to the school . . . they know well enough that the complains are as black as the night." Ringle also added that if "the people cannot have the privilige of hiring their own Teacher, they will cast their vote against raising any more school money at all."[24]

Of course, language was not the only problem presented by "foreign" scholars. Most of the farmer immigrants in the Midwest were not part of the English reform tradition that so dominated American Protestantism. Scandinavian and German Lutherans, along with German Catholics, were often the objects of suspicion and fear. As post-Civil War litigation continued to secularize instruction, anxiety over foreigners not subject to "proper" Christian socialization in the classroom increased, clearly a legacy of the sectarianism in agrarian ideology.[25] Ultimately, laws were passed in Illinois and Wisconsin designed to severely impair the progress of parochial schools. Passed as compulsory attendance bills, Illinois' Edwards Law of 1889 and Wisconsin's Bennett Law of the same year stipulated that while parochial schools could operate and parents could fulfill their children's schooling obligation by sending them there, parents could do this only if the parochial school was within the boundaries of their legal school district. Also, the instruction given in the parochial schools had to be in English.

When these clauses of the compulsory school laws were discovered, there was a grassroots outcry against them. An Anti-Bennett Law League in Wisconsin drew support from Lutherans and Catholics, creating a rare instance of nineteenth-century Protestant-Catholic cooperation. Many Republicans who enacted the restrictive school legislation in 1889 found themselves voted out of office in 1890. The Bennett Law was then promptly repealed, while Illinois did the same to the Edwards Law in 1893. The party of Calvinist clerics that dominated the common school movement and legislatures in the states of the Middle West began to show cracks by the late 1880s. There would be defections to the Democratic camp as well as to the growing People's Party. Yet the states of the Old Northwest would remain largely in the Republican fold, while the states of the trans-Mississippi West leaned in the opposite direction.

The struggles over religious instruction in common schools inevitably led toward greater secularization. This trend may have been complemented by Darwinian thinking. Many common school advocates sought to apply the "rigor" of science to the education enterprise. The Protestant legacy of schooling for spiritual advance was rapidly falling by the wayside. Curiously, Lutherans and Catholics, outside mainstream American Protestantism, were perhaps just as disillusioned with the growing secularization of public schools as popular pietist groups were.

Catholic Archbishop John Ireland urged those gathered at the National Education Association convention in St. Paul in 1889 "'to permeate the regular state schools with the religion of the majority of the children of the land be it as Protestant as Protestantism can be . . . it is no honor to the American republic that she be more than any other nation foremost in efforts to divorce religion from the schools.'"[26] But Ireland also advocated the view that because parochial schools were providing the secular education for the state, they deserved appropriate support from the state's school fund. This suggestion was less hardily endorsed than the first. Many Lutherans and Catholics, outside America's religious mainstream, saw the secularization of common schools as a catalyst to create their own church-affiliated schools.

For example, most North Dakota counties, but not all, operated with a township district system. District 7 of Mercer County contained four country schools. In 1916 the county superintendent of schools discovered that one of these was down to an average enrollment of six, another was at about eight, a third consisted of a teacher with no pupils, and the "fourth building had neither teacher nor pupils." District 7 created a German Lutheran school that averaged between forty and fifty pupils per day in the fall. Classes were held in a church building. E. R. Thomas, Mercer County's school superintendent, inspected the school and found that it was taught by a Reverend Buck, a Lutheran minister; that Buck had no American credentials that would give him the right to teach; that German was the primary language of the school and English, secondary; and that "Buck is more German than American and that his bias and prejudice in favor of Germany prevents him from teaching patriotism and love for our country—American ideals and standards."[27]

World War I escalated tensions in Mercer County and elsewhere concerning the German language and religions and the German presence in parochial schools. In some districts, however, the German population so dominated a geographic area that there was no aggrieved minority population to confront teachers like Buck and Ringle. In these instances, the insecurity produced by America's entrance into the Great War helped to drum up opposition artificially. One interested Nebraska citizen took note of which country schools were not properly displaying the American flag. In an anonymous letter to the county superintendent, someone thought it necessary to ask, "Will you kindly notify school districts #15, #97, of the kind of poles. Hight of poles. & the days the flag must fly. If these districts are *not patriotic* it is time we are finding out." Late in 1917 the Nebraska State Council of Defense sent a circular to all county superintendents requesting information concerning "the parochial and religious schools of the county."[28]

Scandinavian Lutherans appear to have been more amenable to American public schooling. Certainly, they were concerned about proper religious instruction for their children. But generally, they were willing to utilize the vacation periods of public schools to conduct their own "Norwegian school." There were times, however, when this was not possible. Norwegian students in District 84 of Pleasant Grove Township in Olmsted County, Minnesota, were leaving the school for over a month in October to attend the Norwegian school. Because state funding hinged on average daily attendance, the school board evidently discussed ways to combat this situation. Soon a Norwegian woman was hired as teacher, and "one hour each day [was] given for the study of Norwegian."[29]

Sometimes Scandinavians held numerical majorities in rural districts. In Minnesota, for example, it is almost as common to find school board minutes in Norwegian as it is to find them in German. This was true even beyond the turn of the century, although finding minutes in any language other than English is rare. [30] Sometimes confrontation between ethnic groups was not precisely over school matters. The residents of District 34 in Chippewa County, Minnesota, "voted that the Black Duck Lake Scandinavian Temperance Society should not be allowed to use the schoolhouse for their meetings."[31]

School board members were charged with the protection of school property. Sometimes this was construed to mean denying certain groups the convenience of meeting in the local schoolhouse. Some state statutes were very casual about groups' using the school for public meetings. Illinois and Michigan stipulated that board members could open the schoolhouse to whatever groups they "may deem proper." Indiana was more cautious and demanded that board members give "equal rights and privileges to all religious denominations and political parties, without any regard whatever to their numerical strength" in the district. [32]

The use of the schoolhouse for public meetings was not a significant issue until after the Civil War across the Middle West. Even then it was not particularly troublesome, although as the century progressed there were objections raised here and there over the use of a public school building for Sunday school. As a consequence, legislators addressed the question and clearly sided with religious groups who wished to use public school property for Sunday school instruction. The legality of various religious groups utilizing the school for this purpose was well established in the Middle West before the turn of the century. Sunday school was sometimes conducted on a weekday evening, a weekend, or sometimes after regular school hours on a weekday. One district in North Dakota dismissed Catholics early on Friday and then conducted Sunday school lessons. [33]

This practice was not always popular. A lively board meeting was held in Spencer Brook Township of Isanti County, Minnesota, on 20 September 1894. The meeting was called specifically to address the question of whether the District 7 schoolhouse ought to be used for public meetings. The first order of business was to stipulate "that every one that whished to speek on closing the schoolhouse for meetings should be given a *chance*." After much discussion it was finally voted that the schoolhouse should remain closed for all meetings.[34]

Some twelve years later, however, there was a group using the house for Sunday school instruction. The school board in this district received a petition asking that the schoolhouse be closed for all meetings once again. This time a board member advised the Sunday school advocates to offer their own petition received a petition asking for the use of the building. At the next board meeting "a petittion signed by a majority of the leagle voters in the District sworn to by Lilly Goodwin was Presented. Asking to have the school House used for Divine worship Sunday School . . . after considering said petittion on motion it was resolved that we grant the Petittion . . . with the understanding that Parties arraging said meeting furnish their own wood for heat." Then, perhaps as an afterthought, the clerk added, "and also [fuel for] light."[35]

In High Forest Township, Olmsted County, a petition signed by five school district residents asked the local board not to allow political meetings in the schoolhouse. The petition was considered on the evening of 19 October 1872. Three votes were taken before the petitioners acquiesced, and a majority decision was reached allowing the schoolhouse to be opened to various groups. Sometimes the decision to allow such meetings was made more palatable by charging an interested group a fee of, for example, "$1 per night for activities," although in Dane County, Wisconsin, the use of the schoolhouse was made "free for church activities." Most often, however, no fees were charged, and it was simply stipulated, as in Isanti County, that groups must "furnish their own wood."[36]

It is likely that the Chippewa County residents who voted to restrict the use of the schoolhouse by the Black Duck Lake Scandinavian Temperance Society were German in national origin. This supposition is consistent with Minnesota settlement patterns. It is also likely that the Scandinavians and Germans in this district were participating in a temperance debate while scarcely cognizant of the cultural foundations from which it came. As the debate gained strength during the 1830s and 1840s due to the ghettoization of Boston and other large seaboard cities, the temperance movement coincided with the birth of America's common school movement. In both, Protestant clergy played leadership roles. Significantly, the Methodists and Baptists that so dominated the population of the midwestern states were as conspicuous in their leadership of the temperance movement as in their absence from leadership of the common school movement.

This may be partially explained by differing ideological adaptations to changes in political and economic circumstances both in England and the United States. Unlike the situation in England, American Baptists and Methodists were not forced to come to grips with the ramifications of industrialism until after the Civil War. Given their century-long tradition of suspicion reserved for education-based religious structure, it is not surprising that these groups spent their reform energies in another arena. The Women's Christian Temperance Union and its male counterpart, the Anti-Saloon Law League, were both begun and maintained by fervent Methodists. Because of the American Methodists' emphasis on simple theology, they were at the same time well-equipped to win souls on the frontier and ill-equipped to orchestrate state departments of education. Indeed, American Methodist preachers wholeheartedly embraced Wesley's dictum from his first discipline, "You have nothing to do but save souls." Temperance crusades, unlike common schools, worked directly to that end. [37]

Old-line American Puritanism became less and less distinctive in its opposition to the spread of evangelism in American Protestantism. Virulent inter-Protestant debate dissipated in the last quarter of the nineteenth century as Catholic court action against Protestantism in the schools resulted in more and more secularization. These circumstances seemed to have worked catalytically on the evolution of pan-Protestant common school agenda evidenced by the introduction of temperance study into the common school curriculum. By 1895 all the states of the Midwest required that some portion of the school day should be given to the study of the evils of alcohol. [38]

It is interesting that even a reform that one would think

would engender very little inter-Protestant division (at least when compared to something as potentially explosive as dominion over the curriculum of free schools) such as temperance did in fact do just that. While the temperance agenda (like the common school agenda) was ostensibly nondenominational and counted representatives from all religious groups among its advocates, the temperance movement nonetheless was not immune to charges of promoting sectarianism by trying to advance the interests of a particular denomination. The Methodists embraced the movement to a great degree, as did popular Baptists. But certain groups, like anti-mission Baptists, often forbade their members to participate in temperance societies. Young Presbyterians and Congregationalists were swept up in the evangelical fervor that surrounded the movement, but church fathers noted that many congregants were heavily involved in the liquor traffic, making it difficult to make a denominational stand. According to John Allen Krout, some claimed that temperance reform was "a cloak for the activity of certain sects which were busily engaged in gathering the membership of temperance societies into their own ranks."[39]

The eventual embrace of temperance by old-line Calvinist denominations marks the final stage, in my view, of the evolution toward Protestant unity on common schooling. The Puritan religious tradition espoused by so many antebellum common school advocates declined dramatically in the postbellum Middle West. Old-line Calvinist denominations became increasingly indistinguishable from other evangelical or pietistic groups, enhancing the temperance movement's national power base. From this position, temperance advocates could successfully transfer elements of the movement into the common school curriculum. At this point it is reasonable to cast the religious scene on education as something generally two-sided: Protestants versus Catholics. Since popular perception seemed to maintain that alcohol abuse was the near-exclusive province of a few ethnic groups, notably Germans and Irish Catholics, and since the use of alcohol remained an integral part of the Catholic mass, it is fair to suppose that a small measure of anti-Catholicism remained behind these curricular reform proposals. Temperance instruction during the 1890s, therefore, should be viewed in the context of other anti-Catholic developments, such as the growth of the American Protective Association across the states of the Middle West.

A group of Scandinavian farmers in Chippewa County did not simply meet and decide to form a temperance society, just as other residents in the district did not simply meet and decide not to let them use the schoolhouse. These occurrences were historically grounded in the ideological traditions of various groups—the strength of which may very well have overridden any inclination to consider the matter democratically.

The school board men of the rural Midwest served as community guardians in their local neighborhoods. Together with other taxable residents, they had the power to make sure that the school promoted intergenerational stability. The various forms of intolerance that were manifested in decisions about where to locate the school, who would be allowed to vote in a school meeting, who could use the schoolhouse during non-school hours, who was eligible for instruction in the school, and what language this instruction would be in were not based on arbitrary likes and dislikes. These decisions hinged on traditions that evolved according to what certain farmers supposed would be the best set of neighborhood circumstances. Institutional manipulation at the local level was a small part of the process whereby a minority population came to own land and possess the ability to pass it on to their descendants.

In any given rural district during a ten-year span, ten families may have lived in and owned ten separate households. Conservatively, we might hypothesize that three additional households were rented by tenant families. If we suggest that the three tenant families moved on after two years and were replaced by three new families who in their turn moved on after a couple of years, it is possible that within the ten-year span the district was occupied by fifteen tenant families as opposed to ten land-owning families. Some tenant farmers stayed longer than two years, but many moved after one.

Faragher's work describing the settlement and persistence

rates of rural Sangamon County, Illinois, suggests that the above illustration is far too conservative. To demonstrate how mobile Midwest society was, he indicates that within a one-hundred-square mile vicinity along a creek in Sangamon County, only three families in ten listed on the 1830 census were still there ten years later. Rather than improving, the persistence rate dropped to two families in ten after the 1850 and 1860 censuses. These data suggest the magnitude of the gatekeeping chore entrusted to the school board men of the rural Midwest.[40]

Faragher does not focus on the manipulation of schooling as an instrument of community guardianship, but recognizes that manipulation could probably occur. Acknowledging the primacy of maintaining intergenerational stability within the rural neighborhood, Faragher concluded that subscription schools served the landowners of midwestern society by "discriminating against settlers too poor to pay the teacher."[41] This was so common in the antebellum Midwest that McGuffey discussed it in a matter-of-fact essay about a poor boy who abruptly stops attending school. "'Why?'" a classmate asks. "'Poverty,'" replies the teacher.[42]

The resistance of rural neighborhoods to the notion of free schools is more easily understood if one is able to view this resistance in the context of schooling as a vehicle to promote intergenerational stability. The purpose of denying women the right to participate in local affairs also becomes clear. Estate settlements would have become impossibly complicated if female as well as male heirs had a stake in the dispersal of family land. This type of patriarchy, along with the intolerance reserved for those with a different religious orientation, or those who spoke a different language, or even those with a different skin color, were all expedient, acceptable tenets of midwestern rural ideology.

When change was forced upon them in the guise of free schooling for all, the persistent families of Midwest society found ways to conserve their capacity for community guardianship. As noted earlier, schoolhouse location was used, restrictions on the number of people who might vote in school affairs was used, but perhaps nothing was quite as successful as the rural school board's refusal to provide free textbooks to all the students of the district. In this, as in other matters of equity, the states of the trans-Mississippi West led the way. As former victims of the exclusive dimensions of local manipulation in school affairs, the school legislations of the Great Plains states might predictably differ in structure from those of the Old Northwest states. In 1897 Nebraska became the first to require local districts to purchase free textbooks for all. A few other states earlier required local districts to purchase textbooks for "indigents." Of course, this type of publicly announced welfare was probably little utilized by those in need. [43]

The free textbook issue evolved naturally from the earlier question of text standardization. Concern over standardizing schoolbooks had been an integral feature of the free school debate in Massachusetts during the 1830s. It was far from resolved in the rural school districts of Iowa in 1882. In that year the Fairview Township district in Jones County decided to standardize textbooks in the district and were immediately forced to confront the complaints of families that already owned schoolbooks and were not inclined to buy additional titles. In the end they settled on "McGuffey's readers and spellers, Ray's Arithmetics and Monteith's Geography's finding said books can be had on equitable terms." In answer to the parents who opposed this standardization, they worked out an arrangement so that other books could be exchanged toward the purchase of the required books at "Hama's Store." In Lucas Township of Johnson County, the voters simply bypassed this debate with a "10 to 1 vote against standardizing textbooks." For many midwestern farmers, supplying free textbooks was just one more cost they would have to bear for the children of transients. [44]

The Farmers' Alliance that grew to a position of considerable strength in the Great Plains states during the 1880s consistently advocated legislation mandating the purchase of free textbooks. This issue had been a concern of the Grange movement a decade earlier. Some Kansas school districts were providing free textbooks for all children as early as the 1870s. In North Dakota, the Mandan *Pioneer* claimed that many "children of the state are kept from schools because of the cost of books." In response to Alliance agitation of this sort, most states in the Midwest dealt with the issue the same way they handled the question of prohibition, that is, "local option." Local option enabled some districts to refuse to provide textbooks for all students until well into the 1920s. Using specific decisions concerning free textbooks in the states of Wisconsin, Minnesota, and Nebraska as examples, we may see that the trend toward earlier equity in the newer states is immediately and rather strikingly apparent. [45]

It was common in rural Wisconsin school districts for the voters to decide "not to furnish free texts." Requests came as early as 1889, but such motions inevitably failed. It was not until the very end of the period under study that a few Wisconsin districts began to acquiesce on this issue. The earliest district record found indicating a district's willingness to supply free textbooks in Wisconsin is from 1909. [46] In Minnesota it is possible to find records that indicate an earlier acceptance of the free textbook issue. It is common to uncover information on districts that adopted a plan outlined by the state legislature in 1893. However, as in Wisconsin, the local districts were left to decide whether to adopt the plan. In Isanti County, one district "voted not to inforce the Free Textbook Sistem." Still, districts in Minnesota appear to have been more willing to do this. [47] Even before Nebraska's legal mandate for free textbooks in 1897, some local districts had earlier made provisions to supply them. District 35 in Harlan County "voted to supply the district with textbooks" at its annual meeting in 1880. This was far in advance of any such action in Minnesota or Wisconsin. [48] The large area of Nebraska land protected from taxation by homestead law makes this action in Harlan County even more significant.

The agenda of the typical school district meeting in the small rural district was not particularly complicated. Each year the three-year term of one of the three board members expired, and an election was required to fill the vacancy. Next, the treasurer would report how much money was on hand and how much the district could expect during the coming year from the state school fund. The amount needed over the sum of these totals was the amount the residents had to tax themselves. Of course, a very long list of variables could affect the amount levied. Should the district hire a male or female teacher for the next term? Should this teacher possess a third-, second-, or first-grade certificate? How many months would the next term be? Should they repair the old fence around the yard or build a new one? Should the schoolhouse be insured? If so, for how much? Should the schoolhouse be painted, or could it go one more year? How about building a privy "for the convenience of the scholars?" What about hiring someone to start the fires for the teacher, or should the teacher manage this herself? Should the district hire an older boy to haul water to the school or should they have a well dug? How much should they pay for supplying the winter fuel? What might be done about the plaster falling from the ceiling? Do the scholars need maps or a globe? When these questions were answered by a vote, a total dollar figure was projected, and the county superintendent of schools levied this amount according to the county assessor's valuation of local property.

During the period under study, the aesthetic value of a quaint schoolhouse in the country seems to have been of little concern. The people in small, nonconsolidated rural districts typically built frame houses after 1860 in the Old Northwest states and after 1890 in the newer states (although in some locations on the Great Plains sod houses continued to serve as schools into the twentieth century). Many of the consolidated districts in Indiana and Ohio, however, had the resources to build a schoolhouse of brick. Stone schoolhouses also existed, but generally, these were constructed in the vicinity of quarries where the proximity of the building material made it an inexpensive option for local school districts. Like the farmhouses and barns that dotted the rural landscape, the country schools were typically painted either white or red. The size of the school lot varied from a half-acre to two acres. Because there was a general unwillingness to allow the schoolhouse and yard to utilize prime farm ground, the site of the schoolhouse was often located on highly erodible ground at the top or bottom of a hill, or near a low-lying swampy area, or on some irregular, perhaps triangular patch created by the intersection of a field, a stand of timber, a rail line, or a winding gravel road.

Due to the less productive nature of the soil at the schoolhouse site, the schoolyard was often surrounded by pasture rather than cropland. This explains the prevalent concern with fence matters in the school records of rural districts. Though at least one historian has interpreted this concern as an effort to beautify the school site, it appears to have had more to do with an effort to protect the house and outhouses from cattle or sheep that could do considerable damage, say, to the stairs leading up to the house, or to the door of a privy, or to newly planted shade trees. The school board in one rural Wisconsin district decided that "the owner of [the] flock [of sheep?] found on the school yard shell be fined $2 per head for said flock and over half of [the] fine is [to] go to the person making the complaint." In another district the board "moved and carried that the peoples cattle that are caught within the inclosure of the school yard be liable to a fine of $1 Dollar for each such offense."[49]

In 1879 the Waveland Township board in Pottawattamie County, Iowa, grew tired of complaints about livestock getting into schoolyards. The board decided to pass the following resolution: "Resolved that it is hereby made the duty of each subdirector to have of all school property in his subdistrict, keeping the same in good and sufficient repair, and in those subdistricts where the schoolhouse is fenced, to keep said fence at all seasons of the year in a condition to turn all kinds of stock, and in case he shall at any time find any stock unlawfully within said fence or enclosure, he shall treat the same as estrays."[50] Within the schoolhouse a blackboard was deemed to be standard furniture, although teachers working without them sometimes painted a black rectangle on the wall and used it as a blackboard. A disillusioned county superintendent once commented after visiting a poor district school that "the blackboard is painted *Red.*"[51] In the early years, most districts used rough lumber to make crude benches for the scholars. However, as funds and conditions permitted, rural districts soon provided manufactured school desks.

Though a lime-base whitewash was sometimes used to "paint" the interior of the house, more often some color or another of actual paint covered the walls. The Minnesota Public Health Association Director suggested a "light tan, chrome yellow, or light grey" for the schoolhouse interior. In subdistrict 3 of Pleasant Valley Township in Johnson County, Iowa, it was ordered that the inside of the schoolhouse be painted "a lead coulour or something very near that coulour." A district clerk in rural Wisconsin was not so particular. He wrote in the board minutes that the inside of the house was to be painted "a light drab color." Painting was seldom a high priority in rural districts. Sometimes the residents of a district would request that the board members see to it that the schoolhouse be painted. The next year the request would be repeated. The residents in Joint District 9 of Dane County, Wisconsin, asked the board to see to the painting of the schoolhouse at the annual meeting in 1892. Twelve months later they "moved and carried that the board be fined for neglecting to paint the schoolhouse." Apparently after some discussion, however, they "moved and carried that the board be *excused.*" Another vote followed asking the board, once again, to see to the painting.[52]

This sort of disillusionment with the local board was not uncommon. In one instance in Johnson County, Iowa, Pleasant Valley Township board member William Bartholomew was given a contract in 1858 to build a schoolhouse in subdistrict 4. At the 16 July 1859 meeting of the township board, after hearing questions about why the schoolhouse was not yet completed, Bartholomew made a motion to extend the deadline for completion of the building from May to November. Some members of this subdistrict expressed their disapproval of this motion and their belief "that they had no hopes of ever getting a schoolhouse while said Bartholomew had the building of the same and wished the board not to extend the time on said house." Despite this protest, Bartholomew's motion carried.[53]

Until very near the turn of the century, the schoolyard received little attention. Swings and other outdoor amusements were the products of a Progressive era concern with physical education. They appeared in rural schoolyards during the 1910s and 1920s. Before this time the yard was allowed to grow without much care. If it was of considerable size, the district might ask someone to mow the yard in exchange for the wild hay it would yield. If not, they might pay someone to mow the yard. Again, beautification was not the primary concern. It was important to "keep down the weeds" or to "cut the burdocks" to reduce the danger of spreading noxious weeds to clean fields. This type of maintenance also eliminated potential nesting spots for snakes and rodents. Vermin of this sort were often a problem in schoolhouses. Teachers frequently commented in their diaries about the smell of rodent nests emanating from below the floor or behind the walls. Also, it was not uncommon for a scurrying mouse to disrupt the school. Rural Iowa teacher Sarah Huftalen remarked in her diary on 6 March 1886, that she had her "first encounter [with] a mouse and what a race over and under desks and behind stove and table we had."[54]

Another chore the school board regularly attended to was "banking the schoolhouse." To increase the stability and the life expectancy of a wooden frame schoolhouse, it was necessary to build it upon a stone foundation set beneath the frost line. In this way the wood portions of the building did not come into contact with the earth, thus reducing the risk of decay. However, stone is a poor insulator. The cold air beneath the building inevitably came up through the floor, making it difficult to keep the schoolhouse warm in winter. One popular solution to this problem was to "bank" the stone foundation with some type of material such as dirt or straw. In Rock County, Wisconsin, board chairman Lawrence Barrett was paid $2 to "draw dirt from the woods" for banking the schoolhouse. In Sauk County, George Danley was paid $1.75 to "bank the schoolhouse with manure."[55]

Prairie fires posed a significant threat to schoolhouses in the early years on the Great Plains. Entrusted with protecting district property, school board men devised various ways to guard against this possible loss. In Isanti County, Minnesota, in 1891, Hans Larson was instructed "to attend to burning against prairie fires around the school house."[56] This process was sometimes called backburning. On a day when the wind was blowing in the appropriate direction, a person could burn a large enough path around the schoolhouse so that a prairie fire would stagnate when it reached the previously burned ground. The problem with this method, however, is that grasses were sometimes quick to grow back, returning the danger from prairie fires. A more popular device was to "plow the fire brake." The principle was the same as backburning; however, by cutting deep furrows one could extend the period of protection before regrowth brought back the danger from fire. Paying someone to plow the firebreak was a common expense in the states of the trans-Mississippi West.[57]

The treeless prairies of the Great Plains states indicated that schoolhouses subject to prairie fires in the summer were subject to the full force of sub-zero winds in winter. Because the arid Great Plains soils were less productive than the lands of the older Midwest states, settlement was sparse. Instead of having three or four neighbors less than a mile distant, residents may well have had no neighbors so close. As a result, school districts were large, and many children had to travel over four miles to get to the schoolhouse. One way to ease the burden was to have older children drive the younger ones in some sort of cart, buggy, sleigh, or wagon. Of course, this meant that there might be several horses standing outside the schoolhouse all day in the winter winds. In Washington County, Nebraska, the District 30 school board decided to protect these animals by motioning "to build a stables large enough to accommodate the patrons." Small barns or stables were often built along with the schoolhouses in the Dakotas, Nebraska, and Kansas.[58]

The matter of the schoolhouse's location was particularly troublesome for the districts of the Great Plains states. The sparse settlement made it difficult to find a site that would please everyone. Often, as people moved from the district, another location instantly became more equitable for those who remained. The location of the schools often changed as a result. Arbor Day programs designed to encourage districts to plant trees sometimes went unheeded. Few wished to bother planting a shelterbelt if the schoolhouse site would change every few years. Some districts did not plant trees because they had not yet fenced the yard and there was no way to keep livestock from destroying the seedlings. [59]

With no trees for shelter, many schoolhouses were unbearably cold during the winter. Since trees were scarce, wood fuel was frequently not an option for local districts. In the very early years on the Great Plains, twisted prairie grass and buffalo chips were often the fuel of the sod schoolhouses. As railroads entered these states, however, coal became available but had disadvantages. If it was piled outside the schoolhouse during winter, it inevitably became wet from the snow. Igniting the wet coal was a difficult operation. Dusty and dirty as it was, coal was not suitable for storage inside the school. Many districts were then faced with determining how to store the coal. A frequently utilized option in the states of the trans-Mississippi West was to construct a coal shed to keep the fuel dry during the winter. [60]

School districts in the older states shared the problem of wet fuel during the winter. The prevalence of timber in most counties of the Old Northwest states meant that the school district fuel bill was not contingent upon the fluctuation of rail freight rates. Another advantage was that wood was cleaner than coal so that small amounts could be stored inside the schoolhouse. Wood sheds, therefore, were not as necessary as coal sheds. Yet some districts apparently felt the advantages outweighed the costs. [61]

Delegating the wood contract at annual school meetings across the Middle West was often a contentious, divisive affair. Of the odd jobs parceled out to district residents each year, delivering the winter supply of wood was the most lucrative. Before the advent of tax-supported schools, wood was brought "by the scholar," that is, "one load for each man sending one schollar . . . more than one schollar two loads of wood." [62] There were problems with this system, of course. Some kinds of wood were better fuel than others. A cord of oak was worth more than a cord of elm. To reduce local tensions over the woodpile, advocates of common schools felt that a plan to have one individual supply the fuel on a "lowest bidder" basis should be adopted. School boards estimated the amount of wood they would need according to what was used in previous years and then announced that the district would accept bids from individuals hoping to supply the wood. This was accomplished on an appreciable scale only by states that utilized township district organization.[63] Contracting for wood meant that a cash sum might be obtained by the individual willing to supply the schoolhouse with wood at the lowest price. And cash was always in short supply in the rural Midwest.

Consistently allowing the long-standing families to dominate local school affairs, state legislators were not particularly concerned with the issue of conflicting interests. There were general references in state statutes restricting the interest of board members in the purchase of textbooks and school furniture, but small contracts were presumably considered local business. In an undue percentage of instances, therefore, school board members walked away from the annual meeting with the contract to supply winter fuel. If a fence was to be built, or the staircase to the school needed repair, chances are good that the contract went to a board member or to a relative of a board member. Some districts were so accustomed to this practice that they simply stipulated in their board minutes, as one clerk wrote, "that the director get the wood."[64] An event in Iowa shows how blatant school boards could be in awarding contracts. The Scott Township board in Johnson County decided in September 1870 to construct a schoolhouse for subdistrict 1 and another for subdistrict 8. Three bids were taken. Thomas Cherry's bid of $1,625 was lowest. M. A. Westcott's bid of $1,640 was next. Township board member John Downs entered the highest bid at $1,700. Not surprisingly, however, a motion to have Cherry build both houses lost, while "a motion to have John Downs build both houses for $1625 won."[65]

This power possessed by school board men was easily applied to the selection of the teacher for the district, perhaps one of the most controversial of all board duties. Generally, the school board men preferred to hire female teachers when they could, despite their assumption that males could naturally do a better job. A female teacher cost the district between 30 and 50 percent less than a male teacher. During winter term, however, when older males attended school regularly, it was generally acknowledged that the superior strength possessed by males (presumed to be an attribute for keeping good discipline) made them a more appropriate choice for teacher.

The board clerk in District 3, Township 11, of Clark County, Illinois, kept a record of every teacher hired between the fall of 1862 and the spring of 1879. During the seventeen-year period there were two terms each year, summer and winter. Thus, thirty-four teacher contracts were signed. Of these, twenty were signed by men, fourteen by women.[66] All fourteen female teachers taught summer terms. No women were hired to teach a winter term during this seventeen-year period. Twenty-one of the teachers taught one term and never returned to teach in the district. Four males and one female taught more than one term, but none of these teachers taught two terms in succession. Over the seventeen-year period, the average monthly salary for male teachers was thirty-three dollars. Female teachers over the same years averaged seventeen dollars per month. In this particular district there is no record of debate concerning the gender of the teacher to be hired. Records in other districts suggest that such debate was common.

Predictably, there was a contingent at the annual school meeting who favored acquiring a female teacher for both winter and summer terms. The circumstances in a joint school district that lay partly in Dane and Jefferson County, Wisconsin, provide a good example. Prior to the 1872–73 winter term, the district residents decided "that the board be authorized to hire a first class female teacher for the winter school unless they can get a male teacher for nearly the same wages." The assumption, of course, was that a male teacher with any qualifications was superior to a "first class female teacher." After hiring a female teacher for the winter term with no unfortunate ramifications, they decided to go with a "female teacher for both terms" in the school year 1874–75. This time, however, their experience with a female winter teacher were not as positive. A few of those who attended the 1876 annual meeting asked that the board hire a male teacher for the coming winter. The motion failed. Still upset, some of the district residents filed a petition to reconsider the matter at a special meeting. This time they got their way. A male teacher was hired for the winter of 1876–77. But a few years later this district was back to hiring a female teacher for winter term. In fact, district treasurer George Turner wrote the drafts to be paid to Annie Turner, their teacher. George Turner, like many of his counterparts in rural districts across the Middle West, wrote short, cryptic remarks about the quality of the teaching supplied by those to whom he wrote out checks. Though the money paid to Elisha Mattbey was "fooled away" according to Turner, that which went to Annie Turner was "well earned."[67]

As with wood and work contracts, the nepotism displayed by school board men hiring family members to teach in the local school was blatant and frequent.[68] It was so common that teachers came to expect it and dealt with it in a matter-of-fact manner when they confronted it.[69] The situation in District 3 of Albion Township, Dane County, Wisconsin, illustrates the extent to which some district boards would go in hiring family to teach the local school. In May 1854, the board contracted Fanny Coon to teach the summer term. Daniel Coon was then board treasurer. In May 1859, the board hired Lorene Babcock to teach the summer term. H. W. Babcock was board director at the time. Laura Burdick was hired to teach the winter term of 1865–66, a time when the district was in debt to a wealthy resident farmer, Samuel Burdick. Maria Lawton taught the summer term during 1866 while G. F. Lawton served as board clerk. Eliza Coon taught the winter term of 1866–67, and in subsequent years more Coons and Lawtons would sign on to teach in the local district school.

In contrast, there were fewer instances of blatant nepotism apparent in the school records of the trans-Mississippi West. It may well have been that just as the residents of these states were sensitive to unfavorable consideration regarding free textbooks, they were reluctant to draw the ire of neighbors by hiring sons and daughters to teach in the local school. In one rural district in Washington County, Nebraska, "it was proposed by the Director that a petition be circulated to obtain the feeling of the patrons of said district in regard to Dora E. Wright as teacher." Dora was the daughter of the board director. In an effort to minimize the hard feelings sometimes caused by hiring family members to teach school, residents of District 7 in rural Isanti County, Minnesota, "voted to have no one in the district teach school."[70]

To be sure, hiring female teachers saved district residents money. But trying to interpret the degree to which rural school board members were primarily concerned with providing a quality education for their children or with limiting the expenses involved in providing that education is probably asking the wrong question. It is possible to dig up statements by board members to the effect that their intentions were always to save the district money, whether this meant hiring the cheapest teacher, buying the cheapest blackboard, crayons, or books, or repairing the schoolhouse only when it was necessary to keep it standing.[71] There are other glimpses of real devotion to the benefits of formal schooling. Most often these came in the form of petitions presented to the board asking to extend the school term one more month or, as one clerk wrote, "to have as much School as the money in the District would pay for."[72]

What is culturally difficult for us to imagine now is that parents in the nineteenth- and early-twentieth-century rural Midwest generally wanted no more from the schooling provided for their children than that which would prepare them for productive lives in the immediate community. The Progressive reformers around the turn of the century were selling school as a vehicle for breaking away from occupational restrictions, from tradition-bound communities—in short, as the ultimate opportunity for advancement and success. But more and better schooling in the rural Midwest brought no visible signs of enhanced opportunity. For the farmers who served on local boards of education, opportunity lay in the land, not away from it. From our present perspective, we have trouble comprehending how parents could prefer for their children a minimal education and life on the land to high school, college, and the chance to become a doctor, lawyer, or successful city business person. But it is within this culturally foreign notion that the reality of country schooling lies. The kind of education farmers provided for their children was dependent on their view of an ideal society. To understand rural education, one must first understand agrarian beliefs about what the world should look like and how it should run. Though we might wish that it were otherwise, rural Midwest society was marked by various intolerances, the end result of which—when successfully applied to outsiders—left a small community of like-minded owners and tillers of the soil. That rural schools came to reflect these prejudices should not be surprising.

In the matter of choosing a teacher, one can glimpse underlying sexist notions in agrarian ideology. In rural Sauk County, Wisconsin, local residents authorized the board to get a female teacher for the winter "if we cant get a man teacher for a reasonable price." In another Sauk County school, local residents voted to "hire a female teacher as cheap as we can." Still another rural Wisconsin school board was directed to hire the "female teacher most profitable to the district." But some districts tired of the problems encountered when hiring the least expensive teacher. In rural Rock County, Wisconsin, the residents "moved and second[ed] that the board hire no third grade teachers." Another local board, this one in Nebraska, stipulated that it would not hire a teacher unless the individual possessed a second-grade certificate. [73]

Room was made for female schoolteachers in the larger agrarian political economy. Teaching came to be viewed as an acceptable way for women to spend the unmarried adult years. Few questioned the inequity of paying women less for the same work men were paid more for. Male labor, be it physical or mental, was somehow naturally more productive. As a result, women were traditionally assigned the least "productive" roles in agrarian work routines. The affairs of the house, of course, were within the dominion of women. But additionally, women might be asked to glean grain from harvested fields, attend to the productivity of the chickens (which was beneath the dignity of a self-respecting male farmer), or provide care for sick or injured livestock.

Public schools, and to some extent their administration, were deemed to be the limits to which women could participate in public spheres. A disgruntled rural Illinois teacher confided to his diary after attending a Baptist revival led by a woman, "I have no sympathy with strong-minded females who so far forget what is due to themselves and society as to appear in the pulpit or on the rostrum."[74] The strenuous efforts on the part of educators to separate the sexes in the country schools reflects the agrarian divisions between male and female labor. One, by definition, was of greater value than the other. That the country teaching profession was dominated by rural women meant only that the hidden curricula created by agrarian work divisions efficiently and effectively reproduced itself with each succeeding generation of rural schoolgirls who became rural schoolteachers.

This is not to suggest, however, that country teachers inevitably saw eye-to-eye with local school board men. Strong differences of opinion were frequent, but teachers were rarely able to influence local boards of education. Carrie Shephard signed a contract to teach a winter term in the District 4 school of Rock County, Wisconsin. She was paid for one month's work after which the treasurer noted that the school was "closed on account of trouble between teacher and board." There are no details to indicate what this "trouble" was all about, but other records show that the board men in this particular district were difficult to please. A few years later Edna Werner signed a contract to teach a summer term. She was "let off by agreement at the end of three months." Another teacher was hired to teach the last weeks of the four-month term. A year later Harrison Wren began teaching the summer term. He was dismissed after only three weeks "on account of disreputable conduct." Two years later Hattie Whetstone was hired to teach the winter term of 1875–76. Whetstone was "discharged for suffering to teach school by not keeping order in [the] school-house."

Devoted as many of the country schoolteachers were, it should not be surprising that some came to see an education as the goal for schooling as opposed to the mere acquisition of three basic skills. Typically, these were the teachers who bothered local board men most. They constantly lobbied for better school furniture, more library books, a larger black-board, a piano or an organ. Reluctantly, a rural Wisconsin board paid their teacher five dollars for the use of her ency-clopedias but was quick to add in the board minutes that next time "a *good* teacher be hired." Another teacher in rural Wis-consin tried to generate support for the purchase of an organ for the local school. Considering the notion superfluous, local residents voted "not to assist the teacher to [buy] an organ for the school."[75]

Issues such as these often divided the board itself. In one district a fight broke out when the wives of two board members earned a few dollars for cleaning the schoolhouse before the beginning of a new term. The fight ensued because the wife of the third board member was left out. If the school was fortunate enough to purchase a new set of encyclopedias, the matter of who was to keep the old set was particularly divi-sive. In one instance one board member received volumes A through I, another received volumes J through Q, and the last received volumes V through Z as the only alternative to hard feelings. In Fairview Township District of Johnson County, Iowa, the township secretary asked for ten dollars more for his annual salary "in view of the fact that I have to do more than ten times as much work for my official labor as does the treasurer" and because, he claimed, his becoming secretary "was a malisious act on the part of a certain member of the board."[76] Other disagreements between board members were caused by one member making a verbal agreement to hire a teacher who did not meet with the approval of the others. Sometimes this resulted in a teacher beginning the school year without a contract.

In theory, teacher contracts were designed to protect the teacher from arbitrary dismissal. County superintendents warned teachers of the danger inherent in accepting positions without a signed contract. Still, young and inexperienced teachers sometimes found this out the hard way. A rural Burleigh County, North Dakota, teacher taught for three months on a verbal agreement before the board dismissed her. The teacher appealed her case to the county superintendent but received little more than a curt "I told you so."[77]

Contractually, teachers were always at a disadvantage during the period under study. Contract forms were generally provided by publishing companies in the business of selling school district record books, but there were always blank lines that allowed local boards to add their own clauses and caveats. Most often those lines were used to excuse the district from paying the teacher when "disease in the district" shut down the school for extended periods. Whooping cough, scarlet fever, and measles are just a few diseases that accomplished this often. One district, however, used the blank lines of the printed contracts to stipulate "that if a majority of the School Board shall be dissatisfied with the School or the management thereof, the Board reserves the power to annull this contract at any time."[78] Of course, this restriction almost defeated the purpose of the contract, but it is a good description of the reality of teacher-board relations in the rural schools of the Middle West. As teaching became more and more feminized, teachers held an increasingly subordinate position in rural agrarian society. In the view of most boards of education, the ideal teacher kept excellent discipline, made do with whatever books or equipment were on hand, maintained a secluded personal life in the community, and moved on to a different school when the term was over.

Forced to adapt to a free school system, the board men of the Midwest found themselves with a great deal of latitude with which to maneuver schooling to serve community ends. The schoolhouse location, the control over who would be allowed to use the schoolhouse, the power to deny certain residents a voice in school affairs, the choice of textbooks, the power to forestall the movement to provide free textbooks, the choice of teacher, and the power to arbitrarily dismiss the teacher or even to close down the school all contributed to the efforts of board men to create a community conducive to the needs and desires of a minority population in the rural Middle West.

Wish as we may that rural schooling in the Midwest encompassed all things good and democratic about humankind, the evidence does not permit such an interpretation. In our efforts to convey American history to the next generation, we fall into a trap by creating an artificial dualism where if circumstances moving in one direction are clearly bad, the other direction is clearly good. To be sure, Progressive-era centralization in city school governance had some undemocratic consequences. In light of this, it is comforting to look upon the American rural school experience as the epitome of democracy in all its splendor. Rural localism, however, had its undemocratic aspects, too. In fact, a measure of centralization was necessary to produce an effort to curb the undemocratic intolerances built into agrarian ideology and perpetuated by rural schooling. A close-up look at the experiences that made up this kind of schooling is the focus of the next chapter.

4

Recess, Recitation, and the Switch

Students and Teachers in Midwest Country Schools

Their day began long before school was called. On the plains, hills, and valleys of the Middle West, children rose with the sun to complete their chores amid the flurry of morning activity on the typical farmstead. Often, there were cows to be milked, and if the children were too small to help with this, there were calves and chickens to be fed, eggs to collect, a woodbox to fill, cream to be separated, skimmed milk to be fed to the pigs, and an evening's collection of manure to be piled outside the barn or in the spreader. Breakfast generally followed this phase of intensive labor, concluding the first segment of the farm day.

After leaving the breakfast table, schoolchildren gathered a few books and a tin pail (often the emptied container of a prior purchase of syrup or molasses) that generally contained a few sandwiches for lunch at school. The long trek to the schoolhouse began. No two families lived equidistant from the schoolhouse. Some had to walk quite far, particularly during the early years of statehood. In the heavily settled states of the Midwest, such as Michigan, Ohio, and Illinois, only rarely did a rural pupil have to walk a distance greater than three miles after the establishment of tax-supported common schools. In the states of the trans-Mississippi West, such as the Dakotas and Nebraska, distances of more than three miles were common. In many districts throughout these states, construction of a stable to shelter horses ridden or driven by scholars was preceded only by the construction of the schoolhouse itself. Privies could wait. In fact, older scholars were sometimes paid by the district to collect children from outlying farms. [1]

In good weather, the walk might be enjoyable. A group of schoolchildren from one household might meet up with a group from another and talk or sing on their way to the schoolhouse. Frequent opportunities for excitement or mischief opened in this portion of the children's day. Gardens and orchards sorely tempted schoolbound rural youth, as did the inclination to cut through a forbidden pasture to shorten the trip. If a bull grazed therein, boys might take an opportunity to exhibit bravado in front of the girls or the younger students. Similarly, staring down the barking watchdog of a farmstead along the path toward the school was the incumbent duty of the older scholars. Some Ohio children on their way to school during the early 1850s were confronted by a rabid dog. Unable to escape its attack, the oldest boy, just twelve, fought with the animal and was eventually able to hold it down until a farmer nearby could bring a shotgun to kill it. The boy was bitten several times and died painfully within a few weeks. [2]

For most of the nineteenth century, schooling occurred in two terms: winter and summer. Planting in the spring and harvesting in the fall were phases of the agrarian calendar that required the hands of the entire household. The walks to and from school during the summer term were frequently pleasant occasions. But this was only if conditions were right. Rain often made rural roads impassable, rendering a three-mile walk to school an arduous, painstaking activity. Schools were sometimes closed under such circumstances. [3]

During winter term other difficulties existed. Although extreme cold was rarely an obstacle for school attendance, large accumulations of snow often made the walk to and from school impossible. On such occasions neighbors frequently took turns harnessing a team to a bobsled to transport the schoolchildren. Fast-developing winter storms were a constant worry in the countryside. Sometimes an entire class of students became snowed in and were forced to spend the night in the schoolhouse. Rural North Dakota teacher Charles Hubbell remarked in his diary on 12 January 1888 that he had witnessed the "worst storm" he had ever seen. It "hit during the day—only a few scholars—some tried to leave but had to go back to the schoolhouse." James Shields, a teacher in rural Minnesota, commented in his diary that on 4 January 1886 he had "to walk through drifts two feet deep to reach the school."[4]

A rural teacher in Iowa noted in her diary that 31 December 1863 began "cloudy and cold, the wind blowing fierce from the northwest and it was snowing some and filling up in drifts." A relative had stopped at school early in the morning and built a fire for her. Still, "there were but a few scholars." As the day progressed "the storm increased its fury and by noon it snowed and blowed so that George Andrews went and brought dinner." Gradually, it became so cold that the group "could scarcely keep fire enough to keep warm. At about the middle of the afternoon Uncle Tom and Charley came with the oxen and sled . . . we all got home safe."[5]

Sometime in mid-March, 1920, Hazel Miner, age sixteen, was driving a buggy home from school outside of Center, North Dakota. Her younger brother and sister (aged nine and eleven) accompanied her. The Miner children were caught in extreme cold, and when the buggy overturned, conditions were so bad that help could not get to them. Hazel put her brother and sister in the shelter provided by the overturned buggy, but this did not stop the wind from blowing off the blankets they used to cover themselves. Finally, she used her own overcoat to cover her siblings, and additionally, she laid her own body over them. The next day, Hazel was found frozen to death, but her siblings survived. The story of Hazel Miner has reached almost mythic proportions in present-day North Dakota.[6]

There is much talk about old-timers who walked "three miles in the snow, barefoot, just to get to school." It is often said that Abe Lincoln suffered this fate stoically. While it is true that attending school barefoot was commonplace in the nineteenth-century Midwest, existing diaries and memoirs of rural school days offer virtually no references to walking barefoot in snow. However, now and then such walks may well have happened. Shoes were a large expense and a poor investment for parents whose children seemed to outgrow them before they outwore them. Children were often attending school barefoot at the beginning of winter term in November and shed their shoes in the spring as early as March when snow during the course of the day remained a real possibility. One Ohio resident remembered regularly running off a group of lazy cows who often were lying in one corner of a pasture as the children were on the way to school. Quickly, the children stood where the cows had lain to warm their feet for a while before continuing their journey to the schoolhouse. [7]

Some students had to walk through dark stands of timber or cross dangerous creeks or streams. Encountering snakes in the prairie grass was a frequent and often unnerving experience. Anna Webber, a teacher in rural Kansas in 1881, confided to her diary that she and several students "saw two wolves and it frightened us some." Two early Illinois schoolgirls, while walking with a group of students on a return trip from school, remembered seeing wolves at which point, in practiced fashion, "the oldest ones would form a front and rear guard, and put the smallest in the middle, and hurry them along, all nearly scared to death." An early Iowa student sat through an afternoon of school while it rained heavily outside. That evening she wrote in her diary, "When I came to the little creek it was swollen so that I could not jump it and taking off my shoes and stockings I waded through it. They were much surprised at seeing me at home as they thought the creek so high that I could not cross it." An Indiana schoolboy wrote in his diary of a similar experience: "I commenced going to school in company with cousin James, and two other neighborhood boys, but was compelled to abandon it, inconsequence of a suden swell of the river, which cut of [sic] our communication with the neighborhood of the school." With respect to the diverse topographical conditions of the Midwest states, reaching a compromise on the location of the schoolhouse was a difficult enterprise. [8]

The varying directions and distances from which students approached the schoolhouse meant that all rarely assembled at roughly the same time. If a special farm chore was reserved for a particular day of the week, it might mean that members of one family got a late start walking to school on that day. Unlike developing urban school systems, clocklike regularity in calling school was a luxury few rural schoolteachers enjoyed. More typically, the quorum system was used. Teachers and students relaxed until "a quorum was collected and the house called to order." In a rural school near Oxford, Iowa, teacher Sarah Jane Kimball awaited her students on the first day of summer term, 1867. "I went to school and the first scholar was little Barney Eldridge. After that six more came and I waited till after 9 oclock and commenced school with 7 scholars."[9] If conditions were right, school was called at 9:00 A.M. and dismissed at 4:00 P.M.. However, during winter term it was often as late as 10:00 or even 11:00 before the schoolhouse warmed sufficiently so that lessons might progress with a minimum of suffering.

The age of pupils attending midwestern country schools ranged widely. Toddlers aged two or three years might walk along to school with grown men aged twenty-five years. Rural Indiana teacher Julia Merrill described the difficulties dealing with a toddler in school in a letter to a friend. While hearing recitations, she explained, "Little Timmie, a dirty little rogue, stretched out on a bench sound asleep." Timmie was behind Merrill as she listened to a group of pupils. "I heard whispering and supressed laughter and then a real loud burst that could be withheld no longer. I turned around prepared with a long face to scold, but lo! there sat Timmie with his foot stretched to his mouth sucking his dirty toe!"[10] Sometimes toddlers and older students were discouraged from attending school by district trustees because the district's share of the state school fund was predicated on the number of children (frequently white children) between the ages of four and twenty-one who attended regularly. Students younger or older than these ages simply meant an added drain on available resources.

Rural schooling was an individualized activity. For most of the period under study, textbooks were not provided by the school district and there was little standardization of texts.

Teachers might encounter as many different readers, spellers, and geographies as pupils. Many of these books were family heirlooms handed down from parent to children to grandchildren. If a family possessed no schoolbooks, the children usually did not attend school. Not until the late 1880s and early 1890s, prompted by Farmers Alliance agitation for textbook law reform, did midwestern legislatures begin requiring local districts to supply books that the poor were unable to purchase. From these books rural schoolchildren were drilled on the mechanics of reading, writing, and arithmetic.

The "basics" are often nostalgically looked upon as the backbone of country school curricula. This is supported by the inspection of teacher lesson plans, which reveal that classes in reading, arithmetic, and writing (if "writing" is liberally construed to be synonymous with grammar and penmanship) amounted to anywhere from 75 to 90 percent of the instructional day. Often overlooked, however, is the fact that this instruction was inexorably linked to pupil textbooks. And nineteenth- and early twentieth-century textbooks were filled with such non-basics (from a present-day standpoint) as lessons in religion, politics, and moral philosophy. A mere glance at any of these books reveals the obvious Protestant religious bias, making understandable the incentive for Roman Catholics to write their own texts. Ruth Miller Elson's *Guardians of Tradition: American Schoolbooks of the Nineteenth Century* stands as the best systematic historical treatment of the contents of American school texts.

The rejection of Enlightenment notions of equality in antebellum society, particularly in the Midwest and the South, reached into these texts of the common schools. Borrowing from Elson's analysis, we may describe the socialization received by countless schoolchildren about the poor, the American Indian, and blacks.

Clearly, school textbooks sought to rationalize the coexistence of the poor and the wealthy in the United States. Elson describes the circumstances this way: "Throughout the century there are constant references to one's 'rank' or 'station in life' as a frame for daily activities as well as a mold to one's future." She goes on to describe a few passages from typical readers. The first begins with

> a dialogue between a mother and her daughter Sally, entitled "On Different Stations in Life." Sally, who has come from visiting a rich friend, asks her mother why they cannot have a coach and the accoutrements of wealth, since they seem to be as worthy as the family of her friend. The mother replies by saying that since they have no extra money, their lives must be different: "Everything ought to be suited to the station in which we live, and the wants and duties of it."

The second example is still more telling, for it centers on the objectives inherent in the schooling process:

> a mother explains to her complaining daughter that she must study household accounts, reading, and writing rather than music, dancing, and drawing: "Because, my dear, it is the purpose of all education, to fit persons for the station in which they are hereafter to live; and you know there are very great differences in that respect both among men and women."[11]

Far and away, the most successful nineteenth-century textbook entrepreneur was Reverend William McGuffey, a Presbyterian cleric from Ohio. McGuffey's texts dominated sales throughout the century. These titles went beyond merely articulating the need to recognize qualitative differences between the rich and the poor. McGuffey actually included lessons on how to be good poor. In a selection called "The Poor Boy," McGuffey encouraged proper ways for such an individual to view life's circumstances: "When he sees little boys or girls riding on pretty horses, or in coaches, or walking with ladies and gentlemen, and having on very fine clothes, he does not envy them or wish to be like them."[12] Proper poverty in adulthood was prescribed as well. In "The Life of William Kelley,"

McGuffey describes a "habitual drunkard" who found God and became a new man. This passage is one among many in which the anti-Catholicism of nineteenth-century Protestantism appears in school texts. It probably never would have occurred to McGuffey that using William McAlister, a Scottish pseudonym, rather than William Kelley, an Irish pseudonym, would have been less reflective of nineteenth century stereotypes. One former country school student recalled a passage from his reader in later years: "We must educate, we must educate, or we shall perish in our own prosperity." This sentence is taken directly from Lyman Beecher's *A Plea for the West*, a virulently anti-Catholic tract that suggested that through the common schools the West might be saved from the decadent Irish Catholic hordes who were invading New England. [13]

In an 1843 edition of McGuffey's *Second Reader*, a distinct pattern emerges that Elson has described as typical of post–Civil War texts. The clear differentiation between rich and poor people continued, but in addition to delineating a proper way to be poor, the texts began to document the proper way to be wealthy. An essay discussed briefly in the previous chapter, entitled "Emulation Without Envy," is a good example. Since it was written prior to the successful establishment of common schools in the Midwest, it includes an implicit assumption that the children reading from the book were attending school on a subscription basis. In this selection a widow's son is competing with a rich farmer's son for head of the class. One day the widow's son is absent, and he stays out of school for an extended period. "'Why?' asked the rich farmer's son. 'Poverty,' said the teacher." The essay ends with the rich boy's father paying the poor boy's tuition so that the boys might continue to compete against one another. [14]

Social Darwinism, when taken to its extreme, seemed to make necessary a pious virtue that could temper overt subordination of the poor. It was not considered appropriate for Christians who proved to be among the "fittest" to tread upon those who were not successful in life's battles. In other words, an important element of the socialization process of the Gilded age became the way to be wealthy in a Christian manner.

Meanwhile, the essential evangelistic principle of American Protestantism remained unchanged or perhaps intensified. In his essay "Consolation of Religion to the Poor," McGuffey explained that the poor widow who takes dignity in life out of religion "in death receives health which lasts through all eternity."[15]

Slavery was a troublesome issue for antebellum textbook writers. Few confronted the issue directly until after the Civil War. In general, however, Elson concludes, "The Negro of the schoolbooks must be cared for by whites as one would care for a child; he is not vicious, nor is it necessary to quarantine him. His place in America's future is clear: he will assist the whites from his menial but useful position." A typical postbellum textbook passage is represented by this one: "'The negroes are doubtless happier now then when slaves, but in spite of the efforts to educate them on the part of the whites and some members of their own race, many still remain densely ignorant.'" One textbook author even found a way to express a note of anti-Catholicism in a discussion of the characteristics of blacks. Speaking of the nation of Haiti, William Woodbridge wrote that "'they profess the Catholic religion; and few are acquainted with the Bible . . . they are ignorant and indolent.'"[16]

American Indians received less favorable treatment in American schoolbooks than blacks. The Romanticism of the early nineteenth century that rejected Enlightenment notions of human equality were particularly welcome on the frontier. Wresting land away from the Indians required an explanation that children could understand. They found it in their schoolbooks. The 1880 edition of Noah Webster's "blue back" *Speller* included this statement as a practice sentence: "'It is almost impossible to civilize the American Indians.'" One reader discussed President Jackson's removal plan that relocated Cherokees "'to a fine country west of the Mississippi.'" Several others echoed the scientific claim of antebellum scholars concluding that the "'Indian will not learn the arts of civilization, and he and his forest must perish together.'" However, the books were typically quick to point out that as the allegedly superior race, Caucasians were to do nothing to hasten this process of racial extinction artificially. Contrary to what was prescribed for blacks, Elson concludes that the United States of America taught its children that "the Indian . . . is a force hostile to progress, and is best quarantined" on reservations. [17]

It might be easier to entertain the argument that country school curricula centered on the "basics" if textbooks were not central to instruction. The record, however, indicates that very little or perhaps nothing was accomplished without them. A teacher in rural Greene County, Wisconsin, wrote to the state superintendent of public instruction in 1852 to complain that the school board refused to pay him for his teaching. He explained that the board had examined his register and noticed in a few instances "that there were no studies credited to some scholars." Because of this, apparently, the board decided to deny him his pay. But the teacher explained, "When the children came to school the first day of their entrance, and I asked them what they were going to study, many would say, 'I don't know yet. If I can get such and such books, I will study them.' And at the time I told them I would not set down any study, but wait untill they bought their books; and so I have not thought about it, and returned the register with those blanks unfilled."[18]

Schoolbooks were central to the nineteenth- and early-twentieth-century rural school experience. Textbook authors took great pains to be sure that schoolchildren were equipped to correctly interpret events in the world around them. Perhaps more than anything else, the extremes in wealth and poverty were rationalized and made understandable, for this was a fact of life that Americans lived with daily. Loaded wagons and families on the move were almost a part of the Midwest landscape. Rarely did a nineteenth-century country school term begin and end with the same number of pupils. "Removed from the district" was a typical phrase penciled in the registers of country schoolteachers. Also, as David Schob has demonstrated, boys would often drop out of school to work as hired hands, and girls, too, would occasionally "hire out" to do domestic work. [19] The textbook emphasis on differences between rich and poor gave rural children a framework to interpret stability and mobility in Midwest society.[20] Students might understand, too, why it was okay to play war with make-believe Indians at recess, or why it was necessary to confine Indians on reservations. It also became understandable why there might be "quite an excitement" when "a negro man was found this afternoon in our wood-house," as a fourteen-year-old Illinois girl wrote in her diary in 1870.[21]

If a student came to school at age five equipped with a *First Reader*, most likely this scholar would occupy half of a two-person desk with another of similar sex and age near the front of the room. Single desks were available from school furniture producers, but the price of one two-person desk was always a fraction of the price of two single desks, hence the prevalence of two-person desks. Older students were typically assigned desks behind the younger ones such that the oldest were seated near the back of the schoolhouse. If any toddlers were in attendance, they, too, sat near the back, watched over by an older brother or sister. Most often girls sat on one side of the room and boys on the other.[22]

The legacy of English pedagogue Joseph Lancaster is pronounced in the history of midwestern rural schooling. The seating layout of the typical country school (younger scholars in front graduating to older scholars in back) is simply Lancasterian prescription in reverse. However, both styles were used. References to such circumstances as the rich and poor boys competing for the head of the class were a direct spin-off of the Lancasterian legacy. But Lancaster's impact went beyond classroom layout. His advocation of peer instruction through the monitor system seems to have been emulated to a great degree in the states of the Middle West. Also, the use of awards to provide incentive to achieve academically was widespread.[23] Even the notion that a scholar's continued possession of some external reward was contingent on proper behavior and academic performance seems to have held some currency. Angry at some indiscreet act on the part of certain students, yet unable to prove their guilt, Minnesota rural teacher James Shields confided to his diary that he "will likely withhold the premium from one of the supposed culprits."[24]

In Olmsted County, Minnesota, Ella, Cora, and Elmer Buck were removed from the District 36 school in High Forest Township "because their parents objected to the monitors."[25] Quite commonly in the country schools, older scholars were allowed to supervise the work of the younger pupils. Yet not all midwestern teachers were advocates of an Americanized monitorial system. After hearing a lecture on Lancasterian principles, a Mormon teacher in Nauvoo, Illinois, commented in his diary, "I cannot approve of the monitorial system. Some of the promised evils are, in my estimation, too large schools—a general spirit of rivalry—bad effects ensuing from the employment of those too near the age of the scholars in teaching—and a spirit of tale-bearing and back-biting among the Monitors by carrying tails to the master."[26] The differentiation of gender roles may or may not have been apparent during early morning chores. Young girls frequently worked side by side with young boys. But there can be no mistaking the sex role socialization inherent in the rural school process. Typically, girls were seated on one side of the room while boys sat on the other. Some teachers went to extremes in this regard by actually constructing physical barriers between them.[27] Although this pattern began to disintegrate in the waning years of the nineteenth century, some school boards insisted that propriety depended upon keeping the sexes separate. When in 1871 Joint District 8 in the Wisconsin counties of Columbia and Marquette found that their summer teacher had allowed boys and girls recess time together, the board stipulated at the annual school meeting that the next "teacher is instructed to have recesses separate."[28]

But recess, like breakfast, was preceded by work that was not always considered enjoyable. Most lesson plans obtained in school records across the Midwest indicate that the initial call for school was followed by instruction in reading. A ten-year-old child might spend half an hour preparing to recite a page or two of text while the teacher heard the recitations of older or younger students. Because so much of the day was taken up by student recitations, it was deemed particularly necessary that "communications" or "whispering" be held to a minimum. One county superintendent in Minnesota praised a rural teacher because three-fourths of her students had not whispered in over a month. [29]

As noted earlier, instruction throughout most of the nineteenth century was tied to the textbook. Learning to read was no exception. The records left by teachers indicate that generally the pedagogy was prescribed within the reading textbooks. Some of these, like McGuffey's readers, promoted the recognition and sounding of syllables trusting that students would utilize induction en route to literacy. The "spelling method" was also popular. Students were drilled in the sounds of the alphabet and then pressed to "sound out" in the reading process. Still others started at the level of word recognition, moving from simple to complex. Whole-word recognition became increasingly popular late in the century as Francis Wayland Parker's "Quincy method" became widely publicized. But the pedagogy of the country teacher most often included little more than correcting mistakes, administering punishment if appropriate, and calling for the next reader. [30]

With luck, a break might follow reading instruction, although some teachers kept no morning recess. Back in their seats, grammar lessons were frequently next on the agenda. "Parsing" words aloud or diagramming sentences on the blackboard was a major component of grammar lessons. Penmanship, as well, was commonly an element of the instruction in this phase of the school day. Sometimes there were exercises included in textbooks that the student might be asked to write out on paper. However, the use of paper by the scholars was sometimes controversial. Many parents saw this as a needless expense and advocated the use of slates. As late as 1905, the school board for District 25 of Morrison County, Minnesota, "provided that children are to be allowed to use slates if the parents demand it." [31] And paper was not the only problem. A teacher in rural Benson County, North Dakota, purchased a pencil sharpener for her pupils' use. "Shortly thereafter she received a letter from the president [director] of the school board telling her she would have to remove the pencil sharpener. It seems the children were using up their pencils too fast and the parents were complaining."[32]

Because handwriting was one of the cherished "basics," it is useful to examine what the evidence suggests about writing instruction. Though teacher diaries often speak of correcting or grading homework, there is little or no reference to reading creative work composed by students. One former Kansas common school graduate mused about the writing instruction—or the lack of it—he experienced, "I have no doubt that the grammar we learned was really helpful, but I have wished that we had given less time to dissection and more to the construction of simple English."[33] Writing instruction throughout most of the nineteenth century was not an opportunity for students to be expressive. Rather, it was an exercise in conformity. Sentences needed to be deconstructed according to hard and fast grammatical rules. Handwriting had to utilize the unchanging "seven strokes" so that all learned to write alike. Pedagogy advanced tradition.

During summer term, the lunch break was generally an hour long. Fortunate students who lived close to the schoolhouse might eat with their parents and return for the afternoon's activities. Most students, however, ate their lunch on the school grounds and made the most of their free time playing games. Typically, shorter daylight hours during winter term meant that getting the scholars home somewhat earlier was advantageous. Often the lunch period during winter session was only thirty minutes, allowing a 3:30 dismissal.

Arithmetic lessons very likely followed lunch hour. Board work was common, but a great deal of arithmetic "class" consisted of figuring sums individually while seated. Word problems were sometimes talked through while the reciting scholar worked out figures on the board. Arithmetic was typically considered the most difficult subject for both teachers and students. Textbooks, of course, were predominantly filled with practice items usually preceded by the explication of one law-like algorithm that would enable students to work the problems correctly. Instruction in arithmetic centered chiefly around correcting the students' efforts. Without further instruction and forced to deal with problems equipped with one manner of solution, many rural students, not surprisingly, never worked through their books. It is not difficult, therefore, to sense the pride of the country school teacher in rural Clark County, Illinois, when she commented on the term in her register: "One [pupil] got through the arithmetic and others got very near through."[34] Arithmetic was often followed by lessons in spelling, although it was perhaps just as common for "spell-downs" to end the school day.

At 2:30, or very near there, hundreds of thousands of rural scholars (as they were frequently referred to) across the Middle West jumped from schoolhouse steps into the euphoria of afternoon recess. The worst of the school day behind them, they had time for a ball game, anney-anney-over, or crack-the-whip. Recess during winter term was a chance for sledding, fort-building, or a snowball fight. At times, too, oaths were sworn and fistfights broke out. Some teachers intervened in schoolyard affairs; others considered it beyond their jurisdiction. After witnessing "a little trouble among the scholars," teacher Anna Webber confided that she "was provoked enough to cry." However, as the nineteenth century waned, the rigid distance that existed between teacher and pupils began to disintegrate. Some teachers played just as hard as the scholars during recess, as Webber's confession to her diary suggests: "I was playing with the scholars today, and fell down, flat as a *flounder*."[35]

A male teacher in rural Indiana played ball with his students so often, especially with the older males, that it got him into trouble. A former student recalled that this teacher "would sometimes play an hour over the time to begin school. The school directors finally heard how he was running the school, and turned him off, refusing to pay him for the full term." Like other rural teachers who were denied all or part of their salary for one reason or another, this one petitioned higher authorities in support of his plea for full wages but was denied.[36]

Like schools everywhere, rural schools had their own hidden curricula. Webber's diary is representative of the sort of matter-of-fact racism that permeated Middle Western society during the nineteenth and early twentieth centuries. When the day was hot, it was, in Webber's terms, "warm enough to roast a darkey." In a similar fashion, schoolchildren needed to "catch a nigger by the toe" in order to choose teams for a ball game. In one instance Webber had to punish a "little chap who blacked his face" no doubt as a result of playing "black man," a popular schoolyard game. Black man was a type of base tag where the persons who were traditionally "it" received the inferior racial status of the Negro, ostensibly to increase their motivation to "catch" others. A former rural Iowa student recalled his dismay at always being "'caught first when playing black man.'" A North Dakota teacher remembered black man as the most popular game at the schools where she taught. An Ohio teacher made note of the game's popularity in her area. References from Ohio to Kansas to North Dakota suggest that black man was indeed a common recess activity in the country schools of the Midwest. [37]

Clearly, the result of this sort of playground hidden curriculum was that various local intolerances were perpetuated in and around the community. The exclusivity this generated was a legacy of the intense sectarianism and the devotion to political localism that characterized midwestern ideology. The usefulness of this ideology becomes apparent in light of the importance placed on setting up those in the next generation on farms of their own.

The last segment of the school day was generally reserved for the study of history and geography. [38] As with reading and grammar, lessons frequently consisted of the recitation method. "Chanting" geography was popular. This technique involved the teacher in the front of the room equipped with a pointer. As the pointer was moved from location to location on a map, "the whole class would sing to the chosen tune such facts about its capital [sic], its boundaries, its population, etc., as were on the schedule." [39] Geography was *the* social study of the rural school. It was through geography textbooks that students learned of the various races that made up humankind. In all these lessons the white race was promoted as the most decent, civilized, and sophisticated of all. Religious overtones permeated the geography texts and legitimized the clearly unequal distribution of desirable attributes among the races.

Instruction in history was generally the most informal and least tied to textbooks. Compared with the availability of readers, spellers, geographies, and arithmetic books, histories were rare. Teachers frequently lectured on the subject. The Revolution, of course, was the chief topic of study, but there is little to suggest that history instruction was much more than an unquestioning veneration of America's greatest statesmen.

At 4:00, all but the recalcitrant students were dismissed. The second walk of the day commenced with all the dangers, temptations, and monotony of the first. For some the walk home was conducted at a more leisurely pace than the morning trip. After a sandwich or a snack at home, the evening chores loomed ominously.

Some families ate their evening meal before the second milking, some after. But this activity did not exhaust the evening chores for country boys and girls. Animals needed to be fed and bedded down for the night, and water troughs required filling with many long turns at the pump handle. After a day in the fields, horses needed currying, and the harnesses might require a quick wipe with a rag dipped in harness oil. Frequently, young girls remained in the house to help with the preparation of the evening meal. Then the dishes would need washing, the lamp chimneys might require cleaning, and the floor, a good sweeping. In the hour or two that remained of the day after its work was done, the family might visit nearby neighbors or drive a buggy to town. More likely, the evening would be passed with conversation and reading. Students were frequently expected to practice their lessons.

The phases of the farm day passed rhythmically, governed generally by the rotation of the earth before the sun. School attendance records across the Midwest suggest that although schooling was assimilated into agrarian work rhythms, it was not fundamentally a part of it. Before 1918, on any given day in typical local country school districts across the Middle Western states, one could not expect to find more than one-half or two-thirds of the total number of students enrolled actually in attendance. During the antebellum years the average was no doubt below 50 percent. [40] Near the conclusion of World War I, it was closer to two-thirds. What this suggests is that when the agrarian seasonal work cycle was interrupted, as it frequently was, the schooling of the youth in a household might suffer as a consequence. [41]

At times, clouds could affect the work agenda of the typical farmstead in a way that the sun would not. If a cloudy day dawned threatening to rain on several acres of hay that was cured and ready for storage, it is likely that all hands in the household worked to avoid this possible economic loss. Actually, any number of farm-related exigencies could affect the attendance record of children. A cow might get into fresh corn during the night, die from bloat, and require all hands the next day to butcher the animal before the meat went bad. One mother sent the teacher a note to excuse her daughter's absence because "the stork is due any day now." [42]

A school board clerk in Rock County, Wisconsin, wrote to the state superintendent of public instruction in 1852 asking why it was necessary to keep a record of absence and tardiness. He complained that "in large schools where pupils are entering at all hours, which they have an *undeniable right* to do, it is certainly a severe task, and injurious to the school for the Teacher to be obliged to drop all business and betake himself to his Register, in order to enter therein, every instance of tardiness." [43] Of course, part of the rationale of the common school movement rested on the fact that parents did not have "undeniable rights" with respect to the education of their children. The state had rights in this regard as well.

Records kept by children about themselves are scarce. Diaries of nineteenth- and early-twentieth-century schoolchildren are rare. Those that exist seem to suggest that Elizabeth Hampsten's contention in her history of childhood on the plains, *Settlers' Children*, that "school, not play, was the opposite of work, but for most, work was more taken for granted than school" is indeed accurate. George Coleman kept a sparse diary from December 1869 through June 1870. George was the son of James Coleman, the subdirector of subdistrict 9, Clinton Township, Linn County, Iowa. The diary was kept on the blank pages of an old subdistrict 9 clerk's book. The diary leaves the reader with an appreciation of how a young Iowa farm boy interacted with the institution of formal schooling. [44]

On Monday, 6 December 1869, George indicated that the winter school term had begun. He did not attend, however, because his family needed his help picking and husking corn. But on Thursday of that week he noted in his diary that "it rained last night and nearly all day. I had to go to school." The following day, nevertheless, he was back in the fields: "we husked corn today but it was pretty muddy and sloshy." Four days later the last of the corn was picked. On Wednesday, 15 December, George began attending school on a regular basis.

On 20 December, George confided to his diary: "Sour old Monday has come and with it school." References to anything happening in school trail off at this point until Wednesday, 5 January 1870. "It was very frosty this morning and I built a fire at the schoolhouse. The teacher jerked some of the scholars today." Over the course of the next two months, George displayed little interest in his life at school. He did seem to write favorably about "singing schools" and "spelling schools." These were essentially evening social gatherings at the schoolhouse where adults and children alike could compete in a spelling bee or singing contest. They occurred most frequently during winter term when there was very little else to do in the way of entertainment. On Friday, 25 February, George reported with some relief that the last day of the term had arrived, but he noted with perhaps some disappointment that he "did not get through the book."

After two months away from school, on 2 May, summer term began. George noted, "Our school commenced this morning, had 22 scholars. I commenced where I left of [sic] in all my studies. Except grammar." Two days later he reported: "I was to school as I was every other day." However, from May 9 to 13 he was not sent to school. Rather, he worked with his father "plowing, harrowing, and butchering." After the weekend and two more days' respite from school, Monday arrived. "O dear me School School Forever." The following Monday, 23 May, George was sent to "school this fore noon," but "worked for Jim this afternoon planting corn—we covered four acres." On Tuesday, 7 June, he reported "quite a fuss in school" because of something "some of the boys did." A week later George was again excused from school. "I done my first corn plowing [cultivating] this morning." The diary entries end shortly after this point.

This brief glimpse at the childhood of George Coleman is likely representative of the experiences of many rural schoolboys in the Midwest. This diary, along with other accounts, suggests that the institution of formal schooling in this predominantly agrarian society was something that was accommodated rather than something that was heartily embraced. With an understanding of the centrality of farm labor in the rural Midwest should also come more leverage over the question of why state-sponsored schools and school initiatives were resisted by so many in the countryside.

During the nineteenth and early twentieth centuries, rural schoolteachers, both male and female, generally lived away from their parents in a home situated within the school district where they taught. There is nothing in the available records that would indicate that rural families generously opened their homes to the school "marm" or "master" out of sheer gratitude. School boards were sometimes forced to spell out in detail how they planned to keep a roof over the teacher. In Joint District 8 of Sauk County, Wisconsin, the board "voted to employ a male teacher for the winter term of . . . 1860 and 1861, also that the teacher is to board with those that send to school, the time that each one is to board is as the number of his children sent is to the whole number sent." In other locations it was enough for the board to stipulate that the teacher will "board with the scholars." The most common arrangement during the postbellum years was for the school board to fix a sum to pay any family in the district for boarding the teacher by the month.

By the early twentieth century, in some locations, the teacher's pay was increased to such that the teacher might arrange for his or her own lodging. [45]

Few teachers' complaints among available records concern their experiences living in the homes of district residents. Yet there were frequently problems and prejudices to be overcome. Sometimes teachers taught in districts that made it difficult for them to attend the church of their choice. A devout Lutheran, Almida Goodman found herself teaching in a rural North Dakota township where a Catholic church was the only one in the area. She was asked by her boarders if she wished to attend mass. Said Goodman, "I was told that if a Lutheran came into a Catholic church, when the Lutheran went out, they'd wash the pews . . . I don't want that to happen if I go with you to church." "'Oh my goodness, no,'" replied her host, "'we don't do that.'" [46]

The church issue apparently caused no great hardships for boarding teachers. However, in one instance a teacher complained of contracting head lice while boarding around. [47] Teachers were rarely pressed to participate in the functions of the farmstead economy. Milking and its attendant labors were apparently not the teachers' responsibility. Teachers needed to rise early and begin their labors in the schoolhouse before the children arrived. The case of James Shields is typical.

On the morning of 9 November 1885, Shields awoke at 5:15 A.M. to begin his third term as teacher in a country school. He was lucky, for this job was close enough to his home to make it possible for him to board with his parents. Nevertheless, nothing in his diary indicates that he was compelled to take part in the morning or evening farmstead chores. Weekends, however, were another story. On Saturdays he frequently helped butcher hogs, haul hay, and feed livestock.

At 7:30 A.M. on this Monday, Shields arrived at the schoolhouse, "started the fire, swept, and had all in readiness before nine when with fourteen pupils enrolled [I] formally called the school to order." Next, Shields was to take down the names of the scholars, make note of the textbooks from which they would study, and lay down the "program" regarding how schoolhouse affairs would proceed. According to Shields's account, the day passed quietly, and school was adjourned at 4:00. [48] Shields, like his scholars, walked to the schoolhouse. However, sometimes his father would come by buggy at 4:00 and take him home.

The first duty of the day during winter term was to start a fire in the stove. However, this was not always easily managed. Frequently, the stove was located in the middle of the schoolhouse with a long length of horizontal pipe leading to the brick chimney at the back of the house. No doubt the central location dispersed heat more equitably than if the stove were located at one end of the building, but the long horizontal connection to the chimney sometimes made acquiring the proper draft a tricky affair. When the brick chimney was cold in the morning, it could take several attempts to create a proper draft. In the meantime, the schoolhouse might become quite smoky. After many experiences with this result, a rural Iowa school board decided to "change the flues so as to have a strait pipe." [49] Additionally, if the wood fuel was wet from snow or not sufficiently cured, the fire-starting process was not easily managed. Shields struggled with the fires throughout the winter term of 1885–86. "Had some bother with the fire this morning, but finally got it started," reflects a typical diary entry. Shields had an older male student during this winter term who was apparently eager to help in any way that he could. Later in the term he began coming earlier than Shields, getting into the locked schoolhouse through a window, and starting the fire. Shields commented on 26 February, "On arriving at the schoolhouse this morning found that Harry had got in, and started a fire, of which I was not sorry."

For female teachers, seeing smoke rising from the schoolhouse chimney before their arrival was a signal not to enter the building. Drifters often used schoolhouses as a place to spend the night in warmth. When a teacher encountered such a situation, she generally awaited older male pupils before approaching the house. Most often, the night's occupants were gone. Frequently, however, a man would take his leave with a gruff, "I slept here last night." [50]

Possibly to combat this situation and certainly to ease the burden of getting a fire started, school districts sometimes hired a man to come in early and start the fire for the teacher. And in some instances the teacher's pay was slightly inflated so that she could be "compelled to hire someone" to start the fires for her. In other instances the teacher's contract stipulated that the teacher was to start his or her own fires and do the sweeping. A township board in Iowa decided that all teachers in the district be "bound in their contracts to do their own firebuilding and sweeping." Another Iowa district, after fielding requests from bold teachers who asked for extra pay for these duties, "resolved that we employ no teacher for the present year who make any claim on the district for back service for making fires or cleaning house." Often, however, eager schoolchildren, boys and girls alike, were quite anxious to do the fire starting or the sweeping for the teacher. A rural Illinois teacher nervously confided to his diary concerning the unexpected visit of one of the school board members, "the girls had neglected to sweep and he found a dirty house."[51]

Along with getting the fires started, teachers faced other problems (some seasonal, others not), as revealed by Shields's diary. On Monday, 16 November, one week after winter term officially commenced, Shields found that three new pupils were ready to begin school. After appropriately seating them—boys on one side, girls on the other—classes began. The quiet that prevailed the first day, however, began to wane. On Wednesday, 18 November, he confessed that "the boys were so noisy that I kept them after school for twenty minutes." Teachers could expect a steady influx of male students in the early weeks of winter terms as different families finished the corn harvest.

When the third week of school began, Shields commented that he "had [a] notable acquisition in the person of Harry Davis, noted for his good behavior in school." On the Friday following Thanksgiving, Shields gave his first examination in history. Dividing by gender, he noted the group scores in his diary: "average of girls 88%, of boys 45%. Girls over boys 43%." He typically supplied his diary with similar delineations after examinations throughout the term.

On the fourth Monday of winter session, another male asked for admission to Shields's school. Apparently, Louis Prahl did not share the reputation of Harry Davis, for Shields noted in his diary that "before enrolling him I asked the advice of the Board, receiving him conditionally meanwhile." The next day Shields was given permission to enroll Prahl permanently.

By the time the second month of the winter term had begun, Shields was settling in to his new charge. The students, too, were becoming accustomed to the teacher. At recess, according to Shields, it was common for a student "to favor us with a song." New student Louis Prahl frequently "entertained the school with some music on a mouth organ." On one occasion after returning from lunch with his parents, Shields related that he was surprised to find everyone in the schoolhouse dancing. And although they immediately stopped when they saw him, he encouraged them to continue for a time.

When Monday, 7 December, began the fifth week of the term, Shields found himself with four new pupils and was forced to spend "half an hour getting them arranged." However, the rest of the day seemed to go well. They were treated to "a song by Carrie at noon, and a couple of waltzes at the afternoon recess." The fifth week ended with a visit from the county superintendent. All went well: "The children rose on his entrence and again at his departure and were very good."

Week six began with seven new pupils at the schoolhouse door. Five were admitted, two "were refused on account of being [from] outside the District." After beginning the term with fourteen students, Shields was now teaching twenty-six scholars. However, an interesting occurrence quickly reduced the number to twenty-five. On Monday, 14 December, one of the school board members entered the schoolhouse in the afternoon and, according to Shields, "without even consulting my rights as teacher, rudely expelled (or ordered) Annie Prahl to leave the school." When school was dismissed, Shields went to another trustee's home "to register my solemn protest against the act of today but received no satisfaction."

This expulsion is interesting for it quite obviously had nothing to do with Annie Prahl's behavior or performance in school.

More than likely, it had been determined that Annie had committed some impropriety or some act of immorality somewhere off school grounds. From Shields's earlier comments concerning Louis, it seems likely that the Prahl family had a rather unsavory reputation in the vicinity and consequently that schooling for the family was a tenuous affair, subject to the whims of the district trustees. Invoking political localism, the established farmers who served on boards of education exercised wide powers to manipulate the local school as they saw fit.

By late December the peace and quiet that reigned in the schoolhouse earlier in the term began to slowly disintegrate. New students apparently brought with them old animosities, and on 23 December Shields commented that "there was war to the knife between the clans this morning and I finally had to intervene." This misbehavior spilled over into the classroom. And the intervention of the Christmas holidays seemingly did little to ameliorate tensions. On 28 December Shields confessed that the turmoil in the schoolhouse was such "that the ruler had to be wielded with unusual force."

Things were no better the next day. "The boys were outrageously noisy this morning and a couple of them got a sound flogging which quieted the school somewhat." Still, the noise picked up in the afternoon, and Shields decided to keep "nearly all the boys" after school. However, as Shields explained, "George and Nick Berigan both refused to remain, and forced their way out by main force. After severely censuring the conduct of the others, [I] dismissed them and went up to Berigan's and made a bitter complaint of the two, which (although Berigan got very hot over it) will probably result in their being kept at home, a source of great relief to me, and a good riddance to the school." On Wednesday, Shields was able to relate that "peace seamed to reign in the schoolroom today after the nonarrival of the two scamps."

January brought a great deal of snow to rural Rice County, Minnesota, keeping school attendance quite low and hence troublesome incidents at a minimum. However, on Tuesday, 26 January, the "school was nearly full," and Shields was forced to remark in his diary that "the ruler was wielded lively in the afternoon." On 28 January, "a little scene after dinner . . . served to make me anything but sweet during the afternoon and not a smile crossed my face during that time." By 29 January, Shields was happy to report that "today was not any noisier than usual" and that "the third month of the term closed without any ill feeling."

Clearly, by this point in the term, Shields was somewhat disillusioned with the school or with teaching in general. On 1 February, he remarked that the day "moved on as usual with nothing to relieve the monotony." On 4 February, he noted that "the school was noisy as usual." Shields began once again to rely on his ruler to keep order in the schoolroom. Perhaps this explains why on 11 February he noted in his diary that his ruler had disappeared, "and in spite of every place being searched, it was not found." A day later, his ruler still not found, he brought another "for temporary use." The following week, his ruler reappeared, albeit broken into pieces. Still angry two weeks later, he commented that "woe be to the one or ones who took it if I find it out." In the meantime, his replacement ruler seemed to suffice. On 26 February, he confided to his diary that "Tom Berigan got a good hiding for tampering with the stove." The next day, Friday, Shields "breathed a sigh of relief when four [o'clock] dismissed them."

The term was nearly over. On Wednesday, 3 March, "after starting the fire for the last time," Shields awarded "premiums" to the deserving scholars. In the afternoon he heard the final recitations and sang with the students. He confessed to his diary that while giving his final remarks "my feelings so overcame me that I was able to say but a few words, expressing my affection and wishing them every happiness in the future. After all had gone, my pentup heart showed my sorrow in tears." Overcoming this wave of emotion, he returned his register to one of the trustees, filed his term reports, and left to keep a dinner engagement.

A few days later he went to the home of one of the trustees "to formally return the keys" and discuss with him the possibility of teaching the school during summer term. Shields "obtained his consent if the others were willing," then went to the

home of another board member, "but got no satisfactory answer there." Eight days later Shields remarked in his diary
that he had been informed "that the District wanted a female
teacher," so "without any more talk," he verbally withdrew his
application.

Finding summer employment was difficult for male teachers. Common wisdom held that female teachers could handle
summer terms because the older boys generally were too pre-
occupied with farm work to attend at this time. However, male
teachers were thought to be quite necessary for the winter
term. As a result, men and women alike suffered from dis-
criminatory hiring practices depending on the season. As the
nineteenth century waned, however, it became a greater burden for men to find summer work than for women to find winter work. Country school teaching in particular became thor-
oughly feminized by the century's end. Men turned to teaching
almost out of desperation, often acknowledging privately that
they recognized the work as something less than manly. Robert
Pike, a schoolteacher in rural Washington County, Minnesota,
wrote in a letter to a friend about his decision to "resign his
school." When urged by this same friend not to give up teaching, Pike wrote in his diary that "I cannot consent . . . I will
stand up in my manhood" and leave the teaching profession.
It was more than ten years, however, before he accomplished
this. James Wiley, a rural Indiana teacher, wrote to his brother
in 1835: "I have been constantly engaged in this school for the
last nine months but my school will be out in ten days, and I
wish to quit the business if I can possibly commence the practice of medicine. I understand you have bought the Lockwood
farm if so let me know whether you will rent it to me, if so
I will not go to [medicine] but will follow the farming business." Wiley's words demonstrate how transient the midwestern teaching force was. Few men or women made a life-long
career of teaching. Most men, like Wiley, worked into tenant
farming until the dream of owning land was fulfilled. [52]

The demand for summer harvest labor across the Midwest
provided an avenue to the "farming business," albeit an arduous
one. Depending on local conditions, teachers generally took
a pay cut to work in the small grain fields. At a teachers' meet-

ing in Monroe County, Indiana, in 1843, a participant commented about lay perceptions of the teaching field as well as agricultural versus educational wages:

> The occupation of a teacher is too often compared with that of a common laborer. A laborer can be employed for from $6.00 to $10.00 a month and why should not a man teach school for as little, since teaching school is not as hard as mauling rails, grubbing, plowing, etc. I once heard a farmer say while talking about the price of teaching, that if he were making $10.00 a month he would think he was doing good business, and to give a teacher $20 and $25 a month was entirely too exorbitant.[53]

Summer teaching, then, for most of the last half of the nineteenth century, was the near-exclusive domain of the female teacher. The diary of Anna Webber provides some insight into the experience of a first-time teacher in the trans-Mississippi frontier. From May through July 1881, Webber kept a diary of her experience teaching the summer term in Mitchell County, Kansas.

"My anticipations are great," wrote Webber after her first day of teaching country school. She was filled with optimism despite the conditions in her little frame schoolhouse not being conducive to effective instruction. There were "no desks, benches, seats, black board or writing desks." She wrote the first page of her diary while seated on the floor with her paper on "the Teacher's chair." Boards placed on top of rocks provided the only seating for the scholars.

On Thursday, 12 May, her fourth day of teaching, Webber remarked that "I am getting along splendidly. Now if I only had seats and a black board it would be so nice." On Friday her enthusiasm seemed to wane slightly. "One of the twelve weeks is gone. I am not realy settled to school-teaching yet, because I expect more scholars, and new furniture. I hope it will come, for it seems allmost impossible to get along with nothing to write on, or no place to put books."

Webber lived in the home of William McPeak's family

throughout the term. She regretted that she was too far from home to return frequently and visit her friends, yet she seems to have gotten along quite well in the McPeaks's home. Between school terms, county superintendents from across the Middle West were often barraged by letters from teachers looking to teach in a school "closer to home."[54] Homesickness plagued Webber throughout the term. Her separation from her sister, Nellie, was especially difficult.

On Wednesday, 18 May, Webber noted that "Charlie Anderson broke a window light today. He was playing ball (with a rock for a ball)." Other than this obvious indiscretion, disciplining the scholars was not much of a problem for Webber during the first weeks of the term. She even regretted not having "large scholars who were further advanced." Webber taught eleven pupils during the first three weeks of the term. The oldest was just thirteen.

As the novelty of heading a classroom for the first time began to diminish, melancholy crept into Webber's diary. The quiet of the vast, open Kansas prairie seemed to make her contemplative. On 26 May, she wrote, "It is certainly the most quiet place I was ever in." After seven weeks of school she confessed, "It is getting monotonous. not the school, but the surroundings, just the same quietness, seeing the same objects, and going through the same performances day after day, with no merriment or changes mix in it." As the summer wore on, the rains disappeared. The year 1881 marked the beginning of a lengthy drought in Kansas and in other states of the trans-Mississippi West. Its ramifications were not lost on Webber: "We need rain so bad, evry thing is nearly burned up. O, dear this is a hard place to live, this Kansas is. I wonder what in the world will become of us."

Teachers in the arid states of the Great Plains frequently became inwardly speculative. Many moved into isolated areas from more populated places pursuing their first teaching positions. Often the stark environment combined with little local enthusiasm for education to make teaching in remote areas a difficult occasion for young, inexperienced girls. A rural Nebraska teacher remarked in her diary, "'This is a beastly day!!

Rain and snow and *school*! The fire won't burn and we are all huddled up in our sweaters and the children are complaining because we are here. I really can't blame them. I feel the same way. I had a date tonight, cancelled because of the storm. There is just no end to my *misery*.'"⁵⁵ A former county super- intendent in North Dakota recalled a few young women who took their loneliness out on their students. Once, when this superintendent arrived before 9:00 to visit such a teacher, she found several children locked out of the schoolhouse in freez- ing temperatures. When asked why, the teacher replied, "'I can't stand those kids.'" One professional educator toured 103 North Dakota country schools and described in detail some impoverished educational circumstances. In one instance she wrote about a teacher who "allows no leaving the room. Her beginners have large wet circles in their trousers."⁵⁶

While Webber did not go to extremes in taking out her loneliness on students, circumstances did become troublesome as the summer progressed. Her difficulties with rock-throwing Charlie Anderson increased: "He is such a careless, lazy little rascal. He seems to take no interest whatever in trying to learn. I don't know what to do with him." After a month of teaching school Webber reluctantly related the misfortune of having "to keep a scholar after school." Said Webber, "I don't like to punish a pupil, and I have very little to do of it." But things changed.

A week later she was forced "to keep two after school" but added quickly that "I have no serious difficulties but the mis- chievous little rascals are into some mischief half the time." When a fight among the scholars occurred outside the school- house, Webber confessed that it was enough to drive her to tears. Her ability to discipline the scholars began to diminish, and on 29 June she wrote that she "had the pleasure of giving a little chap a whipping." On 22 July, she confessed, "I had to keep two scholars this evening, and that is not all I did for them, the little rascals." Obviously, she had come a long way from the timid teacher who expressed regret at the first occa- sion of holding a pupil after class.⁵⁷

Webber was convinced that the parents in Mitchell County

cared little for education. When she took the job she had been promised that school desks and a blackboard would arrive shortly after the term began. She expressed dismay in her diary when she learned that the furniture had arrived in the county but the local farmers were too busy to pick it up at the rail station and deliver it to the school. "They are not going after them now until they get their corn planted. Then perhaps it will be, 'not until after harvest,' and I wouldn't wonder if by that time it would be 'Let's build a good house first.'"

A few weeks before Webber's summer term ended, the farmers delivered the school desks. A week later she received a blackboard. Though she was certainly not aware of it, she was fortunate to receive those few amenities. Throughout the 1870s and 1880s in the states of the trans-Mississippi West, teachers labored in deplorable conditions. Since about half the farms of the trans-Mississippi West created between 1862 and 1880 were begun under the provisions of the 1862 Homestead Act, lean years for burgeoning school districts were inevitable. Until homesteaders received proper title after five years of "proving" their claim, their property was not eligible for tax assessment. Consequently, school funds were scarce. One rural Kansas teacher recalled the circumstances of her first teaching position:

> "The schoolbuilding was a sod 'dugout,' about fourteen feet long with dirt floor, unplastered walls, two small windows in front, heated by a small fireplace about one yard across. It had neither blackboard, teachers's desk nor chair. The seats were small logs split and supported by pegs, and were placed at the sides of the room. I taught in five districts and in all there were no outbuildings, but some had teacher's desks and chairs, also blackboards and lights."[58]

In good weather teachers who taught in "soddies" sometimes conducted lessons outdoors because the lighting was always poor inside. During inclement weather, they carried on as best they could indoors. Without a blackboard, innovative teachers used a sturdy stick to etch letters and numbers into the dirt floor.

A public school superintendent of Washington County, Nebraska, kept detailed notes on the schools he visited. When he inspected sod schoolhouses, his usual comment was "the school is in a cave." However, frequently frame or log schoolhouses offered no more in terms of comfort or convenience. The following represents a typical 1870s description by this superintendent: "A poor excuse for a schoolroom, no furniture, no blackboard, badly seated but well ventilated."[59] "Good ventilation" evolved into a humorous phrase used to describe a building's shortcomings. Log schoolhouses required constant maintenance to keep some type of mortar blocking the gaps between logs. Teachers in Morrison County, Minnesota, were asked on their term reports in 1883 how the schoolhouse was ventilated. Typical responses included "by the cracks in the floor," "by the broken out windows," and "by the holes in the walls." Others less sarcastically answered "by opening a window" or "by opening the door."[60]

Questions were also asked concerning the privies on the schoolgrounds. Out of the forty-six teachers' term reports submitted to the Morrison County superintendent, twenty indicated that their district had no privies, twelve districts had one, and nine indicated that their district was equipped with two privies, while five teachers neglected to report any such information. The lack of proper outdoor facilities was one reason why some school boards were adamant about teachers keeping separate recess periods for boys and girls. The county superintendent of Olmsted County, Minnesota, chastised one district in the local paper for having no outhouse while the school was located on the prairie, "making it impossible to get out of view." During the 1870s Nebraska's state superintendent of public instruction wrote that "there are in the state 693 schoolhouses without a shadow of an outhouse. Shame! Shame!! on such districts." By 1918 there were companies who played up the disease potential of "unspeakable outhouses" to convince local boards to convert coat rooms or schoolhouse antechambers into water closets.[61]

Some districts provided outhouses of high quality early on. District 3 of Albion Township, Dane County, Wisconsin, built a brick privy in 1869 and a second one in 1894. Another Wisconsin district went to the trouble of constructing "stone vaults to put the outhouses on." In 1887 District 7 of Spencer Brooks Township, Isanti County, Minnesota, voted to build "two privies with three holes each." Before the 1890s, one outhouse was more typical than two or none. However, during the late 1890s, state departments of education set requirements for the construction of *two* privies separated by stipulated distances. As a result, typical twentieth-century schoolhouses were shadowed by two small outhouses. [62]

If the diaries of nineteenth- and early-twentieth-century rural teachers are any indication, teachers' primary classroom concern was establishing and maintaining proper discipline. Even the methods primers from which they studied suggested that "discipline is the first essential for class teaching, the power to teach is the next."[63] Before the advent of a state-sponsored common school system, teachers who earned their living by subscription wages sometimes determined for themselves the amount of misbehavior they would tolerate. When a scholar exceeded the teacher's tolerance level, the scholar was dismissed, as the circumstances described in the diary of a rural Iowa teacher suggests. Arozina Perkins taught a subscription school near Ft. Des Moines in the fall of 1850. She made arrangements with an older male scholar to start the fire every morning in exchange for his tuition. Now and then, however, he neglected his duty. Perkins wrote, "'This happened so frequently and the boy who pretends to see to it is such a notoriously mischievous and wicked fellow that I decided to tell him not to come to school any longer.'"[64] Although the father of this student was not pleased, parents could make little complaint if the teacher no longer accepted a subscription fee.

As schooling shifted into quasi-state support with some measure of subscription, circumstances changed very little. The sale or lease of school lands as prescribed by midwestern state constitutions, though mishandled terribly, did result in some funds finding their way to local districts. Not coming directly from the pockets of local farmers via a tax assessment, schooling paid for but not received because of a teacher's arbitrary behavior tolerance apparently caused little concern.

When common schools arrived, this changed. Local residents knew to the dollar what the local school levy cost them. If their children were dismissed from school, the amount did not change. School boards were then left to consider what might become a dismissable offense. A township superintendent in the early years of district formation in Wisconsin wrote to the state superintendent of public instruction to ask if districts had "a right to summarily expel disorderly students." Generally, local school board members did not wish to incur the enmity of their neighbors over what might be construed as the capricious dismissal of a son or daughter from the local school. Yet some of the offenses committed by students seemed to require their removal from the schoolroom.

Ultimately, a compromise was reached over the expulsion issue. With few state guidelines to direct procedures, and fewer court cases on which to base these guidelines, expelling a student became a temporary banishment. Frequently, the student was allowed to return after a few days. In June 1859, the Fairview Township board in Jones County, Iowa, resolved to "delegate to each subdirector the power to expel scholars from school in their respective districts for incorrigible bad conduct and also to permit such bad scholars to attend school again when the subdirector is satisfied that the scholar has comended his behavior." The result of the tension created by tax-supported schools and the expulsion question was that local boards looked to hire teachers who kept order among the scholars. Consequently, teachers were allowed, and sometimes encouraged, to use corporal punishment. On 16 July 1892, a district clerk in rural Big Stone County, Minnesota, entered into his record book: "Moved and seconded and carred [sic] that the teacher has liberty to use a swich to govern the school."[65]

In fact, the switch was used often in country schools. Both Shields and Webber relied heavily on "whippings" to create incentive for proper schoolroom behavior. But a litany of disciplinary procedures preceded the resort to violence. As the diaries of Shields and Webber suggest, keeping students after school hours or denying recess privileges was common. If this failed, some teachers would try to embarrass the recalcitrant student into conforming behavior. Although no evidence suggests that the practice was ever widespread, the "dunce hat" has been infrequently referred to.[66] More often students were told to stand in the corner. Boys were frequently commanded to "sit on the girls' side." Sometimes scholars were directed to keep their arms outstretched while standing silently. Or they might be instructed to apologize to the class one hundred times on the blackboard.

Sooner or later, however, teachers had to come to terms with the issue of corporal punishment. There was no principal to whom disorderly students could be sent. The problem child was the teacher's alone to face. The nearest adult might be a mile away. Often, for young women, the fear of older male students was constant. One teacher remarked in her diary that she was teaching older boys before whom she "stood in mortal terror."[67] Generally, the "large boys," as they were frequently referred to, instigated the rural teacher's worst nightmare: being "turned (or "carried") out." This phrase is sometimes thought to be synonymous with "running a teacher off," but the latter phrase was something quite different. Running a teacher off generally meant that the students gave the teacher such a rough time that she or he would not consider teaching there another term. Or it might mean that a teacher simply quit before the term was over. This happened more frequently than one might imagine. Being turned or carried out, however, meant just that. In such instances the students simply took the teacher out of the building by force and then retreated inside with the door locked. This was rare, but it happened now and again. Edward Eggleston's fictional teacher in *The Hoosier Schoolmaster* scurried to the roof of the building and placed a cap on the chimney to smoke out the children after he had been turned out.[68]

Most often, however, the teacher who was carried out went straight to the home of a district board member. In Waveland

Township, Pottawattamie County, Iowa, a special meeting was called to consider such an occasion. After his unfortunate experience, the teacher went to the home of the subdirector of his school. The subdirector went immediately to the school and informed the four main culprits that they had a choice: "take their punishment or be expelled." The students chose to be expelled. On learning of this, however, the parents of these children complained to the township board "that the subdirector of said subdistrict had expelled scholars without cause." The subdirector maintained that the four students "had violated the rules of school, locked the teacher out of the schoolhouse, and committed other offences, tending to injure the school and subvert the teachers authority." The board upheld that the teacher and subdirector acted within the rules and that the students could return "*provided* they submit to punishment for breaking the rules which caused there expulsion."[69]

It is rare to find reasonably rich diary accounts or school district records without frequent references to corporal punishment. Few education historians would quarrel with the assertion that throughout the nineteenth century discipline was viewed as the key to successful teaching. Considerable evidence suggests that in addition to correcting misbehavior, the switch was used as punishment for "imperfectly recited lessons."[70] What one does not find in the available data on nineteenth-century rural teachers is any acknowledgment that some students were less capable of reciting their lessons due to intellectual deficiency. Poor performance translated into an inadequate exercise of will, a moral or spiritual, rather than intellectual, failure. The switch was not spared on students so deficient in character that they could not master or attend to their lessons. The legacy of age-old Protestant demands for schooled congregations lingered in the countryside in a system coopted by an increasingly powerful industrial order. As later development in intelligence testing generated differentiated curricula, it also sparked new questions about the place of corporal punishment in schools. Does it make sense to beat students for poor performance if they do not possess the intellectual power necessary to perform well? After 1918, clearly science, not religion, became the stimulus in educational study for questions of scholars' motivation and performance. In rural schools before 1918, however, older notions of mental sensibilities and will seemed to legitimate lively use of the switch.

Samuel A. Briggs taught in rural schools in De Kalb County, Illinois, during the late 1850s. Upon traveling into the city of DeKalb for a county teachers' meeting one January day in 1858, he wrote in his diary that he "found the people laboring under a great deal of excitement in consequence of the teacher, Mr. Martin, cruelly punishing one of his scholars." Records indicate that now and then teachers did go too far and that parents of the young victims often sought redress by remonstrating the teacher, petitioning for the teacher's removal, or, in some cases, taking legal action. In subdistrict 6 of Waveland Township, Pottawattamie County, Iowa, charges were brought against a teacher by a group of unhappy parents. These charges outlined that the teacher "1) refused to comply with the rules laid down for her government [of the school], 2) for cruel and unusual punishment, and 3) for incompetency, partiality, and dereliction in discharge of duties." On a five to two vote, however, the board voted not to dismiss the teacher. In a neighboring township, board member William McCartney brought a complaint to a township board meeting. McCartney served as trustee for subdistrict 4. The minutes of that meeting read as follows: "A charge was prefered [sic] against J. W. Hempsted teacher in SubDist No4 by Wm McCartney of punishing one of his children in a brutal and unusual manner. After listening to testimony from Miss M. A. McCartney, Miss Jennie Larrington, S. A. Van and Frances Helterbran the Board unanimously justified the teacher." McCartney immediately tendered his resignation as subdirector, which the board accepted. [71]

The situation in DeKalb was apparently quite serious, for Briggs remarked in his diary that Martin "was afraid of being mobbed," yet the circumstances apparently roused little suspicion in Briggs as to the benefits of corporal punishment. [72] Less than a month later he confessed to his diary that he was "obliged to whip Albert Durgers and Albert Jordan to day for setting an ink bottle on its nose on a book." On 12 March, he found himself in a situation similar to that of the DeKalb teacher. Briggs said, "I had occasion to punish Cyrus Croff for striking Elanor Kelsey in the face. James saw what I was doing and ran and told his mother that I was beating Cyrus. She came up and demanded her two boys—I told her of course she could have them—she began to lecture me . . . and that her boys had done with school for this winter."[73] A rural Iowa teacher wrote in her diary about a discipline incident that also drew a parent's ire. Because it suggests much about the day-to-day operation of a rural school, the diary entry is worth quoting at some length. Sarah Huftalen began her 30 November 1906 diary entry explaining that

> when the boys came in at Recess Maurice and Roy whispered loudly while hanging up their hats. Edward (a new pupil) sat half way in his seat with the front half of his feet projecting in the aisle. He not being accustomed to the rules I thought the boys would see it and avoid it but it looked to me as though they both tried to stumble and then say "whew" and make a fuss. Roy kept still when I said "Let us be still" but Maurice kept on and when I spoke more sternly he saucily replied "All Right!" I went to him and asked him if he knew a teacher could not be answered in that way and that it was a way to get punishment and I gave him a couple of spats on the cheek, or rather one on the cheek and one on the hand as he put it up. When school closed . . . I detained him and asked his reason for disorderly conduct and talking back to his teacher—and he could give no reason. The tears came to his eyes and I told him I would not bring him before the school [board] or whip him this time as it was his first offense. His mother sent a note afterward . . . saying or rather threatening that which was scarcely called for and which I do not think she would have written if she had known more about it.[74]

In rural Sangamon County, Illinois, a public meeting was held on a February evening in 1838 to discuss an unusually severe whipping administered by the local schoolteacher. One in attendance wrote that the boy's "back, sides, and hips exhibited incontrovertible proof that he had been placed under the tuition of one who knew how to torture as well as teach." Several angry men attempted to seize the teacher after witnessing the manifestations of the beating. School board members tried to protect him, and "a brief scuffle ensued."[75]

In Wisconsin a district clerk wrote to the state superintendent asking if the school board must financially support their teacher after he was found guilty of assault and battery.[76] In North Dakota a teacher had his license revoked for raising an iron poker and threatening to strike an older male student. The circumstances behind this incident reveal how difficult country school teaching could be and therefore merit further examination. Elmer Thompson, the teacher, was born and raised in Blue Earth County, Minnesota. After a common school education, he attended the normal school at Mankato. When he finished the course of study there, he went on to high school in Garden City. Before he could graduate, however, he took a position as teacher in a Blue Earth County school. From there he moved west and taught several terms in Lac Qui Parle County, Minnesota. After various certificate examinations over the years, Thompson received second-grade credentials.

By the 1890s, county superintendents across the Midwest were granting first-, second-, and third-grade teaching certificates. The particulars regarding what these gradations meant varied from state to state, and even from county to county. Generally, however, success on the toughest exams meant that one would receive a first-grade certificate. Minimally acceptable exam scores entitled one to a third-grade certificate. Second-grade certificates, such as Thompson's, were somewhere in between. Those teachers with the highest certificate level were able to command the highest salary.

When Thompson moved to Richland County, North Dakota, in the fall of 1889, the issue of his certificate grade level became significant. Thompson described what to him was a lackadaisical examination that he received from William House, the Richland County superintendent of schools. It included "a few written examples in arithmetic . . . about 25 words in spelling . . . and a few oral questions, comprising in all less than an hour."[77] Thompson expected to receive a second-grade certificate when the examination was over, as he had on previous occasions in Minnesota. However, writing to North Dakota's state superintendent of instruction, Thompson claimed that House had said "he was entitled to $3." Thompson described the circumstances: "I kept silent because I did not know why I should pay the three dollars, but I have reason to think that if I had handed him the $3 that he would have given me a second grade certificate—but, what was my consternation when he said that he could give me only a third grade certificate."

Dismayed, Thompson apparently arranged to teach the winter term in District 1, Barrie Township, Richland County, by intimating to the district clerk that he held a second-grade certificate. Thompson's decision to deceive the school board concerning his certificate level convoluted later troubles. It was a rough district. More than a few older male scholars continually made things difficult for Thompson. Thompson claimed that parents in the district tried to stir up controversy over the school because of a longstanding neighborhood quarrel. After a little more than a month into the winter term, the schoolhouse mysteriously burned down. A log house was constructed shortly thereafter so that the winter term might continue.

Inside the new school, Thompson's difficulties with the older boys increased. He described the circumstances:

> They formed a league and made their threats that "if the teacher laid his hands on any of the boys they would carry him out." One day I saw fit to pull one of the boys out onto the floor, another boy started forward and said, "hold on there." I told him to "keep still," and he said "I won't do it," at that I raised the stove poker above his head which sent their "sand" down into their boot. I did not intend to strike with the poker, but only meant to scar[e?] them as I knew it would.

Complaints went out to the county superintendent. As a result, the certificate issue was discovered and certain district residents became even more angry with Thompson. Many called for his resignation. Defending himself before witnesses, Thompson called William House, not present at the time, a liar. Word of this got back to House, who went to "visit" Thompson's school. While class was in session, House demanded to know if Thompson had raised an iron poker over the scholars' heads. Thompson replied that he had. House then asked if Thompson had called House a liar. Thompson replied that he "did not know but it might be that during the excitement I did." House wrote out a notice of license revocation and handed it to Thompson, who refused to take it. House then set it on Thompson's desk and left. The notice stipulated that the license had been revoked for "immorality and incompetence."

Thompson appealed to the state superintendent of instruction. Both he and House filed affidavits. Favorable letters of character reference were sent on Thompson's behalf from county superintendents in Minnesota. In the meantime, however, House discovered from school board members that Thompson had told them he possessed a second-grade certificate. This disclosure did not bode well for Thompson. In his official decision on the matter, state superintendent William J. Clapp wrote that "the whole proceedings of the revocation and the appeal in this case, appear to have been quite irregular." Nevertheless, Clapp affirmed the decision of the county superintendent stating that both "patrons and scholars strenuously objected to their teacher and his school." However, Clapp found no justification for the charge of immorality and reduced the cause of the revocation to incompetence. [78]

Difficulties between teachers and county superintendents, like those between Elmer Thompson and William House, were not uncommon. Eliza Dean, for example, began teaching in District 12 of Green Prairie Township, Morrison County, Minnesota, in the summer of 1884. Morrison County superintendent A. Guernon kept detailed records of the schools he visited for a number of years. For two years before Dean's arrival at District 12, the school averaged close to two-thirds attendance on the days of Guernon's visits. It is impossible to say whether

Guernon's visit to the school on 4 August 1884 was a response to complaints about Dean. However, only eight students were in attendance on that particular day, while thirty were officially enrolled. The next day, 5 August, Guernon revoked Dean's second-grade certificate "for cause."[79]

If it came to a contest between the county superintendent and a teacher, the teacher seldom won. Even when such confrontations operated in an ostensibly democratic fashion, county superintendents held all the power. Anson Buttles, the Milwaukee County superintendent during the late 1860s, preferred to stage an open forum where charges could be directed and answered by all concerned parties. After hearing rumors and receiving objections to the teacher in one of his rural schools, Buttles called "the whole district" together to examine the "complaints that were made against the teacher." Though there was apparently much discussion, Buttles ultimately made the final decision and, in a rare instance, pronounced the teacher "not guilty."[80]

Other teachers were not so lucky. North Dakota teacher Cora Lee is a good example. As a married teacher in Cass County, North Dakota, in 1890, Lee represents a characteristic of the trans-Mississippi frontier that one would not likely see at this time in the states of the Old Northwest. The shortage of teachers in the Dakotas made it possible for married women to teach. Lee, however, had difficulty disciplining her scholars. In addition, she had enemies in the community who were not happy to see her teaching the local school. In 1893 her license was revoked by Cass County superintendent J. F. Callahan for "cruelty to children, showing undue partiallity in the school, ingovernable temper, rude language, and an insulting manner."[81]

Like Elmer Thompson, Lee appealed to the state superintendent to rescind the revocation. The testimony got very personal. One district resident testified that she had visited the Lee home shortly after Mr. Lee had apparently choked his wife. Another man testified that he heard Cora Lee call another man a "God damned fool." On her behalf, however, ex-

cellent character references were sent to the state superintendent. Additionally, she received supportive testimony from a
man who claimed that one of Lee's accusers had tried to induce
him "to swear to something damaging to the aforesaid Mrs.
Lee." The man responded by indicating that he knew nothing
that would be damaging to Lee. The accuser then indicated
to this man that "he might make him swear to something."

The state superintendent affirmed the county superintendent's decision to revoke Lee's teaching certificate. She, in
turn, waited three years for Cass County to elect a new superintendent. When it happened, Lee took the certification
exam and scored in the nineties on a scale of one hundred in
all subjects. The new superintendent, however, still refused
to grant her a license to teach. Cora Lee's teaching career was
over. Teachers were held to high standards in their private
lives, women more so than men. However, public drunkenness
from a male teacher was sufficient reason to revoke a teaching
license. And it happened often across the Midwest. Newspapers carried the word to school board members that a teacher
had his license revoked for "immorality, intemperence [sic],
and general neglect of business of the school."[82]

Cora Lee would not have been teaching in most midwestern
states in 1890. Even into the twentieth century the question
of employing married women was a divisive one. Well into this
century, most rural districts preferred to hire young, single
females. Marriage usually meant the automatic forfeiture of a
teaching position. A rural school board in Indiana resolved at a
board meeting in 1844 that for its teacher, "amitive corrispon-
dence and all reciprocity and adaptation [is] forbidden, between the male and female sex, that noblest plant on earth
unsullied." Living up to this kind of standard was doubtless
difficult for many young female teachers. For others, like rural
Indiana teacher Aurora Koehler, these kinds of behavioral pro-
scriptions were no problem at all. Rather than get out of a
buggy or wagon in public, Koehler preferred to get out at the
outskirts of town. She noted in her diary, "Who wants to crawl
out of a wagon in town where the men—hateful things! try
their best to get a sight of your *ankles*."[83]

Nevertheless, held to higher behavioral standards, female teachers as well as males were sometimes found lacking. A teacher in Griggs County, North Dakota, was charged with immorality and had her license revoked. [84] Rural teachers Clara Glumseth and Hugh Fursteneau were accused of having an illicit affair. Both taught in Bottineau County, North Dakota. In this instance the state superintendent reissued their certificates, perhaps on the basis of the written testimony of Dr. J. R. McKay, who submitted "that I have this day examined Miss Clara Glumseth and find absolute proof that she has never had sexual intercourse." [85]

Another rural North Dakota teacher had her license revoked when rumors began to circulate about her relationship with the district clerk. Testimony was introduced that placed Jessie Sellars on a hotel bed with O. A. Dietsche on the evening of a local Halloween masquerade party in 1905. Additionally, Sellars was accused of riding a motorcycle with Dietsche "with her arms around his body."

In Rollette County, North Dakota, eighteen-year-old Lizzie Anderson taught a country school in 1899 that included two older "boys," ages twenty-one and twenty-three. Through the course of the term Lizzie became quite friendly with her scholars. She had grown up near this district and was acquainted with many of the pupils. By all accounts she was quite businesslike about her teaching. However, before school was called, at noon, and during recess she apparently became excessively familiar with her older male students. The district clerk demanded that the county superintendent revoke her license for "permitting the scholars to take liberties with her and others during recess and noon hours unbecoming the proper dignity of a teacher."

The oldest male pupil testified that he and another boy stood the teacher and a few of the older girls on their heads on a few separate occasions. He also stated that once "Miss Lizzie" jumped on his back while he was kneeling before the stove. On a very cold morning he rubbed Anderson's feet while the schoolchildren gathered around the stove to warm themselves before classes. Even this last indiscretion, however, in the judgment of the state superintendent, did not warrant the revocation of her license on the grounds of immorality. Anderson was allowed to continue teaching. [86]

Just as the typical American schooling experiences of the nineteenth- and early twentieth-century was rural, the typical pedagogical tool employed by the nation's rural teachers was recitation. [87] Given the history of education since antiquity, we may be reasonably sure that there was more than enough historical evidence to suggest that the recitation method was not an effective teaching strategy. The roots of this particular pedagogical technique suggest that it served two ends better than others: it enhanced a teacher's ability to assert control over student behavior, and it allowed one teacher to handle many students.

The pedagogy of the country schools was most directly derived from the pedagogy produced to administer charity schooling. The dominant thought about the workings of the mind, however, complemented recitation pedagogy well. Many social scientists in the first half of the nineteenth century were convinced that the exterior of the skull shaped itself in response to the brain that lay beneath it. According to advocates of phrenology, the brain was "the organ of mind." If an individual wished to increase her intellectual capacity, vigorous exercise with difficult subject matter could accomplish this. It was important, however, for the content to be of high quality, for craniometric observations suggested there were limits to the development of various faculties. Protrusions on the skull extended only so far.

Phrenologists mapped and remapped the human skull. Protrusions in certain areas meant that certain faculties were well developed. There were "affective faculties" and "intellectual faculties" that cumulatively defined the personality and intellectual power of the individual. Thus, the phrase *faculty psychology* became popular. Though phrenology had late-eighteenth-century origins, it gained acceptance as a legitimate theory only in the days of the Romantic age when notions of equality were being downplayed and the business of creating a national spirit (whether in Europe or America) via a hierarchy of races was promoted to extremes.

Given the utility of phrenology for rationalizing the quarantine of native Americans and the subordination of blacks, as well as the pressure applied to landless whites to keep them moving on, there is little cause for wonder about the widespread acceptance of phrenology during the nineteenth century. Like Horace Mann, rural Illinois teacher James Monroe was impressed with what phrenology seemed to suggest for education. He shared with his diary that when not occupied with his school he spent his time "reading Fowler's *Phrenology*, a very valuable work in my estimation, and containing much information of special benefit to me in my present capacity, as it enables me to form a better opinion of the tasks, feelings, and powers of my little proteges, and thereby suggest a proper mode of education, and tells me which faculties are necessary to be cultivated and which to be repressed. I think I must make a chart of their heads."[88] The very next day Monroe wrote that he was "fully satisfied with the truth of the science" and determined "to live in accordance with phrenological principles."

While the phrenology fad began to fade after the Civil War, the principles of faculty psychology remained the dominant strand of educational thought. Sharing this way of thinking with the mass of American common school teachers was the job of teacher-training institutions called normal schools.[89] The creation of state-controlled normal schools as promoted by Horace Mann in the early 1840s was a slow process in the states of the Midwest. Only Wisconsin and Minnesota could be promoted as examples of states that took the idea of normal training centers seriously. For the most part, the education required to lift common school teachers above the level of their students was achieved by annual teachers' institutes.

With a few exceptions, county superintendents across the Middle West were entrusted with the duty of sponsoring an institute to advance the education of the county's teachers. Some lasted a period of days; others, a period of weeks. Usually held during the summer in the county seat, the teachers' institute was a big event in small-town America. Townspeople awaited the coming of the teachers whose numbers often transformed a sleepy town into one filled with activity. People made room in their homes to board teachers and pick up a little extra cash. County superintendents tried to make lists of those who were willing to board teachers at reasonable rates in order to help place attending teachers. Because the institutes tended to last longer as the century progressed, more and more male teachers became disillusioned with the requirement. Many of these men were gainfully employed during the summer and found it difficult to take off for a couple of weeks to maintain a teaching license for use during the winter.

Regulations regarding attendance at the teachers' institutes varied from location to location. In most instances, attending meant the renewal of a teacher's certificate without the bother of retaking the certification exam. This was particularly true for the lowest grade license, the third-grade certificate. These generally had to be renewed annually. A superintendent in Lokota County, North Dakota, took special notice of those teachers who failed to attend the institute. When he sent notices of license revocation to the state superintendent, he habitually added that over and above the teacher's failure to attend the institute his own personal motive was to "get rid of an incompetent teacher."[90]

By and large, the teachers enjoyed the opportunity to interact with others facing similar circumstances and to discuss the pros and cons of country school teaching. As well there was a great deal of after hours socializing. Male teachers and female teachers met. Relationships developed. Undoubtedly, marriages ended the teaching career of many young women who attended these institutes and there met their future husbands. Sarah Huftalen, a rural Iowa teacher, wrote about her excitement over the attention of a male suitor while attending a teachers' institute: "Fred Patterson offered me his fan. Ah! I don't see how he knew me. He is nice, too." But the institutes were also a time for the development of relationships of a less acceptable kind. Mashers—the nineteenth-century label given to two women engaging in an intimate relationship—were not limited to the women's academies and seminaries on the East Coast. Again confiding to her diary, Huftalen wrote, "Jessie Heath and Amy are 'mashers' as they call themselves. They flirt & are so boisterous I do not care to associate with 'such.'"[91]

The incredibly high turnover rate in country school teaching meant that each year teachers' institutes were deluged with aspiring young women who were to receive their only training beyond their experiences as students. The records kept by a Johnson County, Iowa, superintendent suggest a fairly typical picture of what took place at teachers' institutes across the Midwest. About seventy teachers attended, 90 percent of whom were female. The average age of all attendees was 19.7 years. The average time taught to that point in their careers was 2.7 terms, that is, just a little more than one year of teaching. Twenty-eight percent of those who attended had been to the teacher's institute the year before. Seventy-two percent were attending for the first time.[92]

Teachers' institutes generally aimed at two goals. The first was to lift the teacher intellectually above what they received as common school students. The second was to articulate methods through which they could improve upon their own experience. The methods advocated by those who spoke at teachers' institutes depended in large part on their philosophy of education. Minnesota county superintendent Sarah Christie Stevens saw education as inextricably linked to religious morality. In her address to the teachers' institute in Blue Earth County in the early 1890s, she stressed that "all the faculties of the mind" were distributed "into three grand departments, the intellect, the sensibilities, and the will: all mental activities are expressed when we say—the mind *perceives*, the mind *feels*, the mind *chooses*." Stevens chose to stress the education of the "sensibilities," or what others called the affective domain. Through proper development of the sensibilities, Stevens maintained, perception and choices were improved.[93]

Stevens was affected by the late-nineteenth-century shift in educational thought away from an emphasis on memory, drill, and recitation. Although this type of pedagogy was strengthened by the tenets of phrenology, the demise of this science led teachers to new ideas about education. It was not at all certain that the vigorous exercise involved in memorizing long passages really helped to strengthen the brain. By slow strides, advocates of the "new education" during the 1880s and 1890s realized that the conformity demanded of recitation pedagogy was not particularly liberating. Though clearly skills were acquired in the country schoolhouses of the Midwest, education was occurring only here and there. Farm children learned to read, write, and manipulate at least four mathematical processes. However, these skills represented only the tools used to acquire an education and were not an education in themselves. To advance beyond simple skills, educators promoted methods that they hoped would provide a deeper understanding of the skills' uses. Drill and practice were downplayed. The connection between life and education was played up. A common branch of study at earlier teachers' institutes, "busy work" for scholars not engaged in recitation, began to receive heavy criticism.

What was critiqued by "new educators" during the late nineteenth century and eventually by pragmatists like William James and John Dewey was a pedagogical tradition based on behavioral control through conformity rather than substantive efforts to educate through creativity. The legacy of mass education for the poor, inherent in the common school system, dictated a pedagogy of control. And this old education died hard. Implementing the methods discussed at teachers' institutes around the turn of the century meant bucking tradition in the local district. But more than this, it meant giving up an effective classroom management technique to risk disorder and perhaps chaos in the classroom.

Although teachers seemingly enjoyed the social aspects of the teachers' institutes, little evidence suggests that they improved their teaching by attending. Few teachers shared in their diaries what advances they garnered from the institute experience. An Indiana teacher who won second prize for his autobiographical essay in a contest sponsored by *World's Work*, a popular periodical during the 1910s and 1920s, had this to say about teachers' institutes: "Those institutes cost money,

but I never got a bit of benefit from them. Whenever I asked
some of the others if they really were benefited, they would
grin and say: 'Yes, a little.' As I got acquainted with other
teachers, I found out that, like myself, they were as limp as a
rag in enthusiasm, and were in it for the money—and that was
all."[94] The number of country schools in the Midwest did not
begin to decline until after 1918.[95] As a result, the first years
of the new century were marked by an ever-increasing demand
for country school teachers. High schools began to include
normal departments to help fill the need for educated teachers.
Additionally, heavily populated counties created their own
normal schools rather than hope that prospective county teachers could make it to regional normal schools that may have
been several counties distant. Rock County Normal School in
Janesville, Wisconsin, was created in 1911. However, given
the decrease in rural population that was induced by the agricultural depression of the 1920s, this school and others like
it had short life spans. Many normal schools closed their doors
during the Depression. The need for country school teachers
would never again be so great.

Students and teachers in midwestern country schools went
about their business without much interference from outsiders. Yet the records left by rural teachers indicate that internal problems of some magnitude often had to be overcome.
The traditional, conservative, recitation pedagogy of the country school built in a great likelihood that discipline problems
would arise. Consequently, the switch was often wielded "lively"
in these schools. Of course, this predisposing structure was
present in urban schools as well. But more numbers presented
urban pedagogues with an interesting option: the "special"
class.

The control features of recitation pedagogy meant that criti-
cal or creative inquiry were nearly nonexistent. In such circumstances, schools were hardly liberating. Rural teachers,
for their part, continually reproduced the rural past. As changes
occurred in the cities, traditions such as pietism, localism, and
pastoralism nevertheless lingered in the country. Those who
controlled most of the real property and power in midwestern

farming neighborhoods had the most to gain from the per-
petuation of the status quo. These men made the decisions
about schooling in the rural Midwest. These school trustees,
or, as one historian referred to them, these "educators in overalls," were left to their own devices in insuring that proper
values, attitudes, behaviors, modes of instruction, and curriculum were present in their schools. If the state department of
education appeared to represent different values or espouse
different beliefs about the function and functioning of schools,
farmers dug in their heels to oppose it. Part of the rural antebellum experience in the Midwest was the contest between
religious views that often was played out in education circles.
The vanguard of clerics with religious millennial aspirations
that engendered resistance in some rural locales were replaced
in the postbellum years by professionals who sought to control
the course of human evolution scientifically and were often
resisted with similar fervor. It is to this tenuous relationship
between rural district boards and higher levels in the common
school hierarchy that we next turn our attention.

5

Rural Meets Urban

*Country Schools, State Departments
of Education, and the Country
Life Commission*

David B. Tyack and Elisabeth Hansot argue that close to
the turn of the century in this country a dramatic shift was
taking place in the administration of public schools. The clerics
who made up the "aristocracy of character" of the antebellum
period gave way "to a new breed of professional managers"
who saw in public schools an opportunity "to bring about a
smoothly running, socially efficient, stable social order" using
education as "a major form of human engineering."[1] There is
very little scholarly disagreement concerning these circumstances. The centralization of school administration during the
Progressive era and the evolution of professional educational
"expertise" are hardly contestable topics. However, if we take
this interpretation and apply it to circumstances in farming
neighborhoods, the result would look like something very close
to the standard interpretation of midwestern rural education.[2]
This popular view is summarized well by Fuller: "arrogant and
overconfident professional educators," striving for legitimacy
on par with "the physicians, lawyers, and clergymen, the three
old and respected professions," went about their business with
"strong antidemocratic tendencies" sure that the "pure democracy" of the local school districts was ruinous to the cause of
education.[3]

Some assumptions underlying this interpretation warrant
further investigation. First, to suggest that nineteenth-century
doctors and lawyers were members of old, respected profes-

sions is a bit of a stretch. Given the low regard for doctors and lawyers at that time, one could reasonably argue that educators received as much respect as doctors and lawyers did. Second, there is the assumption that the administrative progressives who tried to sell the centralization inherent in a township system as a substitute for countless small rural districts did so as a result of their "strong antidemocratic tendencies." But this can be interpreted two ways. If the movement toward township centralization is thought to be undemocratic, then it must be because the movement disempowered some group. Based on a review of available evidence, however, it appears that there was never any attempt by "arrogant and overconfident professionals" to deny the right of allegedly excessively democratic farmers to sit on township boards. What a township board could (and sometimes did) do was insure that children attending school in one part of the township, where land was less fertile, did not suffer from the locale's inability to produce a sufficient tax base. Or it might decide to place a school building in an equitable location that previously had been placed according to neighborhood power dynamics. In short, the "antidemocratic tendency" among "arrogant" professionals could have been, in fact, just the opposite. Given the subordinate status of women and tenant farmers in rural school districts, any reference to "pure democracy" is simply misplaced.

But the issue of centralization is important. Who was responsible for the small amount of consolidation that did take place among rural schools across the Midwest? According to the same historian, "Such centralization as there was in those little districts was brought about only by the county superintendents." The next question becomes obvious: who were the superintendents? While most of them had teaching experience, they rarely had any collegiate training, and many did not have a high school diploma. Clearly, the superintendents could not approach the level of experience implicit in the title "professional educator." On the other hand, these men clearly could not be farmers, either. If they had been, however, their ostensible propensity for neighborhood democracy would have prohibited their embracing centralization. Therefore, the position of county superintendent, according to the conventional view, attracted individuals who differed fundamentally from the democratic farmers who served on rural school boards.

The argument contends further that "impecunious lawyers, part-time preachers, and wounded Civil War veterans . . . were often among the first to fill the county superintendent's office in the 1860s and 70s." Later, according to Fuller, a better sort of individual began to fill this position and to these men he extends the label "educator-politicians." But, almost predictably (in light of the conventional interpretation), these educator-politicians "formed their own associations, read papers, discussed problems that confronted them, and became as arrogant and confident of their expertise as those [the professional educators] who ranked above them."[4] Thus, the conventional interpretation is able to explain why the dynamic of rural resistance to state departments and state department initiatives was just as pervasive for what Tyack and Hansot call "the new breed of expert managers" as it had been for the clerical "aristocracy of character." Of course, what looks like overconfidence and arrogance to one historian may well look to another like a committed responsiveness to harsh realities. It may be better to ask to what degree can individual personality traits be bestowed upon entire occupational groups. It seems likely that there were no more or fewer "arrogant and overconfident professional educators" than there were arrogant and overconfident farmers. A quick review of why the office of county superintendent was created and what it came to entail may shed more light on this issue.

As state departments of education were established across the Midwest, provisions were made for setting up intermediaries between the local district and state officials. It was obvious that a remote state-level department could not handle all the disputes that would arise within and among local districts. As state after state opted for free schools in the 1850s, they typically created the position of township superintendent to settle disputes, license and supervise teachers, conduct teacher institutes, and gather statistical information. In 1858 the Iowa legislature made provisions for county superintendents to do the work of the previous township officers. Kansas followed with similar legislation a few years later, and through the 1860s all the midwestern states, with the exception of Ohio, instituted the county superintendency. Generally, county superintendents were elected for two-year terms, though superintendents in Illinois served for four years.

Handling aggrieved residents in various local districts was a common duty of the county superintendent. When several families on the peripheries of two districts decided to form their own district, the petition went first to the county superintendent. Learning of this, other residents in these districts would send their own petition asking the superintendent not to allow the creation of the new district. County superintendents had to listen to both sides of the argument and then decide the matter. The decision inevitably disappointed one group, and consequently appeals to the state superintendent were common. A typical example took place in Grant County, Wisconsin. In this instance the state department was still operating with township, rather than county, officers. Paris Township superintendent William Richardson wrote to Wisconsin state superintendent Eleaser Root in December 1851. He explained, "Some time last year there was a petition presented to me, signed by several resident citizens of school district no. one praying to be attached to school district no. two (2). I took the matter under consideration, granted their prayer, and notified the board officers of district no. one of the fact according to law. But before the alteration became valid under the law, district no. one took up an appeal."[5] Richardson was writing Root to learn about the state superintendent's decision regarding the appeal. In another example, a new district was requested in an Iowa township district in 1899. The township board declined this petition because it felt the inequalities described therein were exaggerated and because those asking for the new subdistrict were tenant farmers anyway.[6]

County superintendents often had to settle disputes over the location of the schoolhouse, which suggests that as with the township board in Iowa, equity was not consistently a concern of those who held power in the local districts. County superintendents sometimes represented those disadvantaged by school circumstances, but they could never lose sight of being elected officials. Taking a public stance at odds with the long-standing families of local neighborhoods could spell trouble at the next election.

Foreigners rarely received warm treatment from county superintendents. In Ozaukee County, Wisconsin, superintendent William Scott described his "German school" as "backward." He wrote that "Miss Ellen Walsh [the teacher] is earnest in her endeavors to advance them, but, the German language, catechism, and parental interference seem to be an insuferable barrier in her path."[7] Further south in Milwaukee County, superintendent Anson Buttles was particularly rough on his "foreign schools." After breaking up a school meeting on 27 September 1858, Buttles confided to his diary on 28 September, "Learned today that the voters in the school district are incensed at me for destroying their meeting. I do not care— & as long as they get dutch teachers I will keep them in hot water." A week later he commented that "the dutch got my opinion of them in style, they *know nothing*."[8]

Buttles perhaps picked up some of his antipathy for foreign teachers at home. Six years before his election as county superintendent, his father, Cephas Buttles, wrote to the Wisconsin state superintendent to complain about his children having to attend school with "foreigners, mostly Hollanders, some Germans." The elder Buttles further complained that this school was taught by "a teacher who I believe has never been to an English school in her life and who two years ago could not speak the English language Plain enough to be understood."[9]

Like the township officers before them, county superintendents were charged with supervising teachers in the local schools. Getting around to as many as forty schools each term was exceedingly difficult in an era of horse travel and poor roads. A visitation trip might take a county superintendent away from home for days, forcing him to lodge in local hotels or, sometimes, in the schoolhouses themselves. Often the superintendent would arrive at a school and find it closed only to learn later that the teacher was sick, or there was a funeral in the district, or that measles were going around, or that the district was predominantly Catholic and he had mistakenly arrived on a Catholic holiday.[10] When the school was in session, superintendents generally took notes about what they saw. Sometimes these descriptions were included in their diaries or in official record books. Examining these notes, one can get a sense of the reality of the country school experience.

Discipline, of course, was the central attribute of the successful teacher. Some superintendents kept accurate tolls of the incidences of whispering among the students as they visited schools. Others, not content with documenting such infractions only on the days they were in attendance, asked teachers in the county to make daily counts of whispering. A Kansas teacher ended each day with what one of his students referred to as a "'moral roll-call.'" As he read down the list of student names, the students were to reply "perfect" if they had kept quiet all day or "imperfect" if they had whispered.[11] In Nebraska a superintendent noted that there were "26 enrolled in the school, 21 present, and 19 chewing gum." He went on to note that the "pupils are nearly all Irish, and, of course full of fun, and yet they are doing better than the teacher. [I] believe his education is insufficient and he possesses no tact to govern."[12]

Nothing drew the ire of county superintendents more than when they were forced to intervene to bring about order in the classroom. But the conditions of the schoolhouses were also critically appraised. Superintendents checked for proper ventilation, heating, the cleanliness of the privies, and the schoolroom itself. After visiting a school in Eyota Township, superintendent Sanford Niles of Olmsted County, Minnesota, noted, "The few pupils present sat shivering over a cold stove, the wind found its way through cracks between the logs." At a school in High Forest Township he commented, "Teaching has been made difficult by boys who have broken windows, kicked open locked doors, stolen hooks for the window blinds and torn off the clapboards." In Orion Township, Niles found the "most miserable school house, rotten floors, crazy door, yawning cracks, blackboard nailed up to the window to keep out the west wind."[13] If the schoolhouse failed to meet expectations, he might chastise the local board publicly in a local newspaper. If the teacher was consistently deficient, it might mean the teaching license would be revoked. Sometimes a revocation was advertised in a local paper as well.

Back at the county seat, superintendents sometimes prepared a school news article for the local paper, or they compiled statistics or filled out forms for the state department, prepared license examinations, tested prospective teachers, and once a year spent a great deal of time organizing the rural teacher preparation program known as the teacher's institute. For this occasion, guest speakers were contracted, arrangements were made for an auditorium, and a list of local residents willing to board teachers at modest rates was compiled. Fliers and notices went out to alert prospective teachers as well as the local contingent of veterans teaching in the country schools of the county.

The county superintendent became an important part of county politics, and in many areas a candidate's political affiliation may have had as much to do with his success as his experience in the world of rural schools.[14] But, by and large, teaching qualifications were an important consideration. What to make of the county superintendents who went about their business across the midwestern states is unclear. Generally, they were implementors rather than architects of change, but some, too, were staunch defenders of tradition. Fuller's label of educator-politician is a useful description, but his tendency to fit all components of the rural educational scene, county superintendents included, into an "us and them" dichotomy serves only to rationalize the persistence of rural resistance in its best possible light. If one examines the existing records of nineteenth- and early-twentieth-century county superintendents in terms of what they had to do and what they did, however, it becomes difficult to see the arrogance and overconfidence that supposedly worked catalytically on the creation of rural resistance. But taking the arrogance and overconfidence away removes a component of the argument that resistance occurred in the name of neighborhood democracy.

It can certainly be argued that something like a group of "professional educators" developed in the postbellum years analogous to the groups of professional psychologists, sociologists, economists, and historians who came of age around the turn of the century. These educators lobbied for the establishment of education departments on major college campuses across the Midwest. They brought a diverse array of disciplinary backgrounds to their studies of education, but they nevertheless sought unity in professional organizations such as the National Rural Education Association established in 1907. Some of these scholars thought education should be regarded as a discipline, like history or economics, while others felt the established disciplines provided an adequate basis from which to launch systematic inquiries into the nature of teaching, learning, and subject matter. For some, education was an art; for others, it was a science. The quandary was not unlike that debated concurrently by historians: was history an art or a science?

By the 1890s it was apparent that professional educators were advocating a revolutionary change for country schools based in part on the philosophy of Johann Friedrich Herbart, a philosophy professor at the University of Konigsberg in Prussian Germany. Herbart wrote extensively about education in the first third of the nineteenth century, but his ideas were not seriously studied in America until fifty years later. Herbart believed that much could be learned from the systematic study of education, and he was one of the first to set up a practice school to test pedagogical innovations. Those who felt that education ought to be considered a science unto itself looked upon Herbart as a kind of founding father. Herbart argued that real knowledge acquisition took place as the mind assimilated "'new ideas by ideas already in the mind.'"[15] In effect, Herbart and many professional educators specializing in rural schooling came to adopt a main tenet of modern cognitive psychological schema theory. That is, they believed that old knowledge was the key determinant in acquiring new knowledge. Based on this belief, Herbart stressed that education must work to develop a child's interests. Subsequently, many educators began a push to relate country schooling to the concerns of agrarian life.

Hard on the heels of Herbartian-inspired "new education,"

of course, were the primitivist ideas of G. Stanley Hall, the social learning theories of George Herbert Mead, the popularization of the Freudian unconscious, and the connectionist behaviorism of E. L. Thorndike and John B. Watson. Another stream of educational thought evolved among pragmatists such as William James and John Dewey. In short order, the "new education" became "Progressive education," with all the ambiguities and differing interpretations such a title might suggest.

The impact of Herbartians, the new psychologists, and the pragmatists meant that the tradition-conserving pedagogy of autocratic teacher control, memorized recitation, and discipline by the switch was fast disappearing. This was particularly true in urban schools as the "special class" became an option for teachers who wished to take troublemakers out of their room. [16] In time rural schools, too, began to show signs of change. William James wrote cogently about the deficiencies of the old assumption that rigorous recitation in the "three R's" constituted an education. Said James:

> A friend of mine, visiting a school, was asked to examine a young class in geography. Glancing at the book she said: "Suppose you should dig a hole in the ground, hundreds of feet deep, how should you find it at the bottom—warmer or colder than on top?" None of the class replying, the teacher said: "I'm sure they know, but I think you didn't ask the question quite rightly. Let me try." So taking the book, she asked: "In what condition is the interior of the globe?" and received the immediate answer from half the class at once: "The interior of the globe is in a state of igneous fusion." [17]

To make education more substantive, Liberty Hyde Bailey, the famous Cornell horticulturalist, began to push for the inclusion of nature study in the rural school curriculum. Arbor Day programs were designed to beautify rural schoolyards and to keep rural schoolchildren in tune with agricultural principles. Politicians like William Hoard of Wisconsin and Henry

Wallace of Iowa began to lobby for the "uplift" of the rural school as part of the turn-of-the-century search for order.

The acceptance of the new education of the 1890s cannot be separated from larger political and economic circumstances. The notion of society as an organic entity, so directly related to social Darwinism, left many citizens wondering how an urban industrial population could keep from an inevitable labor-capital clash, particularly when the backbone of the nation, the yeoman farmers, were dwindling in overall percentages at an alarming rate.[18] Keeping white Anglo-Saxon Protestant farm children on the farm became the goal of the professional educators who advocated changes in rural education. Their concern was so great that a Committee of Twelve was created by the National Education Association in 1895 to study the problems of the small rural school.

Made up predominantly of leading Midwest educators, the Committee of Twelve unequivocally supported township organization and governance of schools. In its opinion, the substantial difference in the amount spent for schooling rural children versus the amount of money spent on urban children was due in large part to impecunious board members who refused to supply textbooks for schoolchildren, or to create libraries in their schools, and consistently hired, as one local district clerk was fond of putting it, "the teacher most profitable to the district." The Committee found that in 1890 an average of $13.23 had been spent on rural schoolchildren as opposed to the $28.87 spent on individual urban students.[19] More than this, however, the Committee pushed the Herbartian notion that education ought to be driven by children's interests and that in so doing the unstable American society of the 1890s might benefit. Manifesting the organic view of society, the report states that "the schools must not confuse or destroy . . . by trying to 'citify' the country or by seeking to 'countrify' the town. The city and country express the equation of life; a weakness in one member means the ruin of both."[20]

The sentiment expressed in the Committee's report intensified as the first years of the new century brought waves of new foreigners to American shores. Said one historian, "The ideology of rural reform . . . rested on agrarianism with all its accompanying faith in the virtues of rural life."[21] The pastoralism embedded in the dominant American ideology suggested that farmers were the backbone of the nation while it heightened the presumed necessity of keeping America's farm population pure and strong. In 1908 President Theodore Roosevelt reacted to this sentiment with his creation of the Country Life Commission.

The conclusions drawn in historical scholarship dealing with the Country Life movement invariably sound something like this: the urban corporate liberals, nostalgics, and social scientists who conspired to reorganize rural social institutions through the recommendations of the Country Life Commission came face to face with democratic yeoman farmers who refused any imposition on rural traditions or ways of living. A major drawback in this scholarship, however, is that little attempt has been made to frame the analysis in light of larger historical developments during the Progressive period.[22]

The Country Life movement, like Progressivism, is difficult to define. In general, however, it is safe to characterize it as an attempt to improve the standard of living of rural dwellers, primarily through various educational initiatives. The movement began in 1908 when Roosevelt called on Liberty Hyde Bailey to head a commission investigating all facets of the rural "problem." But to begin a discussion of the Country Life movement with 1908, however, would inevitably handicap a student of history, for the movement most certainly was an outgrowth of prevailing political, economic, and ideological factors that evolved during the crisis period of the 1890s.

It was during the 1890s that the United States began to face its urban growth. The overextension of railroad companies contributed to the financial panic of 1893, which was to that point unparalleled in the nation's history. Sixteen thousand businesses failed, seventy thousand strikes occurred, and the nation's unemployment rate reached an unprecedented 25 percent. Statistics, however, tell only half the story. The violence that accompanied corporate strike-breaking activities astonished contemporary observers. Everything that occurred during the Progressive period must be analyzed with this backdrop, including the Country Life movement. Bailey frequently voiced his opinion about the "balance wheel" role of rural America in the conflict between labor and capital.

Rail companies tried to squeeze out a troubled existence during the panic by severely taxing farmers who shipped grain on short hauls. Farmer protest was voiced in a surprisingly unified Populist movement that actually won control of a few trans-Mississippi state assemblies. Although a variety of forces silenced the Populist movement, urban attention to rural affairs continued unabated.

The first—and in some ways most significant—deficiency in current scholarship concerning the Country Life movement is the failure to acknowledge the prevalence of the organic scientific view. [23] The impact of William Graham Sumner's essays explicating social Darwinism on subsequent social science is a matter of record. When the world was viewed in evolutionary terms, it is not difficult to comprehend how the fall of agriculture from the profession of nine-tenths of the population at the nation's founding to one-third in 1900 could be viewed as alarming. [24] Bailey saw the situation this way: "The city sits like a parasite, running out its roots into the open country and draining it of its substance. Mankind has not yet worked out this organic relation of town and country." [25] Others commented that rural communities were "'vital parts of the economic organism of the world.'" [26]

Add to this Frederick Jackson Turner's assertion that as of 1893 the frontier was closed, that the vast expanses of available land had been purchased, and one might be led to ponder what impact this would hold for democracy, which, according to Turner, derived its virility from the frontier experience. Writing somewhat later, Turner expressed some doubt as to whether American institutions "have acquired sufficient momentum to sustain themselves under conditions so radically unlike those in the days of their origins." [27]

The philosophy of William James also had an impact on shaping American questions concerning dramatic shifts in the political economy, at least in intellectual circles. James criticized the excess profit of gilded age capitalists and, as a Harvard professor, legitimized a sort of Thoreauvian conception of the sanctity of manual labor. For James, "lives based on having are less free than lives based either on doing or on being." [28] A contemporary of English agrarian intellectuals John Ruskin and Thomas Carlyle, James provided a philosophical foundation for lamenting the decline of agriculture as a profession and inspired the generation of "urban agrarians," as one historian referred to them, who would become the standard-bearers of the Country Life movement. Most notable among them, of course, was James's pupil at Harvard, Theodore Roosevelt. In a speech delivered in Lansing, Michigan, in 1907, President Roosevelt betrayed the influence of James by referring to a tiller of the soil as "the one person whose welfare is vital" to the nation as a whole. [29] Roosevelt's speech in Lansing became the verbal rationale for the creation of the Country Life Commission.

But other factors were involved. In 1899 sociologist Thorstein Veblen published *The Theory of the Leisure Class*. Like James, Veblen criticized the decadence, affluence, and "conspicuous consumption" of the wealthy classes. For many Americans, Veblen's work crystallized the polarization of moral agrarianism and decadent industrialism. Ray Stannard Baker, a respected midwestern journalist, became a popular novelist just after the turn of the century using the pen name David Grayson. Grayson's books built upon the implications of the work of James and Veblen. In 1906 he published *Adventures in Contentment* and followed this with a series of similar novels and short stories. Grayson idyllized the agrarian simple life and revitalized a temporarily dormant pastoral impulse among many Americans. *Three Acres and Liberty*, written by Bolton Hall in 1907, was a prescription for urbanites who wanted to partake of the virtues involved with working the soil. Books in this vein demonstrate the pervasiveness of urban concern with the condition of rural America.

Many factors, however, served to highlight the American rural-urban differentiation near the turn of the century. On one hand, the political economy of a rapidly industrializing society led many people to question the stability of traditional American values and institutions. For such individuals, the tenets of industrialism seemed morally bankrupt when compared with the tenets of agrarianism. We might expect a person harboring this notion to favor the Country Life movement.

On a more scientific level, the decrease in the number of farmers on a percentage basis within the population sounded an alarm among social evolutionists. The publication of Wilbert L. Anderson's *The Country Town: A Study of Rural Evolution* in 1906 clearly spoke of the dangers of the new industrial order. Anderson spoke prophetically when he commented that "the first effect of farm machinery" will be the "departure of the farmer's boy from the home."[30]

Rural population, more than any other circumstance, was at the heart of the Country Life movement. To have a healthy society, many believed that a prosperous rural population was a necessity. If Turner, James, Veblen, Baker, Hall, and others had merely provided rationale for idyllizing agrarian life, there would have been no need for the Country Life movement. However, each intimated that industrialism was creeping into rural America, threatening to do severe damage. In a Darwinian sense, Country Life advocates believed that it was the fittest who were leaving the countryside for the city and that in time this phenomenon would leave a legacy of mediocrity in rural society. As Anderson put it, "Much has been said, and truly, of the removal of the upper stratum of country society to the city . . . it is the cream that is skimmed off."[31] No more evidence was needed than the tremendously popular stories of Hamlin Garland in the 1890s. *Main-Travelled Roads* was a collection of his short stories that vividly portrayed the migration of rural talent down well-traveled roads to the city. *Prairie Folks* was a less-than-complimentary account of the drudgery of farm life that led to cityward migration. Recalling his days as a country schoolteacher, Garland commented that "'our school house did not change—except for the worse. No one thought of adding a tree or a vine to its ugly yard . . . bare as a nose it stood at the crossroads, receiving us through its drab doorway as it had from the first. Its benches, hideously hacked and thick with grime, were as hard and uncomfortable as when I first saw them, and the windows remained unshaded and unwashed.'"[32] Given widespread circumstances such as those described by Garland, it is hardly surprising that individuals interested in improving country life would focus a great deal of their attention on country schools.

But this is not to suggest that Country Life supporters had no ulterior motives. As a few historians have pointed out, the early 1900s were a time of rising food prices. A Country Life movement that made agriculture more efficient would certainly lower these costs. But there is a problem with suggesting that lowered food costs was the primary motivation of Country Lifers. These reformers urged cooperation to attack and defeat the distribution system, something that would benefit producers as well as consumers. [33] They acknowledged that some country dwellers would always move to the city, but they certainly did not want this number artificially inflated by technological dispossession. In fact, most contended that America "needs more good farmers."[34] This hardly seems to be the position taken by a group interested in lowering food costs. One historian has labeled the Country Life movement as the "genesis of modern agribusiness." This interpretation is curious because the watchword of scientific farming in this period was "diversification," rather than the specialization that agribusiness promotes. While Country Lifers advocated rural electrification, telephony, mechanization, and so on, their reason for doing so was to improve the quality of rural living by transforming agricultural labor into something less physical. This is why Country Lifers were so intent on cautioning farmers against land hunger and greed, attributes some consider to be prerequisites for agribusiness operators. They hoped that country people could content themselves with the virtues of simple living. As one journalist put it, "It is a pity that the money test has come to be, to so many, almost the sole standard of values. The elevation of country life, about which we are beginning to hear a great deal, must be attained, if at all, by a general recognition of the solid worth of other elements in the life work. We must all care more for the things that are worth doing in themselves and less for the immediate earnings in solid cash."[35]

The Country Life movement was not about converting agrarian values along industrial lines, but rather it was about perpetuating existing rural values in the face of rising industrialization. This led one Country Life advocate from Ohio to proclaim that the "Country Life movement is fundamentally religious."[36] Increasing urbanization and immigration in the first years of the twentieth century frightened many observers who believed the strength of the nation was derived from "native stock" in the countryside. As one rural sociologist put it in 1911, "To those who hold the belief that the safety of a nation can be maintained only through sustaining a just communion of all its essential parts, and especially the purity of rural life, does it not seem an ever increasing and pressing necessity that the agrarian rights and powers of a people should be ever more vigilantly guarded?"[37] Bailey agreed, "In the accelerating mobility of our civilization it is increasingly important that we may have anchoring places; and these anchoring places are the farms."[38]

Although some historians suggest that the Country Life movement was urban-based, largely because most of the eight commission members had urban backgrounds, the majority of the real catalyzers in the movement were midwesterners who grew up or lived in places like Crawfordsville, Indiana; De Kalb, Illinois; and Mount Vernon, Iowa.[39] As well, the impression left by current scholarship is that if Country Lifers had "known rural America better," they would not have tried to implement the goals of their commission, which were "perceived through urban glasses."[40] Aside from commenting on whether Country Lifers were right, wrong, good, or bad, however, the evidence suggests that it was because Country Lifers knew rural America intimately that they prescribed their reform agenda. In 1908 Bailey warned that those discussing rural social organization who "approach the subject with the idea that the countryman is unresponsive or incompetent, are not really in sight of the problem and would better let it alone.

One who judges country life by city standards, as many persons do, would also better let the problem alone."[41] The author of such insights scarcely seems to merit the characterization of "ignorance, arrogance, and an undemocratic tendency."[42] The commission report itself urges that "centralized agencies should be stimulative and directive, rather than mandatory and formal." Bailey added later that "no movement educational or philanthropic, has adequate justification unless its one purpose or effect is to allow native individual responsibility and initiative to develop" on its own.[43]

There was essentially no facet of country living that Country Lifers did not comment on. Rural schools, churches, local government, home life and labor, clubs, newspapers, farmers' institutes, mechanization, automobiles, telephones, electric lights, parks, fairs, roads, and ditches—all were a source of discussion and study for people concerned with improving the rural environment. There are two questions worth asking about this movement that receive less-than-adequate treatment in current scholarship: what were the motives behind the movement, and why did farmers resist?

Again, current scholarship suggests that the movement was an attempt to reduce food costs and an opportunity for urban people to voice their notions of rural ignorance that "had lain just under the surface." Rural people resisted because "they were stung" by the suggestion of ignorance and because they were emotionally attached to their system of "neighborhood democracy."[44] But the evidence suggests that the motives of the Country Lifers were far less simplistic. Right or wrong, their chief concern was the diminution of the rural population in the face of rising rates of immigration, industrialization, and urbanization. The harsh terms used by some Country Lifers betray fear as well as the pervasiveness of social Darwinism. For example, Ellwood Cubberly, a leading turn-of-the-century education spokesperson, decried the infiltration of "'non Anglo-Teutonics'" coming to farm in the United States. In "The Influence of Immigration on Agricultural Development," University of Minnesota sociologist John Lee Coulter claimed that in order to improve life in the countryside, the United States "must exclude the undesirables and properly distribute the desirables." Journalist Clarence H. Poe maintained in *The Progressive Farmer* that white landowners needed to watch out and protect against "negro competition."[45]

It is helpful to consider the pervasiveness of the new liberal notion that progress could not be taken for granted and that progressive societies needed planning. Integral to this kind of contemporary social thought was the perception that vibrant rural populations needed to be protected, given the vital role that they played in the overall health of the nation. Although there were some county superintendents or occasionally state department of education officials who revealed some anti-farmer sentiment at NEA or state education conventions, by and large the record of true Country Life supporters reflects genuine concern with rural affairs rather than arrogance and condescension. The Country Lifers were trying to promote rural community life, not tear it down.

To be sure, however, there were some vicious attacks concerning "backward" resistant farmers. But generally the attacks came from urban "antiagrarians," to use David B. Danbom's phrase, who published social science texts in the twentieth century's late teens and early twenties. As these "antiagrarians" were mostly sociologists, it seems a stretch to include these individuals as Country Life advocates. Their references to "rural mental deficiency" or "rural feeblemindedness" were not a vindictive response to rural rejection of the Country Life agenda. Actually, only a few groups escaped these labels prescribed by the country's first generation of creators of mass intelligence tests. That farmers scored very low on army alpha tests in 1917 as well as previous and subsequent IQ exams, however biased the tests were, imbued the farmer's image with these labels for some years to come.[46]

Concerning most issues discussed by Country Lifers, the advocates accomplished much, with a measure of success. Clubs were formed. Boy and Girl Scout organizations came within reach of rural children. The Young Men's Christian Association responded to a directive from the Commission report to extend its work into the country. The 4-H movement got its start from the force of the Country Life movement. [47] The national agricultural extension program initiated by the 1914 Smith-Lever Act was a direct manifestation of the fervor concerning farming and rural life. Rural free delivery programs were expanded, and miles of telephone lines were strung across the countryside. Much experimenting with wind-powered generators for electrifying various farm operations was done.

Despite its accomplishments, the Country Life movement's greatest failure was in the area where Country Lifers desired the most success. Almost all of them agreed that the schools were where the rural "problem" would be most effectively addressed. What was the rural "problem"? Mabel Carney, a rural teacher and later teacher educator, was one of the most active figures in the movement. Carney defined what she called "the farm problem" as the search for a solution to keeping "a standard people" on the land. Bailey viewed the "problem" as figuring out how to develop and maintain "on our farms a civilization in full harmony with the best American ideals."[48]

Again, the thread that seems to tie all Country Lifers is the frightening consequences of fewer and fewer farmers. They believed that in order to stem the tide of cityward migration, they would have to instill in country youth a sense of dignity in rural living and an intellectual attachment to the countryside. This desire is reflected in the numerous creeds and pledges created for rural children. The intent of the rhetoric in this sample is obvious: "I believe the country which God made is more beautiful than the city man made."[49] Carney's "Country Life Creed" maintains that the schools should be "temporarily first in leadership and influence because cooperation is a question of education, and education is the special responsibility of the school."[50] Another country creed contends that "opportunity comes to the boy on the farm as often as to the boy in the city, that life is larger and freer and happier on the farm than in town."[51]

That Country Life supporters were not exclusively concerned with country boys is witnessed by Martha Foote Crow's book-length guide to daily living called *The American Country Girl* published in 1915. It begins with her definition of the problem:

> The reason why the American people care so much for the ideals presented to us in the Country Life Movement is that there is something very deep-seated and permanent within us to which these motives can appeal. We are a Country Life people. The bogy of the overshadowing city, threatening to spread and spread until, like a great octopus, it should suck all the sweet fields into its tentacles and cover the green areas with a complete blackness, has given us a definite fright. The result of our terror is the Country Life Movement. [52]

The assumption in Crow's book is that if the confinement of household labor, intensified by rural isolation, could be overcome by the goals of the Country Life movement, the life of the farm girl would permit her to become all "she is capable of becoming."[53] While the rhetoric might sound attractively feminist, any hint of feminism from the pens of female Country Lifers is inevitably laden with predictable sentiment concerning female domesticity.

How were the schools to dignify rural life and instill an allegiance to rural living? Generally, most Country Lifers concurred with Carney's Herbartian suggestions that "daily farm-life experience should be the backbone of everything in the whole school course. . . . Arithmetic, reading, geography, and all other subjects, though not limited by it, should originate from it and maintain direct connection with it. Agriculture should be taught, in other words, because it is the *basic experience* of country children, and all real teaching builds upon past experience."[54] Another Country Lifer agreed, "Good teaching demands that all learning be based upon experiences and interests of the one receiving instruction. Country people think in terms of agriculture."[55] Nature study and field trips were to be a big part of the rural school experience.[56] Clarence H. Poe added in his article "Farmer Children Need Farmer Studies" that "we must instill a love of nature and joy in country living."[57] Country Lifers worked ceaselessly to infuse the country school curriculum with an appreciation for country life. That they favored graded instruction and the consolidation of township governance has led many historians to conclude that the movement was nothing more than an attempt to urbanize the rural schools. Actually, Country Lifers were horrified by such a thought. Carney contended that "what we need and must have, to solve the problem of rural education, is not an urban school whose influences lead young people of the farms directly away from the land, but a country school, a country school improved, modernized, and adopted to the needs of present country life."[58] Another Country Lifer was convinced that "there is better work done in a [rural] school than is possible in a large system of graded schools in the city."[59]

To fully understand the Country Life position regarding school reform, one should keep in mind that the ultimate goal was to keep cityward migration to a minimum. To urbanize rural schools would have been self-defeating. In fact, the evidence indicates that there was no such desire, although many Country Lifers expressed envy over electrified city schools equipped with laboratories, gymnasiums, central heating, and plumbing.

From the outset, farmers rejected the idea of a presidential commission to study the conditions of rural America. Farm periodicals announced the formation of the commission with some suspicion. The *American Farm Review* commented that "there are those who feel that this is only a long leap in the direction of paternal government. They do not like it. They are too independent to believe that the farmer of a republic like ours needs to be lifted on the back of the President or anyone else."[60] A later issue summarized the work of the commission and popular reaction to it:

> Nobody goes farther than the *American Farm Review* in commending any plan for the improvement of rural life. Any measure having for its object the greater efficiency of country schools, the improvement of roads,

the telephone and rural delivery service, the extension of libraries, and so on, meets with our unqualified approval. But we are of the opinion that farm life can be improved only through the continued material advancement of the farmers. No commission can elevate it, or even show the farmer the way. In the future, as in the past, the farmer must work out his own salvation. [61]

The *Country Gentleman* commented after announcing the formation of the commission, "I wonder if it has ever occurred to the good people who are so solicitously taking us under their wing with the intention of uplifting us, that perhaps we are as good and clean and happy in our modest way as we want to be." Further, it said, "We don't particularly relish being told in one breath that we are the salt of the earth, that on us and our labors rest the foundations of the economic structure of the business and politics of the nation, and in the next breath that we are isolated, lonely, groping in dark ways, and need a commission of professors to inquire into our malady."[62]

The methods used by the Country Life Commission to explore rural conditions included a twelve-question survey, to which the Commission received more than 115,000 responses, and a series of thirty hearings in towns across the country. The hearings were designed to allow farmers to interact directly with commission members. One such hearing took place in Champaign, Illinois, on 14 December 1908. The Champaign *Daily Gazette* covered the event, and its description suggests that while the issue of paving roads in Illinois was unpopular, the real sticking point was discussing the reorganization of rural schools: "The twelve principal questions were asked at the morning session and they brought out a flood of information much of which was not entirely to the credit of the great state of Illinois, that part relating to the country school system, at least."[63]

Essentially, there were but two Country Life prescriptions for the country school: infuse a love of the countryside into an experience-based curriculum, and consolidate small country school districts into a township system. To be sure, some rural residents saw "nature-study" and "physical education" as a lot of nonsense and preferred that their teachers did not "dabble in too many fads."[64] But real resistance was reserved for those who advocated school consolidation.

This is the point where current scholarship breaks down. It would be easy to suggest that farmers opposed consolidation because of its costs. However, many Country Lifers pointed out that such a strategy could save money in time. Others openly admitted consolidation would raise taxes, and well that it should, they said. When they considered that only one child in four in the nation's rural districts was completing the eighth grade, slightly inflated tax rates seemed a small price to pay to raise educational standards.

Certainly, cost was a factor, but the historians who have closely studied the movement do not attribute widespread rural resistance to school reorganization as a matter of economics. They contend that the explanation is entwined with Jeffersonian democratic ideals, such as suspicion of anything that tends toward centralization. But whereas historians have scrutinized the motives behind the use of the term *democracy* by southern agrarians, they have generally failed to do the same for midwestern agrarians. Most have agreed with the characterization of Daniel Webster that farmers are the founders of civilization, or with that of Thomas Jefferson that farmers are the strength of the nation. Historians have not dealt much with the Midwest, the rural Midwest in particular. Precisely for this reason, some historians regard the Ku Klux Klan's regeneration and emanation out of rural Indiana in the 1920s as an accident of history. Rather than being an accident, it appears to be a logical consequence of the historical record dating back as far as Tocqueville's observation in 1835 that "'the prejudice of race appears to be stronger in the states which have abolished slavery than in those where it still exists; and nowhere is it so important as in those states where servitude never has been known [i.e., the Middle West].'"[65]

To date, the matter of interpreting rural resistance to township consolidation and the prescriptions of the Country Life movement has not been well scrutinized. Certainly, resistance was rooted in an effort to protect something. But the evidence relayed in this chapter casts doubt on the traditional explanation that local farmers were resisting township consolidation to protect neighborhood democracy. In fact, what the farmers tried to protect may have been something fundamentally undemocratic.

In many ways the Country Life Commission, as well as many other Progressive era commissions, can be seen as the predictable societal response of a people unsure about the kinds of changes going on around them. The transition from an agrarian to industrial society, and from a rural to an urban society, was neither smooth nor efficient. And among intellectuals of the era, stability and efficiency were high priorities. Contemporary wisdom suggested the creation of a commission to determine how to arrive at these goals. As for the Country Life Commission, it was thought that a little more efficiency in rural schools might enhance the strength of the farmer class, something considered a prerequisite for an increasingly urban, industrial society.

But the agenda of the Country Life Commission became increasingly difficult to sustain as more nations of the world found themselves embroiled in the Great War. The demand for agricultural produce skyrocketed and for the first time, in any great numbers, traction engines were put into fields across the country. The industrial agenda, maximizing production while minimizing costs, anti-community though it was, was increasingly praised as the way to support the war effort. Government and privately sponsored agricultural extension agents became the heralds of scientific techniques designed to increase yields regardless of human costs. A much older agrarian agenda, communally derived stewardship of the soil, began to hold less currency among American farmers. Farm size began to slowly increase. The steady stream of agricultural dispossession, which we continue to witness today, had begun, and with it, the slow demise of the rural one-room school.

Conclusion

When World War I ended, more country schools existed than at any previous time in our nation's history. The number would never again be as high. Electricity, along with the internal combustion engine, changed the history of rural schooling just as it changed rural life and labor. Not all rural people have been happy with the changes. Many have felt that life was more meaningful before modern conveniences eroded away what were once high levels of communal interdependence. Some are quick to label this kind of sentiment nostalgia, and there can be no mistaking the pejorative connotation. But as Christopher Lasch so ably demonstrates, the proponents of progress who condemn nostalgia are guilty of the very same sin. One idealizes the past; the other, the future.[1] In both instances, the quality of the instruction we might take for present action is diminished.

It is fair to say that much of the scholarship attending to rural Midwest educational history has been viewed either through the lens of nostalgia or of progress. Through the former lens, rural schools epitomized all that was good in a social institution; through the latter, all that was bad. I believe Lasch was right about placing too much faith in nostalgia or in progress, and his lesson is easily applied to the historical enterprise: the end result is not helpful.

I undertook this work because it seemed that this is where we were as far as coming to understand the educational history of the rural Midwest. Whether we are farther along now, as a result of this volume, is for others to judge. The only answer I was able to find concerning the large, looming, undeniable feature of rural Midwest education—namely, why there was such pervasive resistance to centralized authority—was because farmers were either villains or saints. I was not inclined to accept either view.

There is an alternative. There were at least two significant components to the anatomy of rural resistance, as I see it, one connected to the highly sectarian religious scene during the nineteenth century, and the other, to the scramble for land ownership in an increasingly market-driven agricultural economy. The relationship of each of these circumstances to the educational history of the region has been understudied. While we may perhaps call the propensity to resist free schools— born of concern for the unmistakable presence of a particular religious tradition in the centralized state department of education—an admirable expression of democracy, the same cannot be said for the propensity to resist free schools because they might give an advantage to the ceaseless stream of transients who entered the community each year looking for a chance to become landowners.

The legally enforced silence of women and transient male farmers on school-related issues speaks clearly of the tight connection between schooling and the larger political economy. Male landowning farmers were not overly disposed to see either of these groups come to own property in the immediate vicinity. Women, of course, were to be kept away from market-related affairs; tenant farmers, the landowners hoped, would push on before they threatened the acquisition of more land by longstanding families.

The promotion of certain forms of democratic policy beginning to emanate first out of the trans-Mississippi West becomes more understandable when we recognize that most trans-Mississippi settlers came there after failing to acquire land elsewhere. Gradually, these states broke with the pattern. They became the first to give women and tenant farmers a voice in the schooling affairs of their children. They were the first to provide free textbooks for all schoolchildren. They had the best record for placing schoolhouses in equitable locations. And they most wholeheartedly embraced the Farmers Alliance, in the process becoming the hotbed of that uniquely American expression of grassroots democracy called populism.

The nation's interior filled as these events unfolded, and partially as a result of this filling, a steady stream of rural youth began leaving the countryside and moving to the city. It did not take long for the social evolutionists to see grave danger in this circumstance. Their concern turned into the Country Life Commission and its major initiative, the reform of rural schooling. Once again, when historical study is undertaken with the view that rural schools epitomized all things good, the Country Life Commission receives less-than-favorable treatment. The commissioners become villains looking to impose an urban, industrial model on small rural schools. In this instance, again, we are left with an interpretation that is not particularly helpful. There is little disagreement that the commission failed to achieve its objective. So what are we left to make of this? How can we say the commissioners failed when all across the country rural schools began to disappear or to look more and more like their urban counterparts? It failed, in fact, because the agenda of the Country Life commissioners was to improve rural communities, to make them more attractive to rural youth and thereby, perhaps, put an end to high levels of cityward migration. This did not happen.

In my view, many useful ideas were buried together with the history of the Country Life movement, ideas that rural schools could use today. But the movement's most significant lesson lay in coming to terms with its demise, particularly since the death of the movement coincided with the genesis of the downward trend among one-room rural schools. That is to say, if we can come to see why the Country Life Commission failed, we will discover why 1918 marks the high point in this history of Midwest rural schooling.

The full significance of the Progressive era cannot be ascertained without an appreciation for the discontent, depression, and violence of the 1890s. Nothing was more clear to emerging capitalist business leaders at the turn of this century than the fact that the unionist impulse in America needed to be broken. The worst nightmare of this increasingly powerful group was a political coalition between farmers and laborers. By the business leaders' digging in their heels, forming sociological departments, differentiating labor tasks, capitalizing on racial and ethnic animosities, hiring shop floor spies, and so on, labor might be beaten. Dealing with discontent among farmers, however, required different measures. Grant McConnell perceptively analyzed the situation this way:

> Although the Populist threat had disappeared, the memory of it was still vivid in the eyes of grain exchanges, heads of farm equipment trusts, and directors of banks. It is even likely that some of these glimpsed the possibility of enlisting organized agriculture, or rather, re-organized agriculture on the side of capitalism. Whether or not there was such a deliberate intention, few better means to accomplish the result could be imagined than the course that was followed. [2]

Perhaps encouraged by the loyalty of the Old Northwest to the Republican party, a considerable number of capitalist business leaders may have believed that farmers could serve as more than just the balance wheel between capital and labor, the idea promoted by Liberty Hyde Bailey, chair of the Country Life Commission. Farmers might actually be persuaded to oppose the interests of organized labor. Championing science, technology, and agricultural education for farmers, those with business interests saw a way to improve their image as well as their economic advantage.

Their opportunity came with circumstances in large parts of the South. The new-century prosperity was not shared by southerners whose cotton crops were ravaged by the Mexican boll weevil. Dr. Seaman Knapp, a former college president and land company business manager, developed a system of crop rotation and diversified farming that minimized the weevil infestation. Knapp utilized demonstration plots out in the field to promote his ideas to skeptical farmers. In time, county agents were deployed in large parts of the South to preach the virtue of Knapp's approach to some of the problems of southern agriculture. In 1903 the United States Department of Agriculture adopted Knapp's model of county extension work. A bigger boost occurred in 1906, however, when the Rockefeller-sponsored General Education Board adopted the extension concept and pressured the colleges of agriculture set up under the 1887 Hatch Act to implement the demonstration work. Shortly thereafter, Julius Rosenwald offered one thousand dollars to the first one hundred counties to employ a county agent.[3]

Bankers soon saw the practicality in the industrial-agrarian rapprochement promoted by these corporate foundations. The committee on agriculture of the American Bankers' Association was created in 1909. Two years later the committee's duties were expanded when it became the Committee on Agricultural Development and Education. The committee was convinced that farmers could be taught to manage their affairs in ways that would be profitable for all. When the Federal Reserve Act passed in 1913, the bankers' committee created a new journal called *The Banker-Farmer* designed to explain the agricultural implications of the Act. The twelve regional banks under the auspices of the Federal Reserve were purported to be cooperatives that would ease the burden for farmers desiring credit. Lawrence Goodwyn contends that they were never designed for anything but providing "easier access to funds for only the nation's most affluent farming interests."[4] Other capitalist attempts to build cordial relations with farmers betray the same bias. To be profitable for agricultural support industries, farming had to be efficient on their terms.

The National Implement and Vehicle Association also created a committee to look into the education of farmers. Its journal, *The Progressive Farmer*, conveniently detailed the advantages of the association's mechanistic innovations.[5] Many railroad companies supported county demonstration work, as did the Universal Portland Cement Company, the American Steel and Wire Company, Wells Fargo and Company, the National Association of Retail Merchants, the Western Retail Lumberman's Association, and the Southwestern Lumberman's Association. These and other groups were conveniently touted in the pages of *The Banker-Farmer* as financial supporters of agricultural extension and education. McConnell points out that these were also organizations that received "populist wrath" back in the days when they were frequently cited as corporate exploiters of the average citizen.[6]

One result of so much attention to the affairs of the farmer, particularly in the midst of uncommon prosperity, was the 1914 passage of the Smith-Lever Act. What this law did was solidify the county agent as the cornerstone of the farmer extension program. It delineated the complicated funding procedure that made the agent an arm of the federal, state, and county government, and of private agencies like the General Education Board and the Rosenwald Fund.

County agents became the agricultural experts who taught ways to improve herds, yields, pest control, and profits. In order for Congress to evaluate their effectiveness, massive statistical reports were compiled and presented annually. Thus, it was in the county agent's best interest to "achieve the quickest and most extensive application of approved methods." Inevitably, this meant working with men who were known to be community leaders or, preferably, with groups of such men. One outgrowth of a decade's worth of county agent work was the development of networks that received the curious name of "bureaus." The networks, or bureaus, were composed of the county's leading farmers, that is, the persistent farmers from key families. Dr. Clarence Ousley, an agriculture professor from Texas, detested the government's role in the creation of these bureaus. Ousley commented "'that this bureau movement was a scheme whereby a progressive body of farmers took advantage of the department [USDA] and the college [of agriculture] in order to exclusively utilize the services of the county agent. If that is what the bureau means, then it is an unwholesome movement.'"[7]

In time, federations of these county bureaus were created, and in 1920, a national organization known as the American

Farm Bureau Federation was formed. McConnell claims that "the county agent became the publicly paid organizer" of the new farmers' association.[8] In time, of course, the Farm Bureau became the most effective agricultural lobby in Washington. It should be no surprise, therefore, that subsequent farm policy promoted the economic advantage of large operators, causing a steady cityward flow of the excluded and dispossessed. Keeping rural schools open became understandably more and more difficult. Gradually, the small rural school boards succumbed to the temptation to disband and bus the kids to town.

We are bringing no more thought to the matter than those who sentimentally wish for the good old days if we accept present circumstances in the countryside as somehow inevitable or as the price paid for "progress." The demise of rural communities served the interest very well of a few—at the expense of the majority. The educational history of the rural Midwest has been inextricably caught up in the convoluted religious and economic history that has brought these circumstances about.

Notes
Bibliography
Index

Notes

1. The Kingdom of God in the Wilderness

1. Richard Jensen, *The Winning of the Midwest: Social and Po-
litical Conflict, 1888–1896* (Chicago: University of Chicago
Press, 1971), 58; Paul Kleppner, *The Cross of Culture: A So-
cial Analysis of Midwestern Politics 1850–1900* (New York:
The Free Press, 1970), 71; David B. Tyack and Elisabeth
Hansot, *Managers of Virtue: Public School Leadership in
America, 1820–1980* (New York: Basic Books, 1982), 74, 10.
Jensen's book recognizes a fair degree of intradenominational
differences on questions concerning ritual, liturgy, and
creedalism.

2. Seventeenth-century Baptists are an exception in this regard,
but these were not the popular Baptists of the American
plains. Their intellectual debt to Calvin was far greater than
their debt to Arminius.

3. There is some disagreement over the origins of the term *Methodist*. Generally, however, it is accepted that the term was
initially a derogatory referent used by established ministers
of the Church of England. See Emory Stevens Bucke, ed.,
The History of American Methodism (New York: Abingdon
Press, 1964), 1:16.

4. T. Scott Miyakawa, *Protestants and Pioneers: Individualism
and Conformity on the American Frontier* (Chicago: University of Chicago Press, 1964), 160.

5. Sydney E. Ahlstrom, *A Religious History of the American
People* (New Haven: Yale University Press, 1972), 444; memoir of Dr. Patrick Henry Jameson, 38, 40, Patrick Henry
Jameson Papers, Indiana Historical Society Library, Indianapolis, Indiana (hereafter cited as IHSL).

6. The early spread of Calvinism in the West was accomplished
mainly by Presbyterians of Ulster-Irish descent. They represented the southernmost extension of Puritanism, and it was
this tradition that moved first into Kentucky, Tennessee, and
Ohio. See Ahlstrom, *A Religious History*, 446; Bernard A.
Weisberger, *They Gathered at the River: The Story of
the Great Revivalists and Their Impact upon Religion in
America* (Boston: Little, Brown and Co., 1958), 40.

7. John Mack Faragher, *Sugar Creek: Life on the Illinois Prairie*
(New Haven: Yale University Press, 1986), 161.

8. See Lloyd P. Jorgenson's *The State and the Nonpublic School 1825–1925* ([Columbia: University of Missouri Press, 1987], 25) for a discussion of the spread of Baptist and Methodist denominations in the Midwest. Jorgenson contends that pietists "were often skeptical of the value of any education beyond the rudimentary level." T. Scott Miyakawa concurs with the analysis in his book *Protestants and Pioneers*, cited earlier. It contains a chapter devoted to attitudes toward formal education within the popular denominations that shaped frontier Protestantism.

9. Quoted in Dickson D. Bruce, *And They All Sang Hallelujah: Plain-Folk Camp Religion, 1800–1845* (Knoxville: University of Tennessee Press, 1974), 53.

10. Quoted in Miyakawa, *Protestants and Pioneers*, 126, 164–65; Charles A. Johnson, *The Frontier Camp Meeting: Religion's Harvest Time* (Dallas: Southern Methodist University Press, 1955), 53.

11. Timothy L. Smith, "Protestant Schooling and American Nationality, 1800–1850," *Journal of American History* 53 (March 1967): 690. It is safe to assume that the reference here to Presbyterians could be more accurately construed as a reference to the Cumberlands and other pietist spin-offs from the main Presbyterian polity.

12. Carl F. Kaestle, *Pillars of the Republic: Common Schools and American Society, 1780–1860* (New York: Hill and Wang, 1983), 77–78. Kaestle's reference to "Protestant cosmopolitans" seems to include midwestern Puritans like Beecher, Stowe, Pierce, and so on, as well as non-Puritan New Englanders like Barnard and Mann. In this regard the reference is similar to Tyack and Hansot's depiction of the "aristocracy of character" in *Managers of Virtue*, cited earlier.

13. Ahlstrom, *A Religious History*, 465n.

14. For an interesting commentary on the Beecher clan, see Lyman Beecher Stowe, *Saints, Sinners, and Beechers* (Indianapolis: Bobbs Merrill, 1934). Also see Charles H. Foster, *The Rungless Ladder: Harriet Beecher Stowe and New England Puritanism* (Durham: Duke University Press, 1954); and Kathryn Kish Sklar, *Catharine Beecher: A Study in American Domesticity* (New Haven: Yale University Press, 1973). Catharine was closely connected to the Ladies Society for Promoting Education at the West created specifically to send to the Old Northwest states "competent female teachers,

of unquestioned piety, belonging to the Congregational churches in New England." She was also instrumental in the promotion of the National Board of Popular Education, which was ostensibly nonsectarian, although part of the training for the young female "missionary teachers" included writing "out their views on regeneration and to state the reasons why they thought they had undergone that change." This requirement could have effectively eliminated the participation of women belonging to the Episcopalian church or other ritualistic faiths (Colin B. Goodykoontz, *Home Missions on the American Frontier* [Caldwell, Idaho: Claxton Press, 1939], 370, 373).

15. Mayo is quoted in Jorgenson, *Nonpublic School*, 32. Samuel Lewis and William Larrabee, Indiana's first state superintendent of instruction, also a Methodist minister, represent the two most conspicuous exceptions to Calvinist dominance of early state departments of education. But it is important to note that both of these individuals served very briefly in that capacity and both were succeeded by men from the Calvinist tradition who became more prominent in midwestern educational history.

16. Beecher is quoted in Wayne E. Fuller, *The Old Country School: The Story of Rural Education in the Middle West* (Chicago: University of Chicago Press, 1982), 23–24.

17. Ruth Miller Elson, *Guardians of Tradition: American Schoolbooks of the Nineteenth Century* (Lincoln: University of Nebraska Press, 1954); Barbara Finkelstein, *Governing the Young: Teacher Behaviour in Popular Primary Schools in the Nineteenth-Century United States* (New York: Falmer Press, 1989); Jorgenson, *Nonpublic School*, 60–68.

18. Tyack and Hansot, *Managers of Virtue*, 31. Also see R. Freeman Butts, "Public Education and Political Community," *History of Education Quarterly* 14 (Summer 1974): 167.

19. Quoted in Carl F. Kaestle, "The Development of Common School Systems in the States of the Old Northwest," in *Schools and the Means of Education Shall Forever Be Encouraged: A History of Education in the Old Northwest, 1787–1880*, ed. Paul H. Mattingly and Edward W. Stevens, Jr. (Athens: Ohio University Libraries, 1987), 35.

20. Fuller, *Old Country School*, 38. See also Timothy Smith's passage, cited earlier.

21. Patricia Albjerg Graham makes note of this in her analysis of

rural Johnson County, Indiana, in *Community and Class in American Education, 1865–1918* (New York: John Wiley and Sons, 1974). The county seat, Franklin, was dominated by pietistic Presbyterians (very likely Cumberlands), Baptists, and Methodists. Graham comments that "the churches in a community like Johnson County where Protestantism was so strong had educational commitments of a much lower order than their inspirational, missionary, or moral ones" (67). I believe she is right on target. The Methodists and Baptists, so conspicuous in their absence from the leadership of the common school crusade, were by contrast conspicuous in their domination of organizations like the Anti-Saloon League, the Women's Christian Temperance Society, and the American Protective Association.

22. Quoted in Andrew A. Sherockman, "Caleb Mills, Pioneer Educator in Indiana" (Ph.D. diss., University of Pittsburgh, 1955), 118. Sherockman noted that Mills believed "a man of sterling worth and religious principle could not be obtained for the state superintendency without awakening denominational prejudices and sectarian bigotry to such an extent as to preclude success" (119).

23. Samuel A. Briggs Diary, 13 February 1858, Manuscript Division, Illinois State Historical Library, Springfield, Illinois (hereafter cited as ISHL).

24. Alexis de Tocqueville, *Democracy in America* (New York: Century Co., 1898), 1:395n.

25. The early Kentucky resident is quoted in Thomas D. Clark, *A History of Kentucky* (New York: Prentice-Hall, 1939), 305; John Donald Pulliam, "A History of the Struggle for a Free Common School System in Illinois from 1818 to the Civil War" (Ed.D. diss., University of Illinois, 1965), 108; Cartwright is quoted in Miyakawa, *Protestants and Pioneers*, 186. Also see Rosemary Ruether and Rosemary Skinner Keller, eds., *The Nineteenth Century*, vol. 1 of *Women and Religion in America* (San Francisco: Harper and Row, 1981), 23.

26. Peter Cartwright, *Autobiography of Peter Cartwright*, ed. Charles L. Waller (1856, reprint, New York: Abingdon Press, 1955).

27. Peter Cartwright, *Fifty Years as a Presiding Elder*, ed. W. S. Hooper (Cincinnati: Walden and Stowe, 1871), 96–141.

28. Washington Gladden, *Recollections* (New York: Houghton Mifflin Co., 1909), 34.

29. Quoted in Miyakawa, *Protestants and Pioneers*, 127; and Ahlstrom, *A Religious History*, 444.
30. Edward Eggleston, *The Circuit Rider: A Tale of the Heroic Age* (1873, reprint, Lexington: University of Kentucky Press, 1970), 180.
31. Lyman Beecher, *A Plea for the West* (Cincinnati: Truman and Smith, 1835), 44. For references to Beecher's sermons and the Ursuline convent, see Ahlstrom, *A Religious History*, 561; Weisberger, *They Gathered*, 69; and Lawrence A. Cremin, *American Education: The National Experience 1783–1876*, (New York: Harper and Row, 1980), 36.
32. Perhaps the best account of the resurgence in Catholicism during this period is Ralph William Franklin's *Nineteenth-Century Churches: A History of the New Catholicism in Wurtemberg, England and France* (New York: Garland Publications, 1987). The most direct manifestation of this renewed interest in Catholic liturgy in America was probably the Mercersberg Movement among the German Reformed churches of Pennsylvania; see James H. Nichols, ed., *The Mercersberg Movement* (New York: Oxford University Press, 1966). Also see Ahlstrom, *A Religious History*, 621–29.
33. Ahlstrom, *A Religious History*, 610–13, 425.
34. Frederick Packard is quoted in Raymond Culver, *Horace Mann and Religion in Massachusetts Public Schools* (1929, reprint, New York: Arno Press, 1969), 55.
35. Jorgenson, *Nonpublic School*, 13. In *Culture on the Moving Frontier* (Bloomington: Indiana University Press, 1955), Louis B. Wright suggested that the appearance of Sunday schools may have slowed the adoption of free schools in the Midwest. Jorgenson's position, and I agree with this, is that Sunday schools had virtually the opposite effect.
36. Edward D. Neill, *The Nature and Importance of the American System of Public Instruction* (St. Paul: Owens and Moore, 1853), 8.
37. Henry Barnard was an Episcopalian, while Horace Mann, though born into a Calvinist family, rejected the strict orthodoxy of Congregationalism in favor of Unitarianism. While the label of ritualist may not be a perfect fit, particularly with Mann's Unitarianism, both Unitarians and Episcopalians were confessionalistic-rationalistic bodies at odds with the brand of pietism emerging among Calvinist groups and practiced by the popular denominations. Edith Nye MacMullen,

in her comprehensive biography of Henry Barnard, *In the
Cause of True Education: Henry Barnard and Nineteenth-
Century School Reform* (New Haven: Yale University Press,
1991), relayed Barnard's "disgust" for religious revivalism (22–
23). Mann conveyed a similar sentiment toward revival-in-
spired conversions in a letter to Frederick Packard that became a catalyst for claims by Calvinist clergy that Mann was
trying to spread Unitarianism in Massachusetts common
schools (see Culver, *Horace Mann*, 63–64). Mary McDougall
Gordon distinguishes between Boston's Unitarians and the
much larger group of Massachusetts Calvinist clergy. According to Gordon, however, Unitarians "were caught up in their
own version of evangelicalism" and had no apparent difficulty
with Calvinist thought concerning human nature, education,
and so on. I find this argument less than convincing given the
volumes of scholarship devoted to the ramifications of the
"Unitarian schism." See her "Patriots and Christians: A Reassessment of Nineteenth-Century School Reformers," *Journal
of Social History* 11 (Summer 1978): 557.
38. Clarence J. Karier, *Man, Society, and Education: A History
of American Educational Ideals* (Glenview, Ill.: Scott, Foresman and Co., 1967), 59.
39. Ahlstrom, *A Religious History*, 401.
40. Reverends Emerson Davis and Thomas Robbins were the orthodox clergy appointed to the board. It should be pointed
out, as many of their opponents did, that these men worked
in parishes quite distant from Boston, and they were outnumbered as well (eight to two) by Unitarians on the board.
Still, they seem to have accepted Mann's designs as valuable
rather than as a threat to the Puritan heritage. The presence
of orthodox clergy increased in the composition of subsequent boards. See Cremin, *American Education*, 136–39, and
Culver, *Horace Mann*, 100–101.
41. Carl F. Kaestle and Maris A. Vinovskis, *Education and Social
Change in Nineteenth-Century Massachusetts* (Cambridge:
Cambridge University Press, 1980). Kaestle and Vinovskis provide an insightful chapter concerning the pro-common school
and anti-common school agendas surrounding the 1840 legislative attempt to disband Mann's board of education. Their interpretation (which runs somewhat counter to Culver's) is
that in Massachusetts "party affiliation rather than religious

affiliation seems to be the key to the vote [on whether to abolish the board]" (227). I agree with this view because there were pressing social and economic circumstances on the East Coast and in New England in particular that seemingly demanded concerted political action. The school question in many ways seems to have been just one more issue to consider in Whig or Democratic terms. Despite the liberal religious views of Mann and many of the first board members, Unitarianism was not a threat to the religious hegemony of Puritanism in Massachusetts. Also see Michael B. Katz, *The Irony of Early School Reform: Educational Innovation in Mid-Nineteenth Century Massachusetts* (Cambridge: Harvard University Press, 1968). On Irish immigration and industrialization, see especially pp. 5–11. Albert Fishlow ("The American Common School Revival: Fact or Fancy?" in *Industrialization in Two Systems: Essays in Honor of Alexander Gerschenkron*, ed. Henry Rosovsky [New York: John Wiley & Sons, 1966]) contends that the common school crusade did not result in higher levels of literacy or school attendance in antebellum New England and in New York, thus denying the claims of functionalists who argue that the advances in education produced a corresponding advance in economic productivity. Kaestle and Vinovskis's work modifies, to some extent, Fishlow's analysis; see Kaestle and Vinovskis, in particular pp. 11–24.

42. I focus briefly on Peck and Cartwright because they represent two non-Calvinist clergy sometimes cited as common school founders. It should be be noted, though, that the New England Baptists who sent Peck to the West as a missionary were far more Calvinistic than the Baptists who filtered through backwoods Virginia into Ohio, Kentucky, and Tennessee. Also, in a heavily cited account of Protestant schooling on the plains, Timothy L. Smith contends that such "rough-hewn frontier preachers" as Peck and Cartwright "prepared western soil for Yankee seed" (Smith, "Protestant Schooling," 692–93). I contend, however, that something quite different was going on. Yankee ministers, in fact, before accomplishing their successful drive for free schools, often competed with ministers of the popular denominations in the creation of subscription schools. Reverend Isaac Reed, a Presbyterian minister from Indiana, started ten different schools before Indi-

ana's free school system was established in 1852; see "lecture on education," 1 August 1853, Reverend Isaac Reed Papers, IHSL.

43. Peck's career is interesting because he is supposed to have been an advocate of common schools, yet his biographer Helen Louise Jennings and others who have worked on Illinois educational history do not provide instances of Peck's unqualified support of a free-school system. There are vague references to Peck's support of the common schools, but the extant record of his work suggests that denomination-based education was his first allegiance. Indeed, John Pulliam observed that when Illinois attempted its first free school law in 1825, there was "no indication that [Peck] took an active part in securing" its passage. Later, he was involved with state officials in gathering data from the public concerning the demand for common schools, but this is hardly evidence of unqualified support (see Pulliam, "A History," 37). The greatest part of the energy and drive from both Peck and Cartwright was devoted to the establishment of denomination-based schools and colleges. This was a reality in "an era of intense sectarian conflict," as Lawrence Cremin has described it (*American Education*, 409). These men did not particularly support or resist the concept of free common schools. More important in their minds was the day-to-day work of saving souls on the frontier. Common schools made sense to antebellum midwesterners who counted some advantage through their creation. Outnumbered as they were in the Midwest, the legatees of the Puritan heritage saw significant advantages to adopting a common school system. Generally speaking, both an obvious measure of utility and the education-based religious structure were absent from the world view of the Protestant groups (especially Methodists and Baptists) that were experiencing greater success on the frontier.

44. Quoted in Helen Louise Jennings, "John Mason Peck and the Impact of New England on the Old Northwest" (Ph.D. diss., University of Southern California, 1961), 41, 149, 103, ii. The emphasis on "*deplorable ignorance*" is Peck's.

45. Tyack and Hansot, *Managers of Virtue*, 23, 29; Kaestle, *Pillars of the Republic*, 116. Also see Faragher's description of an early subscription school connected to a group of Cumber-

land Presbyterians in the Sugar Creek vicinity in *Sugar Creek*, 120–29.

46. Quoted in John Cook, *Educational History of Illinois* (Chicago: Henry O. Shepard, 1912), 29. Also see Pulliam, "A History," 29–30.

47. Richard Boone, *A History of Education in Indiana* (1892, reprint, Indianapolis: Indiana Historical Bureau, 1941), 42; Paul Monroe, *Founding of the American Public School System: A History of Education in the United States* (1940, reprint, New York: Hafner Publishing Co., 1971), 250; Fuller, *Old Country School*, 51.

2. Transience and Free Schooling

1. This quotation is attributed to Lord Bryce in Fuller, *Old Country School*, 25.

2. Kaestle, "Common School Systems," 31–44.

3. Tyack and Hansot, *Managers of Virtue*, 46. The historical work on tenancy in the Midwest is voluminous, and I make no attempt here to add new data to the story. My point is simply to demonstrate the pervasiveness of tenancy in the Midwest agrarian order to better understand the utility of agrarian institutions (namely, schools). Allan G. Bogue's work in Iowa and Illinois shows that widespread tenancy was in place from the first days of pioneer settlement; see Bogue, *From Prairie to Corn Belt: Farming on the Illinois and Iowa Prairies in the Nineteenth Century* (Chicago: University of Chicago Press, 1963), 47–66. But this is not to suggest that this feature of Midwest society was static. Clearly, during periods throughout the century, tenancy was more prevalent than at other times. See, for example, Allan G. Bogue, "Foreclosure Tenancy on the Northern Plains," *Agricultural History* 39 (January 1965): 3–16; and Donald L. Winters, "Tenant Farming in Iowa: 1860–1900," *Agricultural History* 48 (October 1974): 130–50. Note, however, that at no time during the century did tenancy cease to be a predictable feature in the midwestern countryside. A study conducted over 1,764 square miles of Illinois during the first decade of the twentieth century—a period of growing prosperity and ostensibly a "window of opportunity" for ownership—showed that 53 percent of the farms in this area were operated by tenants (J. D.

Eggleston and Robert Bruere, *The Work of the Rural School* [New York: Harper, 1913], 20–21).

4. Henry Steele Commager, ed., *Documents of American History* (New York: F. S. Crofts & Co., 1943), 124, 131.

5. Kaestle, *Pillars of the Republic*, 183–84. Also see Cremin, *American Education*, 401. David B. Tyack, on the other hand, has argued that the overall effect of the Ordinances on later educational developments was both positive and powerful. See David B. Tyack, Thomas James, and Aaron Benavot, *Law and the Shaping of Public Education 1785–1954* (Madison: University of Wisconisn Press, 1987), 31–33.

6. Faragher, *Sugar Creek*, 54.

7. Gilbert C. Fite, *The Farmers' Frontier 1865–1900* (New York: Holt, Rinehart, and Winston, 1966), 19. Also see Drew McCoy, *The Elusive Republic: Political Economy in Jeffersonian America* (New York: W. W. Norton, 1982), 252. Paul W. Gates advances the thesis of speculation resulting in high rates of tenancy in *The Farmer's Age: Agriculture 1815–1860* (New York: Holt, Rinehart, and Winston, 1960), 80–88. Subsequent work by Donald L. Winters and others indicates that while there was speculation, it was of far less consequence to tenancy than has been previously supposed; see Winters, "Tenancy as an Economic Institution: The Growth and Distribution of Agricultural Tenancy in Iowa, 1850–1900," *Journal of Economic History* 37 (June 1977): 382–408. Many historians who have posited this explanation for the persistent movement of settlers on the plains have found strength in Alexis de Tocqueville's observation: "It seldom happens that an American farmer settles for good open land which he occupies; especially in the districts of the far west he brings land into tillage in order to sell it again, and not to farm it" (*Democracy in America* [New York: Knopf, 1945], 2:166). Faragher's *Sugar Creek* also discounts the speculation hypothesis (145).

8. James A. Henretta, "Families and Farms: *Mentalité* in Pre-Industrial America," *William and Mary Quarterly* 3d ser., 35 (1978): 29–30.

9. Henretta, "Families and Farms," 9. Also, see Stephen Innes, "Land Tenancy and Social Order in Springfield, Massachusetts, 1652–1702," *William and Mary Quarterly* 3d ser., 35 (1978): 56.

10. There is nothing quite like the frontier thesis for demonstrating the power of historical interpretation. Depending on how circumstances are viewed, related events may be looked at quite differently by different historians. Wayne Fuller, for example, interpreted the prevalence of certain families in the administration of local schools as evidence that speculation theory was ill-founded. Criticizing Hofstadter, Fuller wrote, "That school board members were chosen again and again meant, of course, that many farmers remained in the community in which they had pioneered throughout the rest of their lives, which is in contrast to the picture one historian drew of restless, capitalistic, speculative farmers who moved rapidly across the frontier, never developed community life, and had no real agrarian values" (*Old Country School*, 266). But this dismissal of speculation theory misses the point. Of course there were persistent families; what is significant is that theirs was the minority experience in the Midwest. In this light, the pertinent question becomes whether there was direct or indirect institutional manipulation that worked to keep it this way.

11. Faragher, *Sugar Creek*, 62.

12. Quoted in David E. Schob, *Hired Hands and Plowboys: Farm Labor in the Midwest, 1815–1860* (Urbana: University of Illinois Press, 1975), 38. Schob's chapter entitled "Prairie Breaking" is an invaluable source on the intracacies of creating fields out of prairies.

13. Schob, *Hired Hands*, 96.

14. Henrietta Larson contends in *The Wheat Market and the Farmer in Minnesota 1858–1900* (New York: Columbia University Press, 1926) that in 1861 the mean distance for the farmers of the state to the nearest navigable river was eighty miles (24).

15. Clarence H. Danhof, *Change in Agriculture: The Northern United States 1820–1870* (Cambridge: Harvard University Press, 1969), 32.

16. Faragher, *Sugar Creek*, 59–60. The details on wheat harvesting are from Henretta, "Families and Farms," 18. For an excellent account of antebellum small grain harvesting in the Midwest, see Schob, *Hired Hands*, 67–110.

17. Faragher, *Sugar Creek*, 181, 190, 204. For other significant work that speaks of the prevalence of farm tenancy, see

Schob, *Hired Hands*, 266–270; and Robert V. Hine, *Community on the American Frontier: Separate but Not Alone* (Norman: University of Oklahoma Press, 1980), 93–98.

18. Faragher, *Sugar Creek*, 145.
19. Faragher, *Sugar Creek*, 145.
20. Henretta, "Families and Farms," 16.
21. Faragher, *Sugar Creek*, 252.
22. Faragher, *Sugar Creek*, 30. Also, see Kathleen Neils Conzen, "Peasant Pioneers: Generational Succession Among German Farmers in Frontier Minnesota," in *The Countryside in the Age of Capitalist Transformation: Essays in the Social History of Rural America*, ed. Steven Hahn and Jonathan Prude (Chapel Hill: University of North Carolina Press, 1985), 259–92.
23. Fuller, *Old Country School*, vii.
24. Faragher, *Sugar Creek*, 257.
25. Seth K. Humphrey, *Following the Prairie Frontier* (Minneapolis: University of Minnesota Press, 1931), 131.
26. Quoted in Lawrence Goodwyn, *Democratic Promise: The Populist Moment in America* (New York: Oxford University Press, 1976), 360.
27. Patricia Nelson Limerick, *The Legacy of Conquest: The Unbroken Past of the American West* (New York: W. W. Norton, 1987), 84.
28. Limerick, *Legacy of Conquest*, 83.
29. "Petition to Build School," 8 January 1820, John Armstrong Papers, IHSL.
30. Pulliam, "A History," 96; Smith, "Protestant Schooling," 692.
31. Boone, *Education in Indiana*, 22, 42–77. Also see Andrew A. Sherockman, "Caleb Mills, Pioneer Educator in Indiana" (Ph.D. diss., University of Pittsburgh, 1955), 17–19.
32. Smith, "Protestant Schooling," 692.
33. Quoted in Graham, *Community and Class*, 40.
34. John C. Pulver to Azell Ladd, 26 February 1852, Azell Ladd Papers, Wisconsin State Historical Society, Madison, Wisconsin (hereafter cited as WSHS).
35. J. S. Brown to Eleaser Root, 16 December 1851, Azell Ladd Papers, WSHS.
36. Board of Directors of Joint District 1 to Azell Ladd, 9 March 1852, Azell Ladd Papers, WSHS. For another very similar inquiry, see in the same collection William Coates to Azell Ladd, 14 February 1852.

37. Boone, *Education in Indiana*, 103–4. Boone's work contains a county-by-county breakdown of the 1848 free school vote (106–7). Much has been made of this data. For instance, it has been interpreted by some to be indicative of a propensity for schooling among New English settlers in the north of Indiana and, likewise, a propensity to resist the establishment of schools among southern settlers in the lower portions of the state. Kaestle admirably cautions historians about reading too much into this data; see Kaestle, "Common School Systems," 34.

38. "Addresses on Education," Reel 1, Caleb Mills Papers, IHSL.

39. William P. Heath to John ?, 25 February 1858, William P. Heath Papers, IHSL. As late as 1861, nine years after Indiana's free school system was established, the system's future was still in doubt. Writing to his brother in Indiana from his encampment in Virginia, William Houghton expressed his concern: "I am glad you are going to school, but fear you will not get to continue if it is a public school. I fear this war will be a severe blow to the free school system. Father writes that there is no money for school purposes in Barr Township this winter." Another rural Hoosier, a woman whose husband left her in 1855, wrote to a friend about what was to become of her: "I am thinking of trying to get a school in the spring, but it is uncertain on account of the Free Schools, and if I do not succeed, I don't know what I shall do" (William Houghton to Walter Houghton, 3 October 1861, William Houghton Papers; Mrs. Araminta Marquam to Crane Family, 4 March 1855, Joel Crane Papers, IHSL). The rates teachers were able to charge for subscription tuition varied enormously. In 1838 in Indiana one teacher received $2.20 for teaching a pupil eighty-eight days and $2.51 for teaching another 127 days. Others charged a fee of about $2.50 for a three-month term. In some places parents could expect to pay as little as $1.50 per scholar per term; in other places it was as high as $4.00.

40. As an example, see several tax warrants issued by the superintendent of Dane County schools in the Clerk's Record Book, District 1, Dane Twp., Dane County, WSHS.

41. Thirteen Residents of District 5, Portland Twp., Dodge County, to Azell Ladd, n.d., Azell Ladd Papers, WSHS.

42. This is a general observation based on a review of school board minutes and records in eight states.

43. "Annual Report of W. H. H. Beadle, Territorial Superinten-
    dent of Instruction," reprinted in *South Dakota Historical
    Collections* 18 (1936): 620.
44. Quoted in Reginald Horsman, *Race and Manifest Destiny:
    The Origins of American Racial Anglo-Saxonism* (Cambridge:
    Harvard University Press, 1981), 275.
45. The description of the origins of this district is derived from
    the school records of District 6, Center Twp., Rock County
    Historical Society, Janesville, Wisconsin (hereafter cited as
    RCHS). Where dates are included in the narrative, specific
    details will be found in corresponding entries of the Clerk's
    Minutes.
46. Clerk's Minutes, 17 November 1858, District 40, Elgin Twp.,
    Wabasha County, Minnesota State Archives, Minnesota His-
    torical Society, St. Paul, Minnesota (hereafter cited as MHS).
    The data used in the subsequent discussion of the early cir-
    cumstances in this district can be found in the district's
    school records, Wabasha County. Dated references will refer
    to corresponding entries in the Clerk's Minutes.
47. Data for the following description of early circumstances in
    this district comes from the school records of District 3, Oak-
    wood Twp., Brookings County, South Dakota State Historical
    Society, Pierre, South Dakota (hereafter cited as SDHS).
    Dated references correspond with entries in the Clerk's Min-
    utes.
48. Two of the most widely read accounts of this interpretation in-
    clude Fuller's *Old Country School* and Jonathan Sher, ed.,
    *Education in Rural America: A Reassessment of Conven-
    tional Wisdom* (Boulder: Westview Press, 1977).
49. Clerk's Minutes, 5 November 1886, Fairview Twp. District,
    Jones County; Clerk's Minutes, 5 March 1883, subdistrict 2,
    Lockridge Twp. District, Jefferson County, State Historical
    Society of Iowa, Iowa City, Iowa (hereafter cited as SHSI).
50. Clerk's Minutes, 18 March 1889, Fairview Twp. District,
    Jones County, SHSI.
51. Fuller, *Old Country School*, 124. Fuller scrutinized, or as he
    put it, "finely sifted," through the statistics available in the
    Annual Report of the Department of the Interior, 1901, vol.
    1, (Washington: Government Printing Office, 1902), 71–89.
    Admitting that Indiana did some positive things for its schools
    via the township system, Fuller notes that "perhaps justice
    was served in this way, but improved education was not"

(125). The small degree of "centralization" that occurred when moving from local districts to the township system probably did make circumstances more just, or more democratic. But to suggest that this factor vastly improved the schooling experience in Indiana for the poor, or for blacks, or for anyone, would be as much of a stretch as Fuller's assertion that Indiana's negative statistics show that the township system significantly worsened the school experience in Indiana. Said Fuller, "In retrospect it appears that Indiana's township system retarded the state's educational development more than it helped" (121). This conclusion is drawn primarily from the fact that Indiana consistently ranked near the bottom of Midwest states in average length of school terms and in its adult literacy rates. The differences between states in the various statistics Fuller tapped to denigrate township "centralization," however, are often miniscule and certainly not statistically significant. For instance, much of the force behind Fuller's argument was gleaned from the data provided in the table below:

Percent of the Population Illiterate

	1880	1890	1900
Ohio	5.5	5.2	4.0
Indiana	7.5	6.3	4.6
Illinois	6.4	5.2	4.2
Michigan	5.2	5.9	4.2
Wisconsin	5.8	6.7	4.7
Minnesota	6.2	6.0	4.1
Iowa	3.9	3.6	2.3
North Dakota	4.8	6.0	5.6
South Dakota	4.8	4.2	5.0
Nebraska	3.6	3.1	2.3
Kansas	5.6	4.0	2.9

Source: From the *Report of the Commissioner of Education for the Year 1902* (Washington, D.C.: Government Printing Office, 1903) 2: 2314.

It is difficult to imagine how a historian could look at this table and credit Indiana's poor performance to the township system. For one thing, it ignores a steady record of improvement over the years, something not obtained by all states.

52. For instance, in the school year 1886–87 Indiana required 14,006 teachers to fill 13,500 teaching positions. Iowa, the worst midwestern state in this regard, required 24,232 teachers to fill 14,747 spots. Whereas Indiana's turnover percentage was a low 3.74, Iowa's was 64.32. Obviously, these statistics could fluctuate tremendously from year to year, and therefore it does not seem wise to conclude much from them. Minnesota, for example, so close geographically to Iowa, was second in the Midwest with a 4.11 turnover percentage rate. These statistics can be found in the *Report of the Commissioner of Education for the Year 1886–1887* (Washington, D.C.: Government Printing Office, 1888), 72–73.

53. Boone, *Education in Indiana*, 42.

54. I have argued this point elsewhere; see "The Role of the Common School Concept in the Religious Crusade for the West," *Journal of Religion and Public Education* 18 (Fall 1991): 65–78; and "Democracy and the Origins of Rural Midwest Education: A Retrospective Essay," *Educational Theory* 38 (Summer 1988): 363–68.

3. Community Gatekeepers

1. I use the phrase "school board men" quite intentionally within this chapter. I do not mean to suggest that nowhere in the Midwest did a woman serve as a school board officer prior to 1918. Undoubtedly, there were some. But they were far and few between. In eight states I found reference to only two, one in Iowa who served briefly after 1896, and the other in Wisconsin who served between 1915 and 1918. Wayne E. Fuller calls his chapter dealing with midwestern school board members "Educators in Overalls." Although he failed to acknowledge the significance of this, he would no doubt agree with my assessment that when speaking of rural school board members prior to 1918, we are speaking about men, as the title of his chapter would suggest. The *Report of the Commissioner of Education for the Year 1900* ([Washington, D.C.: Government Printing Office, 1901], 2:2589) includes some data on "women in school administration." Regrettably, there are no statistics concerning women serving on rural school boards. The December 1909 issue of the *School Board Journal* (vol. 39) included an article entitled "Type of Men for School Board Members" that describes rather masculine char-

acteristics as prerequisites for successful school board members (6). There is not the slightest indication that a woman might or should serve as a school board member. The reference to "invaluable laboratories of democracy" is from Fuller's *Old Country School*, 45. The phrase "democratic localists" is often used but is attributable most directly to Michael Katz.

2. Bertha Palmer, "A Brief History of the Department of Public Instruction, 1860–1932," unpublished manuscript included in the Superintendent's Files, Series 386, Box 1, State Archives and Historical Research Library, State Historical Society of North Dakota, Bismarck, North Dakota (hereafter cited as HSND). For references to Wisconsin school statutes regarding women and school districts, see Oliver E. Wells, comp., *Laws of Wisconsin Relating to Common Schools* (Madison: Democrat Printing Co., 1892), 15. For the same in Kansas, see Frank Nelson, comp., *Laws for the Regulation and Support of the Common Schools of Kansas* (Topeka: W. Y. Morgan, 1899), 26.

3. The quotation of Indiana's state superintendent can be found in *The School Law of Indiana* (Hervey D. Vories, comp., [Indianapolis: n.p., 1891], 154). Other information concerning the issue of including or excluding women can be found here as well. The quotation from Ohio school law can be found in *Ohio School Laws* (Edmund J. Jones, comp., [Columbus: F. J. Herr, 1906], 64). Also see *The Illinois School Law 1889–1893* (Springfield: H. W. Rokker, 1893), 95; and *State of Michigan General School Laws* (Frederick C. Martindale, comp., [Lansing: Wynkoop, Hallenbeck, Crawford & Co., 1913], 20). In addition, women who owned taxable property had the right to vote at school elections in the Midwest. It was only upon marriage (or remarriage, for widows) that this right was forfeited. A rare recorded instance in Indiana demonstrates that this right was recognized by the men who dominated school affairs. In District 8 of Township 19 in Henry County, the board clerk noted that "J. Brewer voated for Widow Himes which was not preasant" (Clerk's Minutes, 17 December 1849, IHSL).

4. The Christie family was vehemently anti-Catholic. Stevens's brother, Alexander S. Christie, published a book entitled *Satanic Rome: Impartially Investigated*, which he felt com-

pelled to write lest "our great republic be destroyed by the
Satanic banditti of the vatican." Christie attributed most of
the "research" in the book to his father who first began the
working crusade to expose the "grotesque, hidebound,
bloody, degrading, toe-kissing tyranny" of the Catholic
church. Handwritten drafts of various chapters of Christie's
work are included in the James C. Christie and Family Papers, Box 34, Manuscript Divison, Minnesota State Archives,
MHS.

5. Clerk's Minutes, 1 July 1912, Jt. District 9, Blooming Grove
and Dunn Twps., Dane County, WSHS.

6. Fuller, *Old Country School*, 51.

7. Clarence R. Aurner, *History of Education in Iowa* (Iowa
City: State Historical Society of Iowa, 1914), 2:360.

8. Samuel Fallows, comp., *Laws of Wisconsin Relating to the
Common Schools* (Madison: Atwood & Culver, 1873), 23.

9. Vories, *The School Law of Indiana*, 175; Martindale, *State of
Michigan General School Laws*, 55. Passage on Minnesota's
statute is quoted in David L. Kiehle, *Education in Minnesota*
(Minneapolis: H. H. Williams Co., 1903), 1:34.

10. Quoted in Lewis Atherton, *Main Street on the Middle Border* (Chicago: Quadrangle Books, 1954), 89.

11. Clerk's Minutes, 14 December 1889, District 34, Chippewa
County, Minnesota State Archives, MHS; Clerk's Minutes,
24 June 1912, District 25, Stanton County, Nebraska State
Historical Society, Lincoln, Nebraska (hereafter cited as
NSHS); Clerk's Minutes, 7 August 1900, Jt. District 9, Sun
Prairie and Bristol Twps., Dane County, WSHS.

12. Clerk's Minutes, 20 April 1895, District 5, Twp., 6, Jasper
County, ISHL. A four-year lag occurred between Illinois's
provision for the inclusion of women and their actual participation in this particular district.

13. W. M. Bartholomew to Eleaser Root, 10 December 1851,
Azell Ladd Papers, WSHS.

14. For the incidents cited concerning Nichols and Campbell, see
Clerk's Minutes, 27 September 1869, District 3, Blooming
Grove Twp., Dane County, WSHS.

15. Clerk's Minutes, 26 August 1870 and 18 March 1871, Sugar
Grove Twp. District, Dallas County, SHSI.

16. A partial listing of where the interested researcher could find
references to donations of land in exchange for schoolhouse

location includes: Clerk's Minutes, 17 April 1868, District 3, Blooming Grove Twp., Dane County; Clerk's Minutes, 13 September 1873, Jt. District 9, Blooming Grove and Dunn Twps., Dane County; and Clerk's Minutes, 6 April 1859, Jt. District 8, Excelsior and Dellona Twps., Sauk County, WSHS. Also, see Clerk's Minutes, 20 June 1847, District 6, Center Twp., Rock County, RCHS; Clerk's Minutes, 26 February 1890, District 34, Chippewa County, Minnesota State Archives, MHS; Clerk's Minutes, 19 September 1870, Sugar Grove Twp. District, Dallas County, SHSI; and Clerk's Minutes, 3 September 1892, District 138, Pleasant Grove Twp., Olmsted County, Olmsted County Historical Society, Rochester, Minnesota (hereafter cited as OCHS). An especially interesting discussion concerning the location of a school is in the Clerk's Minutes of District 2 of Oronoco Twp., Olmsted County, between 31 March and 7 April 1868. The district was divided, north and south, by the Zumbro River. There was consequently lengthy debate about whether the school should be placed on the south or north side of the river.

17. Fuller, *Old Country School*, 61.

18. Clerk's Minutes, 15 February 1890, District 34, Chippewa County, Minnesota State Archives, MHS.

19. "The Problem in District #59," *Olmsted County Teacher* 13 (November 1916): 1.

20. Clerk's Minutes, 14 March 1887, Lucas Twp. District, Johnson County; Clerk's Minutes, 1 July 1914, Fairview Twp. District, Jones County, SHSI. For similar cases in Indiana, see Clerk's Minutes, 3 August 1853, and subsequent entries, Washington Twp. District, Washington County, IHSL.

21. Sarah Huftalen Diaries, 7 May 1907, Box 10, Manuscript Division, SHSI.

22. Clerk's Minutes, 5 October 1872, District 36, High Forest Twp., Olmsted County, OCHS; Clerk's Minutes, 24 September 1860, Jt. District 8, Excelsior and Dellona Twps., Sauk County, WSHS.

23. Asa Felt to Eleaser Root, 15 December 1851, Azell Ladd Papers, WSHS.

24. The correspondence concerning the Bartholomew Ringle case from which the above quotations are taken are available in the Azell Ladd Papers, Manuscript Divison, WSHS.

25. Most of the court cases referred to here dealt with the Bible

as a sectarian book, any particular translation of which would
be objectionable to some group or another. These cases generally came from large cities on the East Coast, but *Board of
Education of Cincinnati vs. Minor et al.* (1873) in Ohio
agreed with the East Coast decisions. For more information
regarding this case, see D. F. DeWolf, comp., *Ohio School
Laws* (Columbus: Myers Brothers, 1883), 110. Four other midwestern states followed Ohio in banning Bible instruction
from the schools: Wisconsin in 1890, Nebraska in 1902, Illinois in 1910, and South Dakota in 1929. For more information on this issue, see Jorgenson, *Nonpublic School*, 132–36.

26. Ireland is quoted in Jorgenson, *Nonpublic School*, 198.
27. Affadavit of E. R. Thomas, 7 March 1916, Appeals Case
Files, Series 1176, Box 1, HSND.
28. Anonymous letter to Minnie Knotts, 5 January 1918,
Superintendent's Records, County Superintendent of Schools,
Lancaster County, Box 1, Folder 4, NSHS. A circular from Ne-
braska's war time Defense Council may be found here as well.
29. See the School Registers, 1909–13, District 84, Pleasant
Grove Twp., Olmsted County, OCHS.
30. For an example, see the Clerk's Minutes of District 39,
Meadow Twp., Wadena County, Minnesota State Archives,
MHS.
31. Clerk's Minutes, 17 July 1870, District 34, Chippewa County,
Minnesota State Archives, MHS.
32. See Cornelius A. Gower, comp., *The General School Laws of
Michigan* (Lansing: W. S. George & Co., 1879), 14; J. C.
Thompson, comp., *The School Law of Illinois* (Springfield: Illinois State Journal Co., 1906), 85; and David M. Geeting,
comp., *The School Law of Indiana* (Indianapolis: n.p., 1897),
181.
33. Transcribed interview with Suzette Rene Bieri, 22 November
1980, Box 2, University of North Dakota, Country School
Legacy Collection, Chester Fritz Library, Grand Forks,
North Dakota (hereafter cited as UND-CSLC).
34. Clerk's Minutes, 20 September 1894, District 7, Spencer
Brook Twp., Isanti County, Minnesota State Archives, MHS.
35. Clerk's Minutes, 20 September 1907, District 7, Spencer
Brook Twp., Isanti County, Minnesota State Archives, MHS.
36. Clerk's Minutes, 19 October 1872, District 36, High Forest
Twp., Olmsted County, OCHS; Clerk's Minutes, 5 July 1904,
District 3, Albion Twp., Dane County; and Clerk's Minutes,

27 September 1852, District 5, Christiana Twp., Dane County, WSHS.

37. Sydney E. Mead, *The Lively Experiment: The Shaping of Christianity in America* (New York: Harper and Row, 1963), 118.

38. *Report of the Commissioner of Education for the Year 1894–1895*, vol. 2, (Washington, D.C.: Government Printing Office, 1896), 1833.

39. John Allen Krout, *The Origins of Prohibition* (New York: Knopf, 1925), 114–23, 120.

40. Faragher, *Sugar Creek*, 144. Other historians have chronicled the same pattern of mobility in nineteenth-century Midwest society, though the focus has usually been town or village life. As an example, see Don Harrison Doyle, *The Social Order of a Frontier Community: Jacksonville, Illinois, 1825–1870* (Urbana: University of Illinois Press, 1978), and Peter J. Coleman, "Restless Grant County: Americans on the Move," *Wisconsin Magazine of History* 46 (Autumn 1962): 16–20.

41. Faragher, *Sugar Creek*, 127.

42. William McGuffey, *McGuffey's Newly Revised Eclectic Second Reader* (Cincinnati: Winthrop B. Smith, 1843), 180–81.

43. See James H. Blodgett, "Digest of Laws Relating to Text-Books, Their Selection and Supply," in *Report of the Commissioner of Education for the Year 1897–1898* (Washington: Government Printing Office, 1899), 893–908. Only rarely are there references to school districts buying books "for children who[se] parents are not able to furnish the same" (For reference to this quotation, see the Clerk's Minutes, 21 November 1885, District 5, West Point Twp., Columbia County, WSHS. In this instance five books were purchased for $1.25).

44. Clerk's Minutes, 20 May 1882, Fairview Twp. District, Jones County; Clerk's Minutes, 9 March 1891, Lucas Twp. District, Johnson County, SHSI.

45. Mandan *Pioneer*, 23 January 1891, Scrapbook Series 394, Box 1, HSND. For an example from Kansas, see Marshall A. Barber, *Schoolhouse at Prairie View* (Lawrence: University of Kansas Press, 1953), 48.

46. For an example of early requests for free texts in Wisconsin denied by local district residents, see the Clerk's Minutes, 1 July 1889, Jt. District 8, Marcellon and Buffalo Twps., Columbia and Marquette Counties, Columbia County Series, WSHS; and Clerk's Minutes, 7 July 1890, Jt. District 9, Sun

Prairie and Bristol Twps., Dane County, WSHS. For examples of the earliest acceptance of free textbooks in Wisconsin, see the Clerk's Minutes, 5 July 1909, Jt. District 3, Center and Porter Twps., Rock County, RCHS; and Clerk's Minutes, 1 July 1912, Jt. District 1, Lodi and West Point Twps., Dane County, WSHS.

47. Two examples of districts adopting free textbooks considerably earlier than districts in Wisconsin are Clerk's Minutes, 21 July 1894, District 72, Winfield Twp., Renville County, Minnesota State Archives, MHS; and Clerk's Minutes, 15 July 1893, District 34, Chippewa County, Minnesota State Archives, MHS. The quotation indicating an unwillingness to provide free texts can be found in the Clerk's Minutes, 15 July 1893, District 3, Cambridge Twp., Isanti County, Minnesota State Archives, MHS.

48. Clerk's Minutes, 5 April 1880, District 35, Harlan County, NSHS.

49. Clerk's Minutes, 2 July 1900, Jt. District 2, Albion and Sumner Twps., Dane and Jefferson Counties, Dane County Series; and Clerk's Minutes, 3 July 1905, Jt. District 8, Excelsior and Dellona Twps., Sauk County, WSHS.

50. Clerk's Minutes, 1 July 1879, Waveland Twp. District, Pottawattamie County, SHSI. Fences also required upkeep because those in disrepair often tempted livestock to attempt to get at fresh, untrampled grass. In one instance in Iowa, a horse severely injured itself trying to get through a schoolyard fence. The animal later died, and the farmer demanded damages from the local board. He was refused (Clerk's Minutes, 21 March 1881, Scott Twp. District, Johnson County, SHSI).

51. Records of the County Superintendent of Public Instruction, 9 July 1869, Reel 2, Washington County, NSHS.

52. D. C. Lochead, "Lighting of Rooms: Especially Rural School Rooms," Olmsted County rural schools file, OCHS; Clerk's Minutes, 6 April 1858, Pleasant Valley Twp. District, Johnson County, SHSI; Clerk's Minutes, 11 September 1880, District 5, West Point Twp., Columbia County, WSHS; Clerk's Minutes, 3 July 1893, Jt. District 9, Blooming Grove and Dunn Twps., Dane County, WSHS.

53. Clerk's Minutes, 16 July 1859, Fairview Twp. District, Johnson County, SHSI.

54. For a reference to mowing in exchange for hay, see the

Clerk's Minutes, 5 July 1910, Jt. District 8, Excelsior and
Dellona Twps., Sauk County, WSHS. For references to mowing the yard to control the weeds, see the Clerk's Minutes,
11 July 1904, Jt. District 2, Albion and Sumner Twps., Dane
and Jefferson Counties, Dane County Series; and Clerk's Minutes, 2 July 1894, District 7, Ironton Twp., Sauk County,
WSHS; Sarah Huftalen Diaries, 6 March 1886, Box 7, Manuscript Division, SHSI.

55. Clerk's Minutes, 3 June 1883, Jt. District 3, Center and Porter Twps., Rock County, RCHS; and Clerk's Minutes, 2 July
1888, District 7, Ironton Twp., Sauk County, WSHS. For
other references to banking the schoolhouse, see Clerk's Minutes, 24 June 1895, District 77, Jefferson County, NSHS;
Clerk's Minutes, 7 July 1885, District 7, Spencer Brook
Twp., Isanti County, Minnesota State Archives, MHS.

56. Clerk's Minutes, 11 April 1891, District 3, Cambridge Twp.,
Isanti County, Minnesota State Archives, MHS.

57. For references to fire breaks, see the Clerk's Minutes, 21 July
1888, District 31, Moonshine Twp., Big Stone County, Minnesota State Archives, MHS; Clerk's Minutes, 9 April 1901,
Billings School District, Cavalier County, Box 9, UND-
CSLC; and Clerk's Minutes, 2 April 1883, District 24, Jefferson County, NSHS.

58. Clerk's Minutes, 2 April 1888, District 30, Washington
County, NSHS. Also see the Clerk's Minutes, 23 July 1925,
Billings District, Cavalier County, Box 9, UND-CSLC.

59. See the Arbor Day Reports, Office of the County Superintendent for Public Instruction, Burleigh County, Bismarck,
North Dakota (hereafter cited as BCND).

60. Clerk's Minutes, 30 October 1882, District 3, Oakwood
Twp., Brookings County, SDHS. Also see Barber, *Schoolhouse at Prairie View*, 14.

61. See, for example, Clerk's Minutes, 3 July 1905, Jt. District 1,
Lodi and West Point Twps., Columbia County; and Clerk's
Minutes, 1 July 1902, Jt. District 8, Excelsior and Dellona
Twps., Sauk County, WSHS.

62. Clerk's Minutes, 12 November 1864, District 104, Pleasant
Grove Twp., Olmsted County, OCHS. For another example,
see the Clerk's Minutes, 30 September 1867, Jt. District 2,
Albion and Sumner Twps., Dane and Jefferson Counties,
Dane County Series, WSHS.

63. For an example of bid-reading for wood contracts, see Clerk's

Minutes, 17 March 1890, Fairview Twp. District, Jones
County, SHSI.

64. Clerk's Minutes, 31 July 1902, District 33, Eyota Twp.,
Olmsted County, OCHS. Fuller recognizes in *The Old Country School* that nepotism was widespread among boards of
education in the rural Midwest. However, while he admits
this, he does not address the contradiction inherent in maintaining that Midwest school districts were, on one hand, "the
essence of democracy" and on the other, agents of governmental power where "nepotism . . . was by no means unique" (57,
89). What follows is a partial listing from just four Wisconsin
counties of board minutes that grant wood or work contracts
to school board members: Clerk's Minutes, 5 October 1859,
Jt. District 8, Excelsior and Dellona Twps., Sauk County;
Clerk's Minutes, 27 March 1852, District 3, Blooming Grove
Twp., Dane County; Clerk's Minutes, 6 July 1896, Jt. District 9, Blooming Grove and Dunn Twps., Dane County;
Clerk's Minutes, 31 August 1874, District 5, West Point
Twp., Columbia County; Clerk's Minutes, 7 July 1913, District 7, Ironton Twp., Sauk County, WSHS; Clerk's Minutes,
29 March 1892, Jt. District 3, Center and Porter Twps., Rock
County; Clerk's Minutes, 5 December 1849, District 6, Cen-
ter Twp., Rock County, RCHS.

65. Clerk's Minutes, 8 September 1870, Scott Twp. District,
Johnson County, SHSI.

66. See District 3 Record Book, Twp. 11, Clark County records,
Manuscript Division, ISHL. Seven of the thirty-four positions
were filled by individuals bearing only first and middle ini-
tials. Other records confirm that three of these were male. It
seems likely, then, that the other four were as well.

67. Clerk's Minutes, 30 September 1872, 29 September 1873, 3
August 1874, and 16 September 1876, Jt. District 8,
Marcellon and Buffalo Twps., Dane and Jefferson Counties,
Dane County Series, WSHS; Tresurer's Record Book in-
cluded in the same collection.

68. See, for example, Clerk's Minutes, 20 October 1899, District
72, Winfield Twp., Renville County, Minnesota State Archives, MHS; and Clerk's Minutes, 7 May 1854, 16 May
1859, and 29 November 1866, District 3, Albion Twp., Dane
County, WSHS.

69. See the transcribed interview with Alberta Marie Reger, 28
November 1980, Box 1, UND-CSLC. Complaints about nepo-

tism in hiring teachers are relatively scarce when compared with the incidence of this phenomenon in school records. For an example of one such complaint, see the Mrs. Murphy Folder, Appeals Case Files, Series 1176, Box 1, HSND. Murphy was hired to teach the local school by her husband, a district board member.

70. Clerk's Minutes, 24 August 1891, District 30, Washington County, NSHS; Clerk's Minutes, 7 July 1885, District 7, Spencer Brook Twp., Isanti County, Minnesota State Archives, MHS.

71. Fuller, *Old Country School*, 85.

72. Clerk's Minutes, 27 September 1858, District 3, Albion Twp., Dane County, WSHS.

73. Clerk's Minutes, 1 July 1895, Jt. District 8, Excelsior and Dellona Twps., Sauk County; Clerk's Minutes, 10 July 1882, District 7, Ironton Twp., Sauk County, WSHS; Clerk's Minutes, 25 August 1879, Joint District 2, Albion and Sumner Twps., Dane and Jefferson Counties, WSHS; Clerk's Minutes, 6 July 1897, District 12, Lima Twp., Rock County, RCHS; Fuller, *Old Country School*, 91.

74. Samuel Briggs Diary, 7 February 1858, Manuscript Division, ISHL.

75. For the remarks on various teachers, see the Treasurer's Record Book, District 4, Clinton Twp., RCHS. Clerk's Minutes, 3 July 1916, Jt. District 2, Albion and Sumner Twps., Dane and Jefferson Counties, Dane County Series; Clerk's Minutes, 5 July 1910, District 3, Albion Twp., Dane County, WSHS.

76. Clerk's Minutes, 3 July 1916, Joint District 9, Blooming Grove and Dunn Twps., Dane County, WSHS; Clerk's Minutes, 18 September 1890, Fairview Twp. District, Jones County, SHSI.

77. See the records of the Office of the County Superintendent of Public Instruction, BCND.

78. See any of the teacher contracts in the back of the Clerk's Record Books, District 2, Newark Twp., Rock County, RCHS.

4. Recess, Recitation, and the Switch

1. W. A. Linn to W. L. Stockwell, 12 August 1904, Miscellaneous Subject Files, Box 2, Series 385, HSND.

2. Irene Hardy, *An Ohio Schoolmistress: The Memoirs of Irene*

Hardy, ed. Louis Filler (1906, reprint, Kent, Ohio: Kent State University Press, 1980).

3. As an example, see William F. Scott Diaries, 5 April 1882, Manuscript Division, WSHS.

4. The infamous blizzard that Hubbell refers to has been dubbed the "Children's Blizzard" in Minnesota and the Dakotas because many schoolchildren lost their lives attempting to reach home. Charles Hubbell Diary, 12 January 1888, Series 385, HSND; James Shields Diary, 4 January 1886, Vol. 1, James A. Shields Papers, Minnesota State Archives, MHS.

5. Sarah Jane Kimball Diaries, 31 December 1863, Manuscript Division, SHSI.

6. Elizabeth Hampsten, *Settlers' Children: Growing Up on the Great Plains* (Norman, Okla.: University of Oklahoma Press, 1991), 36–37.

7. Hardy, *Ohio Schoolmistress*, 66. For a reference to barefoot schoolbound youth during the month of March, see Barber, *Schoolhouse at Prairie View*, 23. For another reference to attending school barefoot in summer and with "thick homemade shoes" in winter, see the memoirs, Patrick Henry Jameson Papers, IHSL.

8. Anna Webber, "The Diary of Anna Webber: Early Day Teacher of Mitchell County," ed. Lila Gravatt Scrimser, *The Kansas Historical Quarterly* 38 (1972): 334; Faragher, *Sugar Creek*, 127; Sarah Jane Kimball Diaries, 7 June 1862, Manuscript Division, SHSI; Peter W. Dietz Diaries, n.d., IHSL.

9. James Shields Diary, 11 January 1886, James A. Shields Papers, Minnesota State Archives, MHS; Sarah Jane Kimball Diaries, ? June 1867, Manuscript Division, SHSI. Annual school meetings also awaited a quorum of eligible voters. This not obtained, the meeting was canceled and rescheduled.

10. Julia Merrill to Elizabeth Bates, 4 September 1844, Julia Merrill Moores Papers, IHSL. Also see Leonard Keene Hirschberg, "Should Children Aged Two Years Go To School?" *The American Thresherman* 17 (1914): 68. Hirschberg argues the point in the affirmative. For an example of a twenty-three-year-old man attending country school and the problems this might cause, see the Lizzie Anderson File, Appeals Case Files, Box 1, Series 1176, HSND.

11. Elson, *Guardians of Tradition*, 269–70.

12. William McGuffey, *McGuffey's Newly Revised Eclectic*

Fourth Reader (Cincinnati: Winthrop B. Smith, 1844), 247–48.

13. The student's recollection of a portion of Beecher's work is taken from Fuller, *Old Country School*, 23–24. "The Life of William Kelley" is from *McGuffey's Newly Revised Eclectic Second Reader* (Cincinnati: Winthrop B. Smith, 1853), 92–93. Interestingly, Lawrence Cremin discusses this essay as an example of the religious nature of early school textbooks but ignores the ethnic stereotyping explicit in using an Irish pseudonym for a habitual drunkard; see Cremin, *American Education*, 71.

14. William McGuffey, *McGuffey's Newly Revised Eclectic Second Reader* (Cincinnati: Winthrop B. Smith, 1843), 180–81.

15. William McGuffey, *McGuffey's Newly Revised Eclectic Third Reader* (Cincinnati: Winthrop B. Smith, 1853), 180–81.

16. The quotations are from Elson, *Guardians of Tradition*, 94–95. Woodbridge, a Protestant cleric, perhaps even more than most flooded his geography lessons with anti-Catholic rhetoric. For a thorough analysis of Woodbridge's texts, see Jorgenson, *Nonpublic School*, 64.

17. The quotations are from Elson, *Guardians of Tradition*, 78–80.

18. H. S. Mark to Azell Ladd, 12 March 1852, Azell Ladd Papers, WSHS.

19. See Schob's chapters "Hired Boy" and "Hired Girl" in *Hired Hands and Plowboys*.

20. There are several locations where historians may examine complete records left by rural schoolteachers. A few suggestions include the school records of Joint District 2, Albion and Sumner Twps., Dane County, WSHS; District 7, Ironton Twp., Sauk County, WSHS; District 4, Clinton Twp., Rock County, RCHS; and District 104, Pleasant Grove Twp., Olmsted County, OCHS.

21. Sarah Irwin Bunn Diary, 12 March 1870, Manuscript Division, ISHL.

22. This arrangement was probably the typical nineteenth-century experience. For a detailed description of a class seating arrangement with boys on one side and girls on the other, see Julia Merrill to Elizabeth Bates, 4 September 1844, Julia Merrill Moores Papers, IHSL. Early and late in the century, other pedagogically-based layouts were popular. As an example, see Barber, *Schoolhouse at Prairie View*, 11.

23. See Finkelstein, *Governing the Young*, 101–2.
24. James Shields Diary, 25 February 1886, James A. Shields Papers, Minnesota State Archives, MHS. For more information on Lancaster and Lancasterian schools, see David Hogan, "The Market Revolution and Disciplinary Power: Joseph Lancaster and the Psychology of the Early Classroom System" *History of Education Quarterly* 29 (Fall 1989): 381–417. Also, Carl F. Kaestle, *Joseph Lancaster and the Monitorial School Movement: A Documentary History* (New York: Teachers College Press, 1973). For an interesting vignette on the use of tokens as motivators, see Mark Twain's *Adventures of Tom Sawyer* (New York: Airmont Reprint, 1962), 30–36. Tom trades fishhooks and "lickrish" to obtain the tokens necessary to impress the superintendent.
25. Teacher's Register, 1871, District 36, High Forest Twp., Olmsted County, OCHS.
26. James Monroe Journal, 22 April 1845, Manuscript Division, ISHL.
27. Finkelstein, *Governing the Young*, 127.
28. Clerk's Minutes, 25 September 1871, Jt. District 8, Marcellon and Buffalo Twps., Columbia and Marquette Counties, Columbia County Series, WSHS.
29. County Superintendent Notes, Olmsted County Teacher File, OCHS.
30. For a more detailed analysis of the pedagogy of nineteenth-century schools, see chapters 1 and 2 of Finkelstein, *Governing the Young*.
31. Clerk's Minutes, 24 April 1905, District 25, Swan River Twp., Morrison County, Minnesota State Archives, MHS.
32. "Rock Township History, Benson County, 1904–1976," 1975. Included in Box 5, UND-CSLC.
33. Barber, *Schoolhouse at Prairie View*, 42.
34. District 3 Record Book, Winter term report, 1865–66, Records of District 3, Twp. 11, Clark County, Manuscript Division, ISHL. Finkelstein promotes a similar argument about arithmetic instruction in *Governing the Young*, 72–81.
35. Webber, "Diary of Anna Webber," 330, 322.
36. "Family Memoirs, 1908," Ellen Turpie Harley Papers, IHSL.
37. Webber, "Diary of Anna Webber," 328, 331. The former Iowa student is quoted in Fuller, *Old Country School*, 22. For references to the game in North Dakota, see the transcribed in-

terview with Suzette Rene Bieri, 22 November 1980, Box 2, UND-CSLC. The popularity of this schoolyard game is also cited in Edward Everett Dale, "Teaching on the Prairie Plains, 1890–1900," *Mississippi Valley Historical Review* 33 (1946–47): 302. For an Ohio reference, see Hardy, *Ohio Schoolmistress*, 37.

38. Obviously, the course of instruction varied greatly from lo-cale to locale and from teacher to teacher. What I am depict-ing here seems most typical given the country school records I have observed.

39. Frank T. Clampitt, *Some Incidents in My Life: A Saga of the Unknown Citizen* (Ann Arbor, Mich.: Edwards Brothers, 1936), 16. For other references to "singing" geography, see Joanna L. Stratton, *Pioneer Women: Voices From the Kansas Frontier* (New York: Touchstone Books, 1981), 163; and Anna Marie Keppel, "Country Schools for Country Children: Back-grounds of the Reform Movement in Rural Elementary Edu-cation, 1890–1914" (Ph.D. diss., University of Wisconsin, 1960), 6. Also see Finkelstein, *Governing the Young*, 86; and Barber, *Schoolhouse at Prairie View*, 35.

40. The following table reveals the attendance figures for rural Il-linois counties in 1848. Since the trend is readily apparent, there is little need to reproduce statistics for every county. What follows are figures for the first four counties, alphabeti-cally, for which the appropriate data was collected.

	Number of Children in School	Number of Children under Twenty
Adams	691	12,367
Bond	321	3,585
Bureau	354	2,984
Carroll	600	1,711

Source: From F. G. Blair, *Twenty-ninth Biennial Report of the Superintendent of Public Instruction of the State of Illinois* (Springfield: Illinois State Journal Co., 1913)

Generally, the newer states of the Midwest fared somewhat better in this regard. Attendance figures for Wisconsin coun-ties in 1851 suggest that country school attendance may have been closer to two-thirds; see Eleaser Root, *Report of the State Superintendent of Public Instruction* (Madison: Beriah Brown, 1852), Appendix A.

41. A variety of sources support the suppositions presented here about country school attendance. In particular, see A. C. Monahan, *The Status of Rural Education in the United States*, U.S. Bureau of Education, Bulletin 8 (Washington, D.C.: Government Printing Office, 1913), 22. Monahan's statistics indicate that in the year 1909–10 country school attendance in the states of the Old Northwest was slightly more than half of the eligible schoolchildren. Kansas, Nebraska, North Dakota, and South Dakota, however, averaged considerably more than two-thirds. Teacher term reports from across the Middle West support these figures, as do the remonstrations of various state superintendents in annual reports. Another interesting source for analyzing country school attendance is the record book of A. Guernon, County Superintendent, Miscellaneous School Records, Morrison County, Minnesota State Archives, MHS. Guernon shared no comments or notes about his visits to country schools, but he listed the number of students enrolled versus the number who were in attendance on the day of his visit. His records extend from 1880 to 1885. The average rate of attendance on the days of his visits is somewhere between one-half and two-thirds of the total enrolled. In many districts, the average was much less. Attendance was the worst in Morrison County at the beginning of winter term when there was still corn in the field to pick.

42. Superintendent's Records, Lancaster County, Box 1, Folder 4, NSHS. For another interesting list of excuses for nonattendance, see the Records of the Office of the County Superintendent of Public Instruction, BCND.

43. John N. Pulver to Azell Ladd, 26 February 1852, Azell Ladd Papers, WSHS.

44. Elizabeth Hampsten, *Settlers' Children: Growing Up on the Great Plains* (Norman: University of Oklahoma Press, 1991), 35. The dates and passages that follow refer to the diary of George Coleman, which is located in the Manuscript Division of SHSI. It is listed in SHSI files, however, as the diary of Sadie Stilson. A close reading of this diary indicates that George Coleman was the more likely author.

45. Clerk's Minutes, 24 September 1860, Jt. District 8, Excelsior

and Dellona Twps., Sauk County, WSHS. See Clerk's Minutes, 3 April 1871, Subschool District 1, Decatur Twp., Burt County, NSHS. Also, Clerk's Minutes, 13 August 1892, District 138, Pleasant Grove Twp., OCHS. Frequently, one of the school board members was awarded the stipend for "keeping the teacher." For an example, see Clerk's Minutes, 23 March 1875, District 3, Cambridge Twp., Isanti County, Minnesota State Archives, MHS.

46. See the transcribed interview with Almida Goodman, 18 December 1980, Box 1, UND-CSLC.

47. See the transcribed interview with Winifred Guthrie Erdman, 11 November 1980, Box 2, UND-CSLC.

48. James Shields Diary, 9 November 1885, James A. Shields Papers, Minnesota State Archives, MHS. Subsequent references in the following passages to the Shields diary will be dated in the text, with no further citation. The Shields diary is a valuable source for historians interested in the everyday life of country teachers in the Midwest. Throughout the winter term, Shields was faithful in describing, in some detail, the affairs that dominated his days. Most diary accounts of country school teachers include only brief descriptions of school affairs, such as how many scholars were in attendance, or what time school was called or dismissed.

49. Clerk's Minutes, 7 March 1887, Lockridge Twp. District, Jefferson County, SHSI.

50. Alma Ashley, ed., *Telling Tales Out of School: Retired Teachers of Nebraska* (Lincoln: Augustums Printing, 1976), 43, 88.

51. For an example of a district that compelled the teacher to hire someone to start the fires for her, see Clerk's Minutes, 21 July 1931, District 87, Elmira Twp., Olmsted County, OCHS. Two examples of districts that stipulated that schoolteachers should start their own fires and do their own sweeping are Clerk's Minutes, 10 July 1899, Jt. District 2, Albion and Sumner Twps., Dane and Jefferson Counties, Dane County Series, WSHS; and Clerk's Minutes, 27 June 1892, District 41, Saunders County, NSHS. The quotations from the Iowa school records are from Clerk's Minutes, 19 March 1894, Fairview Twp. District, Jones County; and Clerk's Minutes, 20 March 1871, Scott Twp. District, Johnson County, SHSI. Samuel A. Briggs Diary, 27 January 1858, Manuscript Division, ISHL.

52. Robert Pike Diary, 10 February 1851, Manuscript Division,

Minnesota State Archives, MHS; James Wiley to Jerome
Wiley, 26 June 1835, Jerome Wiley Papers, IHSL.
53. Schob, *Hired Hands*, 81n.
54. Diary entries are from Webber, "Diary of Anna Webber."
Subsequent references in the following passages to the Webber diary will be dated in the text, with no further citation.
For examples of other teachers who experienced homesickness, see the Records of the County Superintendent of Public
Instruction, Lancaster County, Box 1, NSHS. Also see Miscellaneous Subject Files, Box 1, Series 385, HSND. Another
popular letter to county superintendents was the request for
information on the availability of "town positions."
55. Quoted in Mary Hurlbut Cordier, "Prairie Schoolwomen,
Mid-1850s to 1920s, In Iowa, Kansas, and Nebraska," *Great
Plains Quarterly* 8 (Spring 1988): 109.
56. See the transcribed interview with Clara Brown, 2 December
1980, Box 2, UND-CSLC; Superintendent's Files, Box 3, Series 386, HSND.
57. The experiences of Anna Webber with respect to corporal
punishment are quite typical. Picking up any diary of a rural
schoolteacher who begins a term proclaiming an aversion to
striking a child, one can confidently expect the teacher to encounter a change of heart. The journal of Aurora Koehler provides another example of this; see the Hutchins-Koehler Papers, IHSL.
58. Excerpts from the unpublished memoirs of Emma Handy are
quoted in Stratton, *Pioneer Women*, 159.
59. Records of the County Superintendent of Public Instruction,
21 June 1871, Washington County, Reel 2, NSHS.
60. Miscellaneous School Records, Morrison County, Minnesota
State Archives, MHS.
61. The data on Morrison County term reports was taken from
Miscellaneous School Records, Morrison County, Minnesota
State Archives, MHS. County Superintendent's Notes,
Olmsted County Teacher File, OCHS. The pronouncement
concerning Nebraska's outhouses came in the form of an un-
dated circular sent to district officers, found in the Clerk's
Minutes, District 40, Saunders County, NSHS. The Kaustine
Company of Buffalo, New York, was in the business of install-
ing septic systems in rural schoolhouses. Their circular was
found among miscellaneous papers inside the Treasurer's Records, District 121, Elmira Twp., OCHS.

62. Clerk's Minutes, 27 September 1869 and 2 July 1894, District 3, Albion Twp., Dane County; Clerk's Minutes, 5 July 1892, Jt. District 8, Excelsior and Dellona Twps., Sauk County, WSHS. Clerk's Minutes, 18 July 1887, District 7, Spencer Brooks Twp., Isanti County, Minnesota State Archives, MHS.

63. T. F. Baxter and A. H. Garlick, *A Primer of School Method* (New York: Longmans, 1905), 23.

64. Parts of Arozina Perkins's diary are reprinted in Polly Welts Kaufman's *Women Teachers on the Frontier* (New Haven: Yale University Press, 1984). This passage was taken from p. 136.

65. Ira Tremain to Azell Ladd, 23 February 1852, Azell Ladd Papers, WSHS. Clerk's Minutes, 18 June 1859, Fairview Twp. District, Jones County, SHSI. Clerk's Minutes, 16 July 1892, District 31, Moonshine Twp., Big Stone County, Minnesota State Archives, MHS.

66. R. Carlyle Buley, *The Old Northwest* (1950, reprint, Bloomington: Indiana Historical Society Press, 1970), 381. Also see Charles Bloomquist, "Rural School Days," an unpublished manuscript in Box 5, UND-CSLC.

67. "Recollections," n.d., Anna T. Lincoln Papers, Manuscript Division, Minnesota State Archives, MHS.

68. The phrase "turned (or "carried") out" is encountered often in rural school records. For Edward Eggleston's description of the event see *The Hoosier Schoolmaster* (New York: Grosset & Dunlap, 1913), 147–49. One memoir of early school days in rural Indiana contends that this actually happened: "The story Eggleston tells about the tacher [*sic*] who was turned out of the schoolhouse and smoked the children out actually occurred in the neighborhood in which I lived" (unpublished memiors, Patrick Henry Jameson Papers, IHSL).

69. Clerk's Minutes, 10 January 1879, Waveland Twp. District, Pottawattamie County, SHSI. Clerk's emphasis.

70. The short quotation is from Finkelstein, who provides a great deal of data on this topic; see *Governing the Young*, 95–97. The switch was not the only form of punishment used, however. Peter W. Dietz kept a diary as a young schoolboy in Indiana. "Time and time again I have had my ears kuffed," he wrote, because of his awkward handwriting; see the Peter W. Dietz Diary, IHSL.

71. Samuel A. Briggs Diary, 9 January 1858, Manuscript Division, ISHL. Clerk's Minutes, 2 January 1880, Waveland Twp.

District; Clerk's Minutes, 14 December 1874, Walnut Creek Twp. District, Pottawattamie County, SHSI.

72. Briggs Diary, 3 February 1858, ISHL.
73. Briggs Diary, 12 March 1858, ISHL.
74. Sarah Huftalen Diaries, 30 November 1906, Box 10, Manuscript Division, SHSI.
75. The quotations concerning the extent of the boy's injuries are from Faragher, *Sugar Creek*, 122. Faragher provides an excellent description of the ramifications of this incident on the Sugar Creek community.
76. John Hanafin to Azell Ladd, 15 February 1851, Azell Ladd Papers, WSHS.
77. Elmer Thompson to T. Mitchell, 17 February 1890, Appeals Case Files, Series 1176, Box 1, HSND.
78. See the sworn statements of W. J. Clapp and W. M. House, as well as Thompson's statements, in the case file of *Elmer Thompson vs. W. M. House*, Appeals Case Files, Series 1176, Box 1, HSND.
79. School Superintendent's Record Book, Miscellaneous School Records, Morrison County, Minnesota State Archives, MHS.
80. Anson Buttles Diary, 4 January 1869, Manuscript Division, WSHS. Other indiscretions, however, apparently did not merit this form of due process. On 18 February 1868, Buttles wrote in his diary that he intended to revoke the license of a teacher "for sleeping during school."
81. Cora Lee File, Appeals Case Files, Series 1176, Box 1, HSND. All subsequent references to Lee can be located in this file.
82. Miscellaneous Subject Files, Series 385, Box 3, HSND.
83. Clerk's Minutes, 16 December 1844, District 8, Twp. 19, Henry County, IHSL. Journal of Aurora Koehler, n.d., Hutchins-Koehler Papers, IHSL. For an interesting synopsis on the debate over employing married women as teachers, see "Should a Married Woman Teach?" *Independent* 67 (12 August 1909): 361–64.
84. See the Donald Kerr File, Appeals Case Files, Series 1176, Box 1, HSND.
85. Clara Glumseth File, Appeals Case Files, Series 1176, Box 2, HSND.
86. Jessie Sellars File, Appeals Case Files, Series 1176, Box 1, HSND; Lizzie Anderson File, Appeals Case Files, Series

1176, Box 1, HSND. Contrary to Fuller's claim that the country schoolteacher on the Middle Border "was a symbol of rectitude," that "her daily life was above reproach," and that "she virtually never had her teaching certificate recinded for immorality," a more reasonable assumption, given the evidence relayed here, is that female rural teachers were human, not saints. Certainly, acts of immorality were rare, probably more rare than accusations made to that affect. What is most troubling in Fuller's account is his claim that "it said much about her character . . . that her indiscretions with the opposite sex were as rare as the sexual assaults made upon her, even though she taught male students her own age in isolated schoolhouses where such attacks might easily have occurred." The implication seems to be that sexual assault by males can somehow be controlled by the character and deportment of females. The other disturbing conclusion drawn by Fuller is his contention that since there were very few incidents of assault reported, very few actually occurred. See *The Old Country School*, 201.

87. A rural Iowa schoolgirl described a typical afternoon in her diary. The passage is indicative of the centrality of recitation pedagogy and gender separation in rural schools: "After recess it was time for the boys to speak their pieces. Harry Sales spoke first. Next George his brother. William McMullin spoke a long piece. Horace Morrow forgot part of his. After they were through the teacher spoke to show them how they ought to speak. He talked till it was time for school to close" (Sarah Jane Kimball Diaries, 18 May 1858, Manuscript Division, SHSI).

88. James Monroe Diary, 25 April 1845, Manuscript Division, ISHL.

89. The phrase *normal schools* is French in origin and has to do with the acquisition on the part of teachers of society's highest "norms" or ideals and standards of behavior; see Carl F. Kaestle, *Pillars of the Republic*, 129–31.

90. Miscellaneous Subject Files, Series 385, Box 3, HSND.

91. Sarah Huftalen Diaries, 14 August 1884, Box 7, Manuscript Division, SHSI. Also see Fuller, *Old Country School*, 176.

92. Johnson County Teacher's Institute, school records inventory, Box 19, SHSI.

93. "Education and the Sensibilities," unpublished manuscript,

n.d., James A. Christie and Family Papers, Box 1, Manuscript Division, Minnesota State Archives, MHS.

94. H. Gard, "The Autobiography of a Country School Teacher,"
World's Work 20 (May 1910): 12958.

95. See Ivan Muse, Ralph B. Smith, and Bruce Barker, *The One-
Teacher School in the 1980s* (Las Cruces, N. Mex.: ERIC
Clearinghouse, 1987), 2.

5. Rural Meets Urban

1. Tyack and Hansot, *Managers of Virtue*, 106–7.

2. By the "standard interpretation," I am referring to Wayne
Fuller's *Old Country School*, as well as such work as James
H. Madison's "John D. Rockefeller's General Board of Education and the Rural School Problem of the Midwest, 1900–
1930," *History of Education Quaterly* 24 (Summer 1984):
181–99.

3. Fuller, *Old Country School*, 103–9.

4. Fuller, *Old Country School*, 131, 139, 153. Nothing in
Fuller's account supports the assertion that county superintendents were "impecunious lawyers" or anything other than
bona fide rural residents with close familial connections to
farming. Several county superintendents that Fuller intro-
duces in his analysis, like Anson Buttles, William Scott, and
Herbert Quick, do not in any way fit this caricature. It is important to his interpretation, however, that county superintendents were somehow made of different stuff than local farmers or they would not have tried to impose their ostensibly
urban educational agenda.

5. William Richardson to Eleaser Root, 1 December 1851, Azell
Ladd Papers, WSHS.

6. Fuller, *Old Country School*, 129.

7. William F. Scott Diaries, 30 January 1882, Manuscript Division, WSHS.

8. Anson Buttles Diaries, 28 September 1858 and 4 October
1858, Manuscript Division, WSHS. Buttles' emphasis.

9. Cephas Buttles to Azell Ladd, 21 February 1852, Azell Ladd
Papers, WSHS.

10. Examples of all of these circumstances are included in the
William F. Scott Diaries, 6 January 1882, 10 January 1882,
and 19 January 1882, Manuscript Division, WSHS. Also see

the unpublished autobiography of Caswell Ballard, Caswell Aden Ballard Papers, p. 47, IHSL.

11. Barber, *Schoolhouse at Prairie View*, 73.

12. Records of the County Superintendent of Public Instruction, 12 February 1878, Reel 2, Washington County, NSHS.

13. Olmsted County Teachers File, County Superintendent Notes, 1866, OCHS.

14. The use of the male pronoun is intentional because it reflects the typical experience before 1918. However, it should be noted that women were far more likely to hold the position in the states of the trans-Mississippi West than in the states of the Old Northwest.

15. Lewis F. Anderson, *History of Common Schools* (New York: Henry Holt and Co., 1909), 290.

16. Joseph Tropea provides an excellent analysis of this turn-of-the-century phenomenon in "Bureaucratic Order and Special Children: Urban Schools, 1890s–1940s," *History of Education Quarterly* 27 (Spring 1987): 29–53.

17. William James, *Talks to Teachers on Psychology* (New York: Holt, Rinehart, and Winston, 1899), 150.

18. See Richard Hofstadter, *Social Darwinism in American Thought, 1860–1915* (Philadelphia: University of Pennsylvania Press, 1945).

19. Larry Cuban, *How Teachers Taught: Constancy and Change in American Classrooms, 1890–1980* (New York: Longman, 1984), 18.

20. National Education Association, *Report of the Committee of Twelve on Rural Schools* (Chicago: University of Chicago Press, 1897), 152.

21. Keppel, "Country Schools for Country Children," 21.

22. I am referring here specifically to William L. Bowers, *The Country Life Movement in America 1900–1920* (Port Washington, N.Y.: Kennikat Press, 1974) and David B. Danbom, *The Resisted Revolution: Urban America and the Industrialization of Agriculture, 1900–1930* (Ames: Iowa State University Press, 1979).

23. "Current scholarship" refers to Bowers and Danbom cited earlier.

24. Liberty Hyde Bailey, *The Country Life Movement in the United States* (New York, Macmillan, 1911), 33.

25. Bailey, *Country Life Movement*, 20.
26. Wilbert L. Anderson, *The Country Town: A Study in Rural Evolution* (New York: Baker and Taylor Co., 1906), 29.
27. Frederick Jackson Turner, *The Frontier in American History* (New York: Henry Holt and Co., 1920), 4.
28. William James, *The Varieties of Religious Experience* (New York: Collier, 1911), 255.
29. *Report of the Commission on Country Life* (New York: Sturgis and Walton, 1911), 121. Danbom uses the phrase "urban agrarians" in *The Resisted Revolution*, 25–28.
30. Anderson, *Country Town*, 23.
31. Anderson, *Country Town*, i.
32. Garland is quoted in Keppel, "Country Schools for Country Children," 5.
33. See Dwight Drew, "A Program of Community Cooperation," *Rural Manhood* 1 (January 1910): 19–22. Also see Bailey, *Country Life Movement*, 149–64, and Mabel Carney, *Country Life and the Country School* (Chicago: Row, Peterson and Co., 1912), 203–4.
34. Bailey, *Country Life Movement*, 26.
35. "An Old Fashion in Farming," *The Country Gentleman* 78 (September 1908): 910.
36. G. Walter Fiske, *The Challenge of the Country* (New York: Young Men's Christian Association Press, 1913), 111.
37. John W. Bookwalter, *Rural Versus Urban* (New York: Knickerbocker Press, 1911), 292.
38. Bailey, *Country Life Movement*, 17. See also John M. Gillette, "The Drift to the City in Relation to the Rural Problem," *Rural Manhood* 2 (March 1911): 81–82.
39. David E. Shi, *The Simple Life: Plain Living and High Thinking in American Culture* (New York: Oxford University Press, 1985), 202. Also see Bowers, *Country Life Movement in America*, 31.
40. Danbom, *Resisted Revolution*, 81.
41. Liberty Hyde Bailey, *The State and the Farmer* (New York: Macmillan, 1908), 66.
42. Danbom, *Resisted Revolution*, 58.
43. *Report of the Commission on Country Life*, 113; Bailey, *The State*, 75.
44. Danbom, *Resisted Revolution*, 97, 15.
45. Cubberly is quoted in David B. Tyack, "The Tribe and the

Common School: Community Control in Rural Education,"
American Quarterly 24 (March 1972): 13; John Lee Coulter,
"The Influence of Immigration on Agricultural Develop-
ment," *Annals of the American Academy of Political and So-
cial Science* 33 (March 1909): 373; Clarence H. Poe, "Success
Talk for Farm Boys: How Can White Farmers Escape the
Dangers of Negro Competition?" *The Progressive Farmer* 36
(April 1921): 445.

46. Newell Leroy Sims, *Elements of Rural Sociology* (New York:
Thomas Y. Crowell Co., 1928), 85.

47. Franklin M. Reck, *The 4-H Story: A History of 4-H Club
Work* (Ames: Iowa State College Press, 1951), 3–5.

48. Carney, *Country Life*, 2–3. For biographical information on
Carney, see Helen E. Marshall, *Grandest of Enterprises: Illi-
nois State Normal University, 1857–1957* (Normal: Illinois
State University Press, 1956), 256–57.

49. Fiske, *Challenge of the Country*, 35.

50. Carney, *Country Life*, 203.

51. "The Country Boy's Creed," *Rural Manhood* 3 (April 1912):
106. Also see "The Schoolteacher's Creed," *Rural Manhood* 4
(September 1913): 218.

52. Martha Foote Crow, *The American Country Girl* (New York:
Frederick A. Stokes Co., 1915), 15.

53. Crow, *Country Girl*, 31.

54. Carney, *Country Life*, 240.

55. B. M. Davis, "The Correlation of the School and Farm,"
Rural Manhood 4 (September 1913): 219–22.

56. Beginning in 1896, Liberty Hyde Bailey began the Cornell
Rural School Leaflet Project. It was an attempt to distribute
curricular ideas to teachers in New York's rural schools. With
the creation of the Country Life Commission in 1908, the
"leaflets" took on journal form and were generally available at
universities and normal schools across the country until well
into the 1920s. For a particularly telling example of Bailey's
belief in the value of nature study, see "The Point of View,"
Cornell Rural School Leaflet 5 (September 1911): 2–6.

57. Clarence H. Poe, "Farmer Children Need Farmer Studies,"
World's Work 6 (August 1903): 3760.

58. Carney, *Country Life*, 177.

59. Joseph Kennedy, *Rural Life and the Rural School* (New
York: American Book Co., 1915), 36.

60. "Roosevelt's Farming Commission," *American Farm Review* 1 (September 1908): 6.
61. "What the President's Commission is Doing," *American Farm Review* 1 (November 1908): 4.
62. "Lo! The Poor Farmer," *The Country Gentleman* 78 (September 1908): 909–10.
63. "About Life on the Farm," Champaign (Ill.) *Daily Gazette* (14 December 1908): 1.
64. Danbom, *Resisted Revolution*, 77.
65. Tocqueville is quoted in C. Vann Woodward, "White Racism and Black Emancipation," *New York Times Review of Books* 12 (27 February 1969): 7.

Conclusion

1. Christopher Lasch, *The True and Only Heaven: Progress and Its Critics* (New York: W. W. Norton and Co., 1991), 82.
2. Grant McConnell, *The Decline of Agrarian Democracy* (Berkeley: University of California Press, 1953), 20.
3. McConnell, *Decline*, 30.
4. Goodwyn, *Democratic Promise*, 518.
5. McConnell, *Decline*, 32.
6. McConnell, *Decline*, 32.
7. Quoted in McConnell, *Decline*, 49.
8. McConnell, *Decline*, 47.

Bibliography

Archival Sources

Illinois State Historical Library (ISHL), Springfield, Illinois
Indiana Historical Society Library (IHSL), Indianapolis, Indiana
Minnesota Historical Society (MHS), St. Paul, Minnesota
Nebraska State Historical Society (NSHS), Lincoln, Nebraska
Office of the Burleigh County Superintendent of Schools
    (BCND), Bismarck, North Dakota
Olmsted County Historical Society (OCHS), Rochester, Minnesota
Rock County Historical Society (RCHS), Janesville, Wisconsin
South Dakota State Historical Society (SDHS), Pierre, South Dakota
State Historical Society of Iowa (SHSI), Iowa City, Iowa
State Historical Society of North Dakota (HSND), Bismarck, North Dakota
University of North Dakota, Country School Legacy Collection
    (UND-CSLC), Grand Forks, North Dakota
Wisconsin State Historical Society (WSHS), Madison, Wisconsin

Books and Pamphlets

Ahlstrom, Sydney E. *A Religious History of the American People*. New Haven: Yale University Press, 1971.

Anderson, James D. *The Education of Blacks in the South, 1860–1935*. Chapel Hill: University of North Carolina Press, 1988.

Anderson, Lewis F. *History of Common Schools*. New York: Henry Holt and Co., 1909.

Anderson, Wilbert L. *The Country Town: A Study in Rural Evolution*. New York: Baker and Taylor Co., 1906.

Ashley, Alma, ed. *Telling Tales Out of School: Retired Teachers of Nebraska*. Lincoln: Augustums Printing, 1976.

Atherton, Lewis. *Main Street on the Middle Border*. Chicago: Quadrangle Books, 1954.

Aurner, Clarence R. *History of Education in Iowa*. 4 vols. Iowa City: State Historical Society of Iowa, 1914.

Axtell, James. *The School Upon a Hill: Education and Society in Colonial New England*. New Haven: Yale University Press, 1974.

Bailey, Liberty Hyde. *The State and the Farmer.* New York: Macmillan, 1908.

————. *The Country Life Movement in the United States.* New York: Macmillan, 1911.

Barber, Marshall A. *Schoolhouse at Prairie View.* Lawrence: University of Kansas Press, 1953.

Barnard, Henry. *In the Cause of True Education: Henry Barnard and Nineteenth-Century School Reform.* New Haven: Yale University Press, 1991.

Baxter, T. F., and Garlick, A. H. *A Primer of School Method.* New York: Longmans, 1905.

Beals, Carleton. *Brass-Knuckle Crusade: The Great Know-Nothing Conspiracy.* New York: Hastings House Publishers, 1960.

Beecher, Lyman. *Plea for the West.* Cincinnati: Truman and Smith, 1835.

Bell, Daniel. *The End of Ideology.* Glencoe: Free Press, 1960.

Blue, Frederick J. *The Free Soilers: Third Party Politics, 1848–1854.* Urbana: University of Illinois Press, 1973.

Blum, Jerome. *The End of the Old Order in Rural Europe.* Princeton: Princeton University Press, 1978.

Bogue, Allan G. *From Prairie to Corn Belt: Farming on the Illinois and Iowa Prairies in the Nineteenth Century.* Chicago: University of Chicago Press, 1963.

Bookwalter, John W. *Rural Versus Urban.* New York: Knickerbocker Press, 1911.

Boone, Richard. *A History of Education in Indiana.* 1892. Reprint. Indianapolis: Indiana Historical Bureau, 1941.

Bowers, William L. *The Country Life Movement in America, 1900–1920.* Port Washington, N.Y.: Kennikat Press, 1974.

Boylan, Anne M. *Sunday School: The Formation of an American Institution, 1790–1880.* New Haven: Yale University Press, 1988.

Bradford, Mary D. *Memoirs of Mary D. Bradford.* Evansville, Wis.: Antes Press, 1932.

Bruce, Dickson D. *And They All Sang Hallelujah: Plain-Folk Camp Religion, 1800–1845.* Knoxville: University of Tennessee Press, 1974.

Bucke, Emory Stevens, ed. *The History of American Methodism.* 3 vols. New York: Abingdon Press, 1964.

Buley, R. Carlyle. *The Old Northwest.* 2 vols. 1950. Reprint. Bloomington: Indiana Historical Society Press, 1978.

Campbell, Jack K. *Colonel Francis W. Parker: The Children's Crusader.* New York: Teachers College Press, 1967.

Carney, Mabel. *Country Life and the Country School.* Chicago: Row, Peterson and Co., 1912.

Carroll, Anna Ella. *The Great American Battle; Or, The Contest Between Christianity and Political Romanism.* New York: Miller, Orton, and Mulligan, 1856.

Cartwright, Peter. *Fifty Years as a Presiding Elder.* Cincinnati: Walden and Stowe, 1871.

——. *Autobiography of Peter Cartwright.* Edited by Charles L. Waller. New York: Abingdon Press, 1955.

Clampitt, Frank T. *Some Incidents in My Life: A Saga of the Unknown Citizen.* Ann Arbor, Mich.: Edwards Bros., 1936.

Clark, Thomas D. *A History of Kentucky.* New York: Prentice-Hall, 1939.

Commager, Henry Steele, ed. *Documents of American History.* New York: F. S. Crofts & Co., 1943.

——. *The American Mind: An Interpretation of American Thought and Character Since the 1880s.* New Haven: Yale University Press, 1950.

Cook, John. *Educational History of Illinois.* Chicago: Henry O. Shepard, 1912.

Cremin, Lawrence A. *American Education: The National Experience, 1783–1876.* New York: Harper and Row, 1980.

Crow, Martha Foote. *The American Country Girl.* New York: Frederick A. Stokes Co., 1915.

Cuban, Larry. *How Teachers Taught: Constancy and Change in American Classrooms, 1890–1980.* New York: Longman, 1984.

Culver, Raymond. *Horace Mann and Religion in Massachusetts Public Schools.* New York: Arno Press, 1969.

Curran, Francis X. *The Churches and the Schools: American Protestantism and Popular Elementary Education.* Chicago: Loyola University Press, 1954.

Curti, Merle. *The Making of an American Community: A Case Study of Democracy in a Frontier County.* Stanford: Stanford University Press, 1959.

Danbom, David B. *The Resisted Revolution: Urban America and the Industrialization of Agriculture, 1900–1930.* Ames: Iowa State University Press, 1979.

Danhof, Clarence H. *Change in Agriculture: The Northern United States, 1820–1870.* Cambridge: Harvard University Press, 1969.

Davies, John D. *Phrenology Fad and Science: A 19th-Century American Crusade.* New Haven: Yale University Press, 1955.

de Tocqueville, Alexis. *Democracy in America.* 2 vols. New York: Knopf, 1945.

Doyle, Donald Harrison. *The Social Order of a Frontier Community: Jacksonville, Illinois, 1825–1870.* Urbana: University of Illinois Press, 1978.

Eggleston, Edward. *The Circuit Rider: A Tale of the Heroic Age.* 1873. Reprint. Lexington: University of Kentucky Press, 1970.

Eggleston, J. D., and Bruere, Robert. *The Work of the Rural School.* New York: Harper, 1913.

Elson, Ruth Miller. *Guardians of Tradition: American Schoolbooks of the Nineteenth Century.* Lincoln: University of Nebraska Press, 1954.

Faragher, John Mack. *Women and Men on the Overland Trail.* New Haven: Yale University Press, 1979.

———. *Sugar Creek: Life on the Illinois Prairie.* New Haven: Yale University Press, 1986.

Finkelstein, Barbara. *Governing the Young: Teacher Behaviour in Popular Primary Schools in the Nineteenth-Century United States.* New York: Falmer Press, 1989.

Fischer, David Hackett. *Albion's Seed: Four British Folkways in America.* New York: Oxford University Press, 1989.

Fiske, G. Walter. *The Challenge of the Country.* New York: Young Men's Christian Association Press, 1913.

Fite, Gilbert C. *The Farmers' Frontier, 1865–1900.* New York: Holt, Rinehart, and Winston, 1966.

———. *American Farmers: The New Minority.* Bloomington: Indiana University Press, 1981.

Foster, Charles H. *The Rungless Ladder: Harriet Beecher Stowe and New England Puritanism.* Durham: Duke University Press, 1954.

Franklin, Ralph William. *Nineteenth-Century Churches: A History of the New Catholicism in Wurtemburg, England and France.* New York: Garland Publications, 1987.

Fuller, Wayne E. *The Old Country School: The Story of Rural Education in the Middle West.* Chicago: University of Chicago Press, 1982.

Gates, Paul W. *The Farmer's Age: Agriculture, 1815–1860.* New York: Holt, Rinehart, and Winston, 1960.

Gladden, Washington. *Recollections.* New York: Houghton Mifflin Co., 1909.

Goodwyn, Lawrence. *Democratic Promise: The Populist Moment in America.* New York: Oxford University Press, 1976.

Goodykoontz, Colin B. *Home Missions on the American Frontier.* Caldwell, Idaho: Claxton Press, 1939.

Graham, Patricia Albjerg. *Community and Class in American Education, 1865–1918.* New York: John Wiley and Sons, 1974.

Grayson, David [Ray Stannard Baker]. *Adventures in Contentment.* New York: Doubleday, 1906.

Greenberg, David E. *Countryman's Companion.* New York: Harper and Bros., 1947.

Hahn, Steven, and Prude, Jonathan, eds. *The Countryside in the Age of Transformation: Essays in the Social History of Rural America.* Chapel Hill: University of North Carolina Press, 1985.

Hardy, Irene. *An Ohio Schoolmistress: The Memoirs of Irene Hardy.* Edited by Louis Filler. Kent, Ohio: Kent State University Press, 1980.

Hays, Samuel P. *The Response to Industrialism: 1885–1914.* Chicago: University of Chicago Press, 1957.

Heimert, Alan. *Religion and the American Mind.* Cambridge: Harvard University Press, 1966.

Henretta, James A. *The Evolution of American Society, 1700–1815: An Interdisciplinary Analysis.* Lexington, Mass.: D. C. Heath and Co., 1973.

Hine, Robert V. *Community on the American Frontier: Separate but Not Alone.* Norman: University of Oklahoma Press, 1980.

Hofstadter, Richard. *Anti-intellectualism in American Life.* New York: Knopf, 1963.

Hollingshead, August B. *Elmtown's Youth: The Impact of Social Classes on Adolescents.* New York: John Wiley and Sons, 1949.

Horsman, Reginald. *Race and Manifest Destiny: The Origins of American Racial Anglo-Saxonism.* Cambridge: Harvard University Press, 1981.

Hoyt, Charles O., and Ford, Clyde. *John D. Pierce, Founder of the Michigan School System: A Study of Education in the Northwest.* Ypsilanti, Mich.: Scharf Tag, Label, & Box Co., 1905.

Humphrey, Seth K. *Following the Prairie Frontier*. Minneapolis: University of Minnesota Press, 1931.

James, William. *Talks to Teachers on Psychology*. New York: Holt, Rinehart, and Winston, 1899.

—————. *The Varieties of Religious Experience*. New York: Collier, 1911.

Jensen, Richard. *The Winning of the Midwest: Social and Political Conflict, 1888–1896*. Chicago: University of Chicago Press, 1971.

Johnson, Charles A. *The Frontier Camp Meeting: Religion's Harvest Time*. Dallas: Southern Methodist University Press, 1955.

Jorgenson, Lloyd P. *The Founding of Public Education in Wisconsin*. Madison: State Historical Society of Wisconsin Press, 1956.

—————. *The State and the Nonpublic School, 1825–1925*. Columbia: University of Missouri Press, 1987.

Kaestle, Carl F. *Joseph Lancaster and the Monitorial School Movement: A Documentary History*. New York: Teachers College Press, 1973.

—————. *Pillars of the Republic: Common Schools and American Society, 1780–1860*. New York: Hill and Wang, 1983.

Kaestle, Carl F., and Vinovskis, Maris A. *Educational and Social Change in Nineteenth-Century Massachusetts*. Cambridge: Cambridge University Press, 1980.

Karier, Clarence J. *Man, Society, and Education: A History of American Educational Ideals*. Glenview, Ill.: Scott, Foresman and Co., 1967.

Katz, Michael B. *The Irony of Early School Reform: Educational Innovation in Mid-Nineteenth Century Massachusetts*. Cambridge: Harvard University Press, 1968.

Kaufman, Polly Welts. *Women Teachers on the Frontier*. New Haven: Yale University Press, 1984.

Kennedy, Joseph. *Rural Life and the Rural School*. New York: American Book Co., 1915.

Kiehle, David L. *Education in Minnesota*. 2 vols. Minneapolis: H. H. Williams Co., 1903.

Kinzer, Donald L. *An Episode in Anti-Catholicism: The American Protective Association*. Seattle: University of Washington Press, 1964.

Kleppner, Paul. *The Cross of Culture: A Social Analysis of*

Midwestern Politics, 1850–1900. New York: Free Press, 1970.

Krout, John Allen. *The Origins of Prohibition*. New York: Knopf, 1925.

Larkin, Jack. *The Reshaping of Everyday Life, 1790–1840*. New York: Harper and Row, 1988.

Larson, Henrietta. *The Wheat Market and the Farmer in Minnesota, 1858–1900*. New York: Columbia University Press, 1926.

Leonard, Ira M., and Parmet, Robert D., eds. *American Nativism, 1830–1860*. New York: Norstrand Reinhold Co., 1971.

Limerick, Patricia Nelson. *The Legacy of Conquest: The Unbroken Past of the American West*. New York: W. W. Norton, 1987.

Link, William A. *A Hard Country and a Lonely Place: Schooling, Society, and Reform in Rural Virginia, 1870–1920*. Chapel Hill: University of North Carolina Press, 1986.

Madison, James H. *Indiana Through Tradition and Change, 1920–1945*. Indiana Historical Society, 1982.

———. *The Indiana Way: A State History*. Bloomington: Indiana University Press, 1986.

Marshall, Helen E. *Grandest of Enterprises: Illinois State Normal University, 1857–1957*. Normal: Illinois State University Press, 1956.

Marx, Leo. *The Machine in the Garden: Technology and the Pastoral Ideal in America*. New York: Oxford University Press, 1964.

Mattingly, Paul H. *The Classless Profession: American Schoolmen in the Nineteenth Century*. New York: New York University Press, 1975.

Mattingly, Paul H., and Stevens, Edward W., eds. *Schools and the Means of Education Shall Forever Be Encouraged: A History of Education in the Old Northwest, 1787–1880*. Athens: Ohio University Libraries, 1987.

McCaul, Robert L. *The Struggle for Black Schooling in Nineteenth-Century Illinois*. Carbondale: Southern Illinois University Press, 1987.

McConnell, Grant. *The Decline of Agrarian Democracy*. Berkeley: University of California Press, 1953.

McCoy, Drew. *The Elusive Republic: Political Economy in Jeffersonian America*. New York: W. W. Norton, 1982.

McGuffey, William H. *McGuffey's Newly Revised Eclectic Second Reader*. Cincinnati: Winthrop B. Smith, 1843.

————. *McGuffey's Newly Revised Eclectic Fourth Reader*. Cincinnati: Winthrop B. Smith, 1844.

————. *McGuffey's Newly Revised Eclectic Second Reader*. Cincinnati: Winthrop B. Smith, 1853.

————. *McGuffey's Newly Revised Eclectic Third Reader*. Cincinnati: Winthrop B. Smith, 1853.

McMath, Robert C. *Populist Vanguard: A History of the Southern Farmers' Alliance*. Chapel Hill: University of North Carolina Press, 1975.

Mead, Sydney E. *The Lively Experiment: The Shaping of Christianity in America*. New York: Harper and Row, 1963.

Miyakawa, T. Scott. *Protestants and Pioneers: Individualism and Conformity on the American Frontier*. Chicago: University of Chicago Press, 1964.

Monroe, Paul. *Founding of the American Public School System: A History of Education in the United States*. 1940. Reprint. New York: Hafner Publishing Co., 1971.

Muse, Ivan; Smith, Ralph B.; and Barker, Bruce. *The One-Teacher School in the 1980s*. Las Cruces, N. Mex.: ERIC Clearinghouse, 1978.

National Education Association. *Report of the Committee of Twelve on Rural Schools*. Chicago: University of Chicago Press, 1897.

Neill, Edward D. *The Nature and Importance of the American System of Public Instruction*. St. Paul: Owens and Moore, 1853.

Painter, Nell. *Standing at Armageddon: The United States, 1877–1919*. New York: W. W. Norton, 1987.

Paludan, Phillip Shaw. *A People's Contest: The Union and the Civil War, 1861–1865*. New York: Harper and Row, 1988.

Philbrick, Francis S. *The Rise of the West, 1754–1830*. New York: Harper and Row, 1965.

Power, Richard Lyle. *Planting Corn Belt Culture: The Impress of the Upland Southerner and Yankee in the Old Northwest*. Indianapolis: Indiana Historical Society, 1953.

Principles and Objectives of the American Party. New York: n.p., 1855.

Quick, Herbert. *One Man's Life*. Indianapolis: Bobbs-Merrill, 1925.

Reck, Franklin M. *The 4-H Story: A History of 4-H Club Work*. Ames: Iowa State University Press, 1951.

Report of the Commission on Country Life. New York: Sturgis and Walton, 1911.

Rosovsky, Henry, ed. *Industrialization in Two Systems: Essays in Honor of Alexander Gerschenkron*. New York: John Wiley and Sons, 1966.

Ruether, Rosemary, and Keller, Rosemary Skinner, eds. *Women and Religion in America*. 3 vols. San Francisco: Harper and Row, 1981.

Schob, David E. *Hired Hands and Plowboys: Farm Labor in the Midwest, 1815–1860*. Urbana: University of Illinois Press, 1975.

Sher, Jonathan, ed. *Education in Rural America: A Reassessment of Conventional Wisdom*. Boulder: Westview Press, 1977.

Shi, David E. *The Simple Life: Plain Living and High Thinking in American Culture*. New York: Oxford University Press, 1985.

————, ed. *In Search of the Simple Life: American Voices Past and Present*. Salt Lake City: Peregrine Smith Books, 1986.

Sims, Leroy Newell. *A Hoosier Village: A Sociological Study With Special Reference to Social Causation*. New York: Columbia University Press, 1912.

————. *Elements of Rural Sociology*. New York: Thomas Y. Crowell Co., 1928.

Sklar, Kathryn Kish. *Catharine Beecher: A Study in American Domesticity*. New Haven: Yale University Press, 1973.

Stowe, Lyman B. *Saints, Sinners, and Beechers*. Indianapolis: Bobbs Merrill, 1934.

Stratton, Joanna L. *Pioneer Women: Voices from the Kansas Frontier*. New York: Touchstone Books, 1981.

Turner, Frederick Jackson. *The Frontier in American History*. New York: Henry Holt and Co., 1920.

Twain, Mark [Samuel Clemens]. *The Adventures of Tom Sawyer*. 1876. Reprint. New York: Airmont Reprint, 1962.

Tyack, David B. *The One Best System: A History of American Urban Education*. Cambridge: Harvard University Press, 1974.

Tyack, David B., and Hansot, Elisabeth. *Managers of Virtue:*

Public School Leadership in America, 1820–1980. New York: Basic Books, 1982.

Tyack, David B; James, Thomas; and Benavot, Aaron. *Law and the Shaping of Public Education, 1785–1954.* Madison: University of Wisconsin Press, 1987.

Vogeli, V. Jacques. *Free but Not Equal: The Midwest and the Negro During the Civil War.* Chicago: University of Chicago Press, 1967.

Warren, Donald, ed. *American Teachers: Histories of a Profession at Work.* New York: Macmillan, 1989.

Webster, Noah. *The Elementary Spelling Book.* New York: American Book Co., 1908.

Weisberger, Bernard A. *They Gathered at the River: The Story of the Great Revivalists and Their Impact upon Religion in America.* Boston: Little, Brown and Co., 1958.

Wiebe, Robert H. *The Search for Order, 1877–1920.* New York: Hill and Wang, 1967.

Wright, Louis B. *Culture on the Moving Frontier.* Bloomington, Indiana University Press, 1955.

Dissertations

Clutts, Betty Carol. "Country Life Aspects of the Progressive Movement." Ph.D. diss., Ohio State University, 1962.

Jennings, Helen Louise. "John Mason Peck and the Impact of New England on the Old Northwest." Ph.D. diss., University of Southern California, 1961.

Keppel, Anna Marie. "Country Schools for Country Children: Backgrounds of the Reform Movement in Rural Elementary Education, 1890–1914." Ph.D. diss., University of Wisconsin, 1960.

Pulliam, John Donald. "A History of the Struggle for a Free Common School System in Illinois from 1818 to the Civil War." Ed.D. diss., University of Illinois, 1965.

Sherockman, Andrew A. "Caleb Mills, Pioneer Educator in Indiana." Ph.D. diss., University of Pittsburgh, 1955.

Swanson, Robert Merwin. "The American Country Life Movement, 1900–1940." Ph.D. diss., University of Minnesota, 1972.

Government Documents

Annual Report of the Department of the Interior 1901, Washington, D.C.: Government Printing Office, 1902.

Blair, F. G. *Twenty-ninth Biennial Report of the Superintendent of Public Instruction of the State of Illinois.* Springfield: Illinois State Journal Co., 1913.

Blodgett, James H. "Digest of Laws Relating to Text-Books, Their Selection and Supply." *Report of the Commissioner of Education for the Year 1897–1898,* 893–908. Washington, D.C.: Government Printing Office, 1899.

DeWolf, D. F., comp. *Ohio School Laws.* Columbus: Myers Brothers, 1883.

Fallows, Samuel, comp. *Laws of Wisconsin Relating to the Common Schools.* Madison: Atwood & Culver, 1873.

Fought, H. W. *The Rural School System of Minnesota: A Study in School Efficiency.* U.S. Department of Interior, Bureau of Education, Bulletin 20. Washington, D.C.: Government Printing Office, 1915.

Geeting, David M., comp. *The School Law of Indiana.* Indianapolis: n.p., 1897.

Gower, Cornelius A., comp. *The General School Laws of Michigan.* Lansing: W. S. George & Co., 1879.

Illinois School Law. Springfield: H. W. Rokker, 1893.

Jones, Edmund J., comp. *Ohio School Laws.* Columbus: F. J. Herr, 1906.

Martindale, Frederick C., comp. *State of Michigan General School Laws.* Lansing: Wynkoop, Hallenbeck, Crawford & Co., 1913.

Monahan, A. C. *The Status of Rural Education in the United States.* U.S. Department of Interior, Bureau of Education, Bulletin 8. Washington, D.C.: Government Printing Office, 1913.

National Education Association, *Report of the Committee of Twelve on Rural Schools.* Chicago: University of Chicago Press, 1897.

Nelson, Frank, comp. *Laws for the Regulation and Support of the Common Schools of Kansas.* Topeka: W. Y. Morgan, 1899.

Report of the Commissioner of Education for the Year 1886–1887. Washington, D.C.: Government Printing Office, 1888.

Report of the Commissioner of Education for the Year 1894–1895. 2 vols. Washington, D.C.: Government Printing Office, 1896.

Report of the Commissioner of Education for the Year 1897–1898. Washington, D.C.: Government Printing Office, 1899.

Report of the Commissioner of Education for the Year 1900. 2
vols. Washington, D.C.: Government Printing Office, 1901.
Report of the Commissioner of Education for the Year 1902. 2
vols. Washington, D.C.: Government Printing Office, 1903.
Root, Eleaser. *Report of the State Superintendent of Public In-
struction.* Madison: Beriah Brown, 1852.
Thompson, J. C., comp. *The School Laws of Illinois.*
Springfield: Illinois State Journal Co., 1906.
Vories, Hervey D., comp. *The School Law of Indiana.* India-
napolis: n.p., 1891.
Wells, Oliver E., comp. *Laws of Wisconsin Relating to Com-
mon Schools.* Madison: Democrat Printing Co., 1892.

Articles
"About Life on the Farm." Champaign (Ill.) *Daily Gazette* (14
December 1908): 1.
"Affection for the Old Schoolhouse." *Wallace's Farmer* 35 (18
March 1910): 474.
"An Old Fashion In Farming." *The Country Gentleman* 78 (Sep-
tember 1908): 910.
Bailey, Liberty Hyde. "Why Do the Boys Leave the Farm?"
Century 72 (July 1906): 612–17.
———. "The Point of View." *Cornell Rural School Leaflet* 5
(September 1911): 2–6.
"Bankers and Farmers." *Outlook* 101 (August 1912): 997–98.
Baruch, Bernard. "Some Aspects of the Farmers' Problems." *At-
lantic Monthly* 128 (July 1921): 111–20.
Beadle, W. H. H. "Annual Report of W. H. H. Beadle, Territo-
rial Superintendent of Instruction." *South Dakota Historical
Collections* 18 (1936): 616–25.
Bell, John E. "From the Man Who Holds the Plow." *The Out-
look* 91 (April 1909): 826–29.
Bogue, Allan G. "Foreclosure Tenancy on the Northern Plains."
Agricultural History 39 (January 1965): 3–16.
Breen, Timothy. "Persistent Localism: English Social Change
and the Shaping of New England Institutions." *William and
Mary Quarterly* 3d ser. 32 (Spring 1975): 3–28.
Butts, R. Freeman. "Public Education and Political Commu-
nity," *History of Education Quarterly* 14 (Summer 1974):
165–84.
Coleman, Peter J. "Restless Grant County: Americans on the

Move." *Wisconsin Magazine of History* 46 (Autumn 1962): 16–20.

Conzen, Kathleen Neils. "Peasant Pioneers: Generational Succession Among German Farmers in Frontier Minnesota." In Hahn and Prude, *The Countryside in the Age of Capitalist Transformation.*

Cooper, Arnie. "A Stony Road: Black Education in Iowa, 1838–1860." *The Annals of Iowa* 48 (1986): 113–34.

Cordier, Mary Hurlbut. "Prairie Schoolwomen, Mid-1850s to 1920s, In Iowa, Kansas, and Nebraska." *Great Plains Quarterly* 8 (Spring 1988): 102–19.

Coulter, John Lee. "The Influence of Immigration on Agricultural Development." *Annals of the American Academy of Political and Social Science* 33 (March 1909): 373–79.

"The Country Boy's Creed." *Rural Manhood* 3 (April 1912): 106.

Dale, Edward Everett. "Teaching on the Prairie Plains, 1890–1900." *Mississippi Valley Historical Review* 33 (1946–47): 293–307.

Danbom, David B. "Rural Education Reform and the Country Life Movement, 1900–1920." *Agricultural History* 53 (April 1979): 462–74.

Davis, B. M. "The Correlation of the School and Farm." *Rural Manhood* 4 (September 1913): 219–22.

Drew, Dwight. "A Program of Community Cooperation." *Rural Manhood* 1 (January 1910): 19–22.

Dublin, Thomas. "Women and Outwork in a Nineteenth-Century New England Town: Fitzwilliam, New Hampshire, 1830–1850." In Hahn and Prude, *The Countryside in the Age of Capitalist Transformation.*

Englehart, Carroll. "Compulsory Education in Iowa, 1872–1919." *The Annals of Iowa* 49 (Summer/Fall 1987): 58–76.

"The Exodus of Farmers." *Wallace's Farmer* 33 (25 September 1908): 1146.

"Farm Immigrants." *Independent* 73 (September 1912): 631.

Finch, Henry. "Stick to the Farm." *Country Gentleman* 3 (27 April 1854): 268–69.

Foght, Harold W. "The Country School." *Annals of the American Academy of Political and Social Science* 40 (March 1912): 149–57.

Gard, H. "The Autobiography of a Country School Teacher." *World's Work* 20 (May 1910): 12957–67.

Gillette, John M. "The Drift to the City in Relation to the Rural Problem." *Rural Manhood* 2 (March 1911): 81–82.

"Good Farming, Clear Thinking, and Right Living." *Wallace's Farmer* 35 (7 January 1910): 2.

Gordon, Mary McDougall. "Patriots and Christians: A Reassessment of Nineteenth-Century School Reformers." *Journal of Social History* 11 (Summer 1978): 554–73.

Henretta, James A. "Families and Farms: *Mentalité* in Pre-Industrial America." *William and Mary Quarterly* 3d ser. 35 (1978): 3–32.

Hill, Edna M. "The Little Red Schoolhouse a 'Fake'." *Independent* 75 (August 1913): 517–23.

Hirschberg, Leonard Keene. "Should Children Aged Two Years Go To School?" *The American Thresherman* 17 (1914): 68.

Hogan, David. "The Market Revolution and Disciplinary Power: Joseph Lancaster and the Psychology of the Early Classroom System." *History of Education Quarterly* 29 (Fall 1989): 381–417.

Holmes, Roy Hinman. "The Passing of the Farmer." *Atlantic Monthly* 110 (October 1912): 316–18.

Hutchinson, Woods. "Overworked Children on the Farm and in the School." *Annals of the American Academy of Political and Social Science* 33 (March 1909): 116–21.

Innes, Stephen. "Land Tenancy and Social Order in Springfield, Massachusetts, 1652–1702." *William and Mary Quarterly* 3d ser. 35 (1978): 33–56.

Johnson, Keach. "The State of Elementary and Secondary Education in Iowa in 1900." *The Annals of Iowa* 49 (Summer/Fall 1987): 26–57.

Kaestle, Carl F. "The Development of Common School Systems in the States of the Old Northwest." In Mattingly and Stevens, *Schools and the Means of Education Shall Forever Be Encouraged.*

Kulik, Gary. "Dams, Fish, and Farmers: Defense of Public Rights in Eighteenth-Century Rhode Island." In Hahn and Prude, *The Countryside in the Age of Capitalist Transformation.*

"Lo! The Poor Farmer." *The Country Gentleman* 78 (September 1908): 909–10.

Madison, James H. "John D. Rockefeller's General Board of

Education and the Rural School Problem of the Midwest, 1900–1930." *History of Education Quarterly* 24 (Summer 1984): 181–99.

Mattingly, Paul H. "American Schoolteachers Before and After the Northwest Ordinance." In Mattingly and Stevens, *Schools and the Means of Education Shall Forever Be Encouraged.*

Medick, Hans. "The Proto-Industrial Family Economy: The Structural Function of Household and Family During the Transition from Peasant Society to Industrial Capitalism." *Social History* 3 (Spring 1976): 291–315.

Onuf, Peter S. "The Founders' Vision: Education in the Development of the Old Northwest." In Mattingly and Stevens, *Schools and the Means of Education Shall Forever Be Encouraged.*

Poe, Clarence H. "Farmer Children Need Farmer Studies." *World's Work* 6 (August 1903): 3759–62.

—————. "Success Talk for Farm Boys: How Can White Farmers Escape the Dangers of Negro Competition?" *The Progressive Farmer* 36 (April 1921): 445.

Prude, Jonathan. "Town-Factory Conflicts in Antebellum Rural Massachusetts." In Hahn and Prude, *The Countryside in the Age of Capitalist Transformation.*

"Roosevelt's Farming Commission." *American Farm Review* 1 (September 1908): 4.

Ross, Edward Alsworth. "Folk Depletion as a Cause of Rural Decline." *Publications of the American Sociological Society* 11 (1916): 21–30.

"The Schoolteacher's Creed." *Rural Manhood* 4 (September 1913): 218.

"Should a Married Woman Teach?" *Independent* 67 (12 August 1909): 361–64.

Smith, Timothy L. "Protestant Schooling and American Nationality, 1800–1850." *Journal of American History* 53 (March 1967): 679–95.

"Social Side of Farm Life." *Independent* 67 (19 August 1909): 431–33.

Strout, Joseph Woodbury. "The Rural Problem and the Country Minister." *Atlantic Monthly* 110 (September 1912): 353–59.

"Teachers Should Have Common Sense as Well as Book Learning." *Farm Life* 34 (July 1915): cover page.

Theobald, Paul. "Democracy and the Origins of Rural Midwest Education: A Retrospective Essay." *Educational Theory* 38 (Summer 1988): 363–67.

————. "The Role of the Common School Concept in the Religious Crusade for the West." *Journal of Religion and Public Education* 18 (Fall 1991): 65–78.

————. "Country School Curriculum and Governance: The One-Room School Experience in the Nineteenth-Century Midwest." *American Journal of Education* 101 (February 1993): 116–39.

Tropea, Joseph. "Bureaucratic Order and Special Children: Urban Schools, 1890s–1940s." *History of Education Quarterly* 27 (Spring 1987): 29–53.

Tyack, David B. "The Tribe and the Common School: Community Control in Rural Education." *American Quarterly* 24 (March 1972): 3–19.

"Type of Men for School Board Members." *School Board Journal* 39 (December 1909): 6.

Vance, Truman S. "Why Young Men Leave the Farms." *Independent* 70 (March 1911): 553–60.

Webber, Anna. "The Diary of Anna Webber: Early Day Teacher of Mitchell County." Edited by Lila Gravatt Scrimser. *The Kansas Historical Quarterly* 38 (1972): 320–37.

"What the Country School Must Be." *World's Work* 17 (April 1909): 11417–18.

"What the President's Commission is Doing." *American Farm Review* 1 (November 1908): 4.

Wilson, Warren H. "Social Life in the Country." *Annals of the American Academy of Political and Social Science* 40 (March 1912): 119–30.

Winters, Donald L. "Tenant Farming in Iowa, 1860–1900." *Agricultural History* 48 (October 1974): 130–50.

————. "Tenancy as an Economic Institution: The Growth and Distribution of Agricultural Tenancy in Iowa, 1850–1900." *Journal of Economic History* 37 (June 1977): 382–408.

Woodward, C. Vann. "White Racism and Black Emancipation." *New York Times Review of Books* 12 (27 February 1969): 5–11.

Index

"Act to Encourage Learning in White County, An," 29
Addington, Julia, 67
Ahlstrom, Sydney, 12, 16
American Bankers' Association, 181
American Farm Bureau Federation, 182–83
American Farm Review (periodical), 173–74
American Home Missionary Society, 13, 15, 21
American Sunday School Union, 24–25
Anderson, Lizzie, 145–46
Anderson, Wilbert L., 166
Anglicans, 8
Anti-Saloon Law League, 81
Arminianism, 8, 15, 21–22
Arminius, Jacobus, 7
Atheism, 22

Bailey, Liberty Hyde, 161, 163–64, 168–69, 171, 180, 225n. 56
Baker, Ray Stannard (pseud. David Grayson), 165–66
Banker-Farmer, The (journal), 181
Baptists, 6–7, 9–11, 13, 16, 18, 19, 22, 28, 45, 69, 81, 82, 187n. 2; anti-mission, 19, 82
Baptist Tract and Youth Magazine, 45
Barnard, Henry, 26–27, 30, 191n. 37
Barrett, Lawrence, 90
Bartholomew, W. M., 70, 89
Bateman, Newton, 30
Beadle, William, 50
Beecher, Catharine, 16, 188n. 14
Beecher, Rev. Edward, 16, 17
Beecher, Rev. Henry Ward, 16
Beecher, Rev. Lyman, 15, 16, 17, 20, 23–24, 109
Bennett Law (of Wisconsin), 7, 76
Bernard, Nicholas, 74
Bible reading, 51, 53; Cincinnati Bible war, 6–7; in schools, 205–6n. 25
Bill for the More General Diffusion of Knowledge, 59

Black Duck Lake Scandinavian Temperance Society, 80
Black man (schoolyard game), 117
Boone, Richard, 31, 199n. 37
Boston Recorder, 25
Briggs, Samuel A., 138
Brownson, Orestes, 24
Buck, Reverend, 77–78
Bushnell, Horace, 24
Buttles, Anson, 143, 157
Buttles, Cephas, 157

Calvin, John, 7
Calvinists, 8–13, 15, 17, 19, 21–22, 26, 60, 63, 76, 82, 187n. 6; domination of State Departments of Education, 2–3, 17–19, 26, 46, 53–54, 63
Campbell, Alexander, 10, 12
Campbell, Alexander (farmer), 70–71
Campbellites, 13, 19
Carney, Mabel, 171–73
Cartwright, Peter, 14, 16, 21–22, 27–30, 193n. 42, 194n. 43
Catholics. *See* Roman Catholics
Champaign Daily Gazette (Ill.), 174
Child, Z., 74–75
Clapp, William, 142
Coleman, George, 119–21
Committee of Twelve, 162
Confessions of Westminster, 12
Congregationalists, 6, 8–13, 15–17, 19, 25–26, 82
Conzen, Kathleen Neils, 41
Corporal punishment, 126–27, 131, 135, 137–41, 218n. 57, 219n. 70
Coulter, John Lee, 169
Country Gentlemen (periodical), 174
Country Life Movement, 4, 163–76, 179–80, 225n. 56
County school superintendents, 133, 142–43, 155–59
Crary, Isaac, 17
Cremin, Lawrence, 194n. 43
Crow, Martha Foote, 171–72
Cubberly, Ellwood, 169

Dakota Farmers Alliance, 44
Dakota Territory land scheme, 43
Danbom, David B., 170
Danhof, Clarence, 38
Davis, Harry (student), 123, 124, 125
Dean, Eliza, 142–43
Denomination-based schools, 21, 28–
    29, 44–46, 51, 193–94n. 42, 194n. 43
de Tocqueville, Alexis, 20, 175
Dewey, John, 150, 161
Downing, Joshua, 57

Edmondson, S., 71
Edwards, Ninian, 17
Edwards Law (of Illinois), 7, 76
Eggleston, Edward, 22, 136
Eisenhuth, Laura J., 67
Elson, Ruth Miller, 107–8, 109, 110,
    111
Episcopalians, 10, 12, 14, 24

Falling exercise, 14–15
Faragher, John Mack, 13, 34, 36–37,
    39–40, 42, 52, 83–84
Felt, Asa, 74
Female school officers, 66–67, 202–
    3n. 1
Finney, Charles Grandison, 15–16, 24
First Great Awakening, 8, 11
Foot, Ezra A., 54–56, 72
Foreign scholars, 74, 76
4-H movement, 171
Fox, George, 75
Franklin Jacksonian, 46
Fuller, Wayne, 31, 153, 155, 159, 200–
    201n. 51, 222n. 4
Fursteneau, Hugh, 145

Garland, Hamlin, 166–67
General Education Board, 182
Gladden, Washington, 22
Glumseth, Clara, 145
Goodman, Almida, 122
Goodwyn, Lawrence, 181
Gordon, Mary, 30

Hall, Bolton, 165–66
Hall, G. Stanley, 161

Hampsteen, Elizabeth, 119
Hatch Act, 181
Hecker, Isaac, 24
Henretta, James, 35, 37, 39, 52
Herbart, Johann Friedrich, 160
Herbartian influence in education, 161,
    162
Hoard, William, 161
Hofstadter, Richard, 13
House, William, 140–42
Hubbell, Charles, 103–4
Huftalen, Sarah, 139, 148–49

Inclement weather, 103–5; Children's
    Blizzard, 212n. 4
Industrialization, 1–2, 27, 52, 180–82
Inter-Protestant competition, 2–3, 14,
    17–18, 21–23, 45–46, 60, 81–82,
    189n. 21, 190n. 22
Ireland, John (Catholic archbishop), 77
Ives, Levi S. (Episcopal bishop), 24

James, William, 150, 161, 164–65
Jennings, Helen Louise, 28
Jensen, Richard, 6–7, 18, 23, 31, 187n. 1
Jorgenson, Lloyd P., 25

Kaestle, Carl F., 16, 26–27, 32, 192n.
    41, 199n. 37
Karier, Clarence, 26
Katz, Michael, 3
Kimball, Sarah Jane, 106
Kleppner, Paul, 6–7, 18, 23, 31
Knapp, Seaman, 180–81
Koehler, Aurora, 144
Ku Klux Klan, 175

Lancaster, Joseph, 112–13
Larrabee, William, 189n. 15
Larson, Hans, 91
Lasch, Christopher, 177
Leatherman, Joseph, 56–57
Lee, Cora, 143–44
Lewis, Rev. Samuel, 17, 189n. 15
Limerick, Patricia Nelson, 43
Lincoln, Abraham, 45
Log college, 8, 11–12
Lutherans, 6, 76–78, 122

Mandan *Pioneer* (N. Dak.), 86
Mann, Horace, 26–27, 30, 52, 59, 147, 191n. 37, 192n. 40
Martin, Laura, 69
Mayo, Rev. Amory, 17, 19
McCartney, William, 138
McConnell, Grant, 180, 182, 183
McGuffey, Rev. William H., 108–9, 110, 114
McKay, J. R., 145
Mead, George Herbert, 161
Merrill, Julia, 106
Methodist Episcopal Sunday School Union, 24–25
Methodists, 6–14, 16, 18, 19, 20, 21, 22–23, 24, 29, 51, 81–82, 187n. 3; rejection of "Yankee" Methodism, 20
Mexican boll weevil, 180
Mills, Rev. Caleb, 9, 17, 48
Miner, Hazel, 104
Monroe, James, 147
Monroe, Paul, 31

Nebraska State Council of Defense, 78
Neill, Rev. Edward, 17, 25
Nichols, George, 70
Niles, Sanford, 158
Normal schools, 147, 221n. 89
Northwest Ordinance, 33

Ousley, Clarence, 182
Outside scholars, 72–74, 125
Oxford movement, 23–24

Parker, Francis Wayland, 114
Peck, John Mason, 27–28, 29–30, 193n. 42, 194n. 43
Perkins, Arozina, 134
Petit, John (U.S. senator), 53
Phrenology, 146–47
Pierce, Rev. John, 9, 17
Pietists, 6–11, 13, 16–17, 19, 24, 26, 77, 82, 151
Pike, Robert, 128
Plessy v. Ferguson, 68
Poe, Clarence H., 170, 172
Populism, 164, 179
Prahl, Annie (student), 125–26

Prahl, Louis (student), 125
Presbyterians, 6, 8–12, 14–16, 19, 22, 45–46, 82; Cumberland Presbyterians, 10, 12, 16, 29, 188n. 11; "Presbygationalism," 13
Progressive era, 4, 65, 90, 101, 153, 163, 176, 179
Progressive Farmer, The (journal), 181
Pulliam, John Donald, 20
Puritans, 9, 11, 15–18, 20, 22, 30–31, 60, 81–82

Raikes, Robert, 24
Recitation pedagogy, 113–17, 151–52, 221n. 87
Reed, Rev. Isaac, 193–94n. 42
Resistance to state-sponsored schooling, 3–4, 31, 47–49, 52, 54, 63–64, 178–79
Rice, David, 14
Richardson, William, 156
Ringle, Bartholomew, 74–76
Ritualists, 6, 10–11, 26
Rogers, D. F., 71
Roman Catholics, 6, 8, 15–16, 24, 27, 52, 76–77, 79–83, 110, 157–58; anti-Catholicism, 23–24, 45, 82–83, 109, 203–4n. 4, 213n. 16
Roosevelt, Theodore, 4, 163, 165
Root, Eleaser, 156
Rosenwald, Julius, 181; Rosenwald Fund, 182

Schob, David, 111
School attendance, 111, 118–21, 215n. 40, 216nn. 41, 42
School boards, 69–72, 83–84, 88–89, 99, 101; divisions within, 74–78, 99; duties of, 64, 88–91; exclusion of tenant farmers, 67–68; exclusion of women, 66–68; immigrants serving on, 74–78, 157–58; nepotism, 93, 95–96, 210n. 64; preference for male or female teachers, 94–97, 127–28
Schoolhouses, 87; furnishings, 88–89, 123, 218n. 61; location of, 70–72, 88, 204–5n. 16; wood contract for, 92–93

School taxes, 49–50; taxation and subscription, 58
Schoolyards, 90, 92; backburning, 91; coal sheds, 92; fencing, 208n. 50; games, 116–17; privies, 55, 133–34, 218n. 61; stables, 91; wood sheds, 92
Scott, William, 157
Second Great Awakening, 12, 15–16
Secularization of instruction, 76–78, 205–6n. 25
Shephard, Carrie, 98
Shields, James, 104, 122–28, 135–36
Slaughter, Linda, 66–67
Smith, Timothy L., 15, 30
Smith-Lever Act, 171, 182
Social Darwinism, 109, 169
Speculation hypothesis, 34, 36, 197n. 10
Squatters, 34–39; networks of, 37; rights of, 34
Stevens, Sarah Christie, 66, 149, 203–4n. 4
Stone, Barton, 10, 12
Stonites, 13, 19
Stowe, Rev. Calvin, 16
Subscription schools, 45, 48, 56, 84, 134; fees, 44, 52, 134, 199n. 39
Sumner, William Graham, 164
Sunday schools, 24–26, 28, 54, 79–80, 191n. 35

Taylor, Nathaniel, 15–16
Teachers, 123–24; boarding of, 121–22; contracts for, 94–95, 99–100; and homesickness, 130–31, 218n. 54; and license revocation, 140–46, 220n. 80; ministers as, 20–21, 45; salaries, 62, 94, 129; turnover, 62, 202n. 52
Teachers' institutes, 147–50, 159
Temperance instruction, 81

Tenant farmers, 33–37, 40–42, 52, 62, 68, 83–84
Tennent, Gilbert, 8, 12
Tennent, William, 8, 11–12
Textbooks, 85, 107–10; free, 69, 85–86, 207nn. 43, 46, 208n. 47; standardization of, 85
Thompson, Elmer, 140–42
Thorndike, E. L., 161
Toleration Act of 1690, 23
Town, Gurden, 56
Township school organization, 57–63, 200–201n. 51; resistance to, 61, 63–64, 72–73
Turner, Frederick Jackson, 164, 166
Turner, George, 95
Tyack, David, 6–7, 16, 30, 33, 153, 155; and Elizabeth Hansot, 6–7, 16, 153, 155

Unitarians, 10, 21, 24, 26, 191–92n. 37; Unitarian schism, 192n. 37

Veblen, Thorstein, 165–66
Vinovskis, Maris A., 27, 192n. 41

Wallace, Henry, 161–62
Watson, John B., 161
Webber, Anna, 105, 116–17, 129–32, 135–36
Webster, Daniel, 175
Webster, Noah, 110
Wesley, John and Charles, 8–9
Whitefield, George, 8
Wiley, James, 128
Women's Christian Temperance Union, 81

Yale Band, 15, 30
Young Men's Christian Association, 170–71

Paul Theobald is head of the Department of Teacher Education and coordinator of the Program for Rural School and Community Renewal at South Dakota State University in Brookings, South Dakota. He received his Ph.D. in educational history from the University of Illinois after teaching for six years in the public schools of Minnesota. His work has been published in such journals as the *American Journal of Education*, the *Peabody Journal of Education*, the *Journal of Educational Thought*, *Educational Theory*, *Educational Foundations*, and the *Journal of Agricultural and Environmental Ethics*, among others. His forthcoming second book chronicles philosophical conceptions of place and community as they have existed in the countryside through the centuries.